DATE DUE

DEC

THE
YOUNG HEMINGWAY

For

Raymond Douglas Reynolds
and
Teresa Barbara Reynolds

the end precedes the beginning,
And the end and the beginning were always there
Before the beginning and after the end.
And all is always now.

T. S. Eliot

THE
YOUNG HEMINGWAY

Michael Reynolds

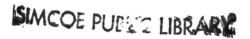

Basil Blackwell

Copyright © Michael S. Reynolds 1986

First published 1986
Reprinted (twice) 1986
First published in paperback 1987

Basil Blackwell Ltd
108 Cowley Road, Oxford OX4 1JF, UK

Basil Blackwell Inc.
432 Park Avenue South, Suite 1503,
New York, NY 10016, USA

British Library Cataloguing in Publication Data
Reynolds, Michael S.
The young Hemingway.
1. Hemingway, Ernest—Biography   2. Novelists,
American—20th century—Biography
813'.52   PS3515.E37Z/
ISBN 0-631-14786-1
ISBN 0-631-14787-X (Pbk)

Library of Congress Cataloging in Publication Data
Reynolds, Michael S., 1937–
The young Hemingway.

Bibliography: p.
Includes index.
1. Hemingway, Ernest, 1899–1961—Biography—Youth.
2. Authors, American—20th century—Biography.   I. Title.
PS3515.E37Z7549   1986   813'.52 [B]   85-22936
ISBN 0-631-14786-1
ISBN 0-631-14787-X (pbk.)

Typeset by Freeman Graphic, Tonbridge, Kent
Printed in the USA

Contents

ACKNOWLEDGEMENTS

Like most books, this biography is built on the past, resting on foundations laid down by others. Some earlier scholars did parts of the life so well that I found nothing substantially new to add. Charles Fenton, for example, did a thorough job on Hemingway's experience in Kansas City and Toronto – portions of the early life noticeably elided in this book. Some earlier books, like Carlos Baker's *Ernest Hemingway: A Life Study*, I have absorbed so completely that it would be impossible to credit every point of debt. Other books, like Bernice Kert's excellent *Hemingway's Women*, were published after I had started writing this biography. I chose to wait until I was finished writing before reading them. If, at times, I do not cite secondary sources, it is because I returned to the primary sources on which earlier scholars drew.

I am most grateful to Mary Hemingway for opening the rich Hemingway Collection at the John F. Kennedy Library to scholars. I am in her debt for previous permissions (1974, 1977, 1980) to quote from this collection, permissions which I have also exercized in this volume. I have also drawn on all excerpts from Hemingway manuscripts and letters previously in print. I am equally grateful to the Humanities Research Center at the University of Texas for permission to quote from their Hemingway family collection. I must also thank the numerous librarians at the Lilly, Firestone and Newberry libraries; the archivists at Mary

ACKNOWLEDGEMENTS

Institute and Washington University in St. Louis; and inter-library loan at North Carolina State University's D. H. Hill Library, all of whom assisted me at crucial stages. Equally important was the collection of Hadley Richardson Hemingway letters which her son John Hemingway made public at the Kennedy Library and for the use of which I am deeply grateful. Her letters are copyrighted in the name of John Hemingway.

I must also thank *American Literature* for previously publishing "Hemingway's Home: Depression and Suicide," which appears here in somewhat different form, and the English Department at North Carolina State, who gave me the time to write this book.

Like most books, this one could not have been written without the support of friends whose contributions can be counted but not measured: Scott Donaldson, who corrected countless errors in substance and style; Paul Smith, whose suggestions for revision were always right, even the ones I did not follow; Jim Hinkle, whose sharp eye picked the nits out; Carlos Baker, whose example, encouragement and help over the years have set a standard in this profession, and who generously shared his rich files with me; Jo August and her successor at the Kennedy Library, Joan O'Connor, whose interest and assistance were priceless; Stephan Chambers at Basil Blackwell, who insisted and persisted when I could not make a decision; and Bob Bradford, who dug out curious details when I had need of them.

Above, beyond all duty was my good wife, Ann Reynolds, who was with me in the research, spotting crucial points I missed, and who lived with me that year in the book when we were very happy. Even better, she was there post-partem when the doubts began. Home, as Eliot told us, is where one starts from, always.

Michael Reynolds
Raleigh, North Carolina

Chronology

1871	Clarence Edmonds Hemingway born September 4.
1872	Grace Hall Hemingway born June 15.
1890	Clarence and Grace graduate Oak Park High School.
1891–95	Clarence attends Oberlin College and Rush Medical School.
1891	Hadley Richardson born November 9.
1892	Katy Smith born.
1895–96	Grace Hall takes voice lessons in New York and visits England with her father.
1896	Marriage of Clarence Hemingway and Grace Hall.
1898	Marcelline Hemingway born January 15.
1899	Ernest Hemingway born July 21.
1902	Ursula Hemingway born April 29.
1903	First rest cure for Clarence's "nervous condition."
1904	Madelaine (Sunny) Hemingway born November 28.
1905	Death of Ernest Hall, Grace's father.
	Suicide of James Richardson Jr. in February.
1907	Hemingway family moves into 600 N. Kenilworth.
1909	Theodore Roosevelt's African safari.
1910	Hadley Richardson graduates from Mary Institute in St. Louis.
1910–11	Hadley attends Bryn Mawr college.
1911	Carol Hemingway born July 19.

1912 Woodrow Wilson elected President in Bull Moose election when Theodore Roosevelt's third-party candidacy split the Republican vote.

Clarence Hemingway takes another rest cure for "nerves." Gives up the Agassiz Club.

1913 Ernest and Marcelline begin high school.

1914 Great European War begins in August.

1915 Leicester Hemingway born April 1.

1916 Wilson re-elected President.

1917 U.S. enters the war in April.

Ernest and Marcelline graduate from high school in June.

Ernest takes job on Kansas City *Star* in October.

1918 Ernest goes to Italy as Red Cross ambulance driver.

July 8 Ernest blown up at Fossalta, Italy.

Fall, Ernest recovering in Milan hospital.

Volstead Act passed by U.S. Congress to usher in Prohibition.

1919 Ernest returns to Oak Park in January.

Prohibition begins.

Grace builds her cottage on Longfield Farm.

Summer race riots in Chicago.

Clarence evicts Ruth Arnold from N. Kenilworth in August.

Ernest summers at Lake Walloon and stays on for the fall.

1920 January, Ernest takes job with Connables in Toronto.

Ernest selling stories to Toronto *Star*.

Ernest returns to Oak Park in May.

After his 21st birthday at the lake, Grace evicts Ernest from the cottage.

Florence Richardson, Hadley's mother, dies in St. Louis.

Ernest returns to Chicago in the fall and meets Hadley Richardson.

White Sox baseball scandal breaks.

Harding elected President.

December, Ernest takes job with *Co-operative Common-wealth*.

1921   March, Ernest visits Hadley in St. Louis. Engagement made public.

September 3, Ernest and Hadley married at Horton Bay.

Sherwood Anderson returns to Chicago from Paris.

Mid-October, fraud closes the *Commonwealth*.

December, Ernest and Hadley sail for France.

1923   Death of Grandmother Adelaide Hemingway.

1926   Death of Grandfather Anson Hemingway.

1928   Suicide of Clarence Hemingway, December 6.

1951   Death of Grace Hall Hemingway.

1961   Suicide of Ernest Hemingway, July 2.

Introduction

TIME WAS

THERE was a time when the Village had no squirrels, but Uncle George took care of that deficiency. As soon as the editor of *Oak Leaves* pointed out that Oak Park, the best suburb in the entire United States, had no squirrels for its trees, a beautification committee was formed with George Hemingway at its head. In no time at all fifty Oak Parkers subscribed five dollars each to buy pairs of Arkansas grey squirrels, which came with instructions for building snug housing. By the next year some owners complained that their squirrels would not stay in their own yard, but generally the Village was pleased with this touch of class. Ten years later they were complaining that there were too many squirrels; that they nested in attics, not in their proper housing; that they ate flower buds and killed song birds. In short, they were not at all genteel squirrels. But by that time the Great War was starting and no one remembered to blame Uncle George. Today there are no Hemingways left in Oak Park, but there are plenty of grey squirrels.

In those days when the distances were different, Oak Park was an island on the Illinois prairie, safe from Chicago. Cows grazed in vacant lots that now have disappeared, and dogs ran freely in summer dusty streets where there were more horses than dogs. At the Fourth of July picnic, young and old ran foot-races, cheered at the baseball game and applauded the band. There were prizes then for the fattest lady and the oldest man. Many Oak Parkers were old men who had fought in the Civil War. On Memorial Day they put on their faded blue uniforms to march the school children down the main street. The Grand Army of the Republic was never grander than in the eyes of grandchildren who heard old stories enlarged by memory and passing time. For a boy like Ernest Hemingway, born in the last year of the last century, these stories became part of his mythology, a standard measurement.

As he passed through childhood to puberty and old veterans died off, the local paper detailed the deeds of those pioneers and soldiers who had founded Oak Park. Colonel Brinkerhof's adventurous life must have seemed in those days as daring and as remote as the Trojan War. After the Civil War, the Colonel had fought on the frontier with real Indians, shot real buffalo, escaped from breathless crises to fight again in the Philippines. Those times would not come again; the great tasks had all been done. When Ernest was three, the Spanish-American War ended. There was no longer an American frontier to cross, no wilderness to conquer except in books. Ernest's uncle Leicester Hall, escaping Oak Park, had gone to the gold fields of California and Alaska, found them boring, and become a lawyer in Bakersfield. Hemingway's father, the Doctor, told of Carolina bear hunts in his youth, but nowhere in Illinois or upper Michigan at the summer place were there any bears left. The giants were all dead and the wars all fought. For his generation, there was only the world of business to conquer, only an urban world to explore. As the founding fathers died off and a new generation came to power in Oak Park, Ernest was one who did not give up his dreams of valor. Always he could find it in books and in his imagination. With wooden guns and birthday-present uniforms, Ernest Hemingway played at war and stalked his prey. Except for his mother, no one who knew him then took special note of his interests.

In those days everyone knew everyone else in Oak Park. Certainly everyone knew the Hemingway family. His grandmother, Adelaide Hemingway, was known as a born teacher, a trained botanist who passed on exact knowledge and terminology to children and grandchildren. When neighbors consoled her on the ragged state of her lawn she replied: "I am not raising grass; I'm raising boys." Grandfather Anson Hemingway, the patriarch, was a deeply religious man whose opinion was valued in local political issues. A student at Wheaton College and a Civil War officer commanding Negro troops, he had then given ten of his best years to forming the Chicago Y.M.C.A. before he turned to Oak Park real estate, selling houses and lots to all the best families. There were a great number of best families then, for the south side of the rail tracks was not yet developed. The six children of Anson Hemingway were Oberlin College graduates. His two daughters – Nettie and Aunt Grace Hemingway – were accomplished ladies; Grace toured for several summers on the national Chautauqua circuit that brought culture and entertainment to rural America. His four sons – Willoughby, Clarence, George and Tyler – were young men of great promise: the first two doctors; George, the real-estate man; Tyler, the Kansas City business man. That was just before the real-estate boom began, just before George began pushing apartments, which Oak Parkers knew could never be homes. The flats came in with the telephone, electricity and the automobile, changing Village life, first slowly and then very quickly.

In that world before the war, young Hemingway grew up in the heart of a secure, prosperous, educated and admired family, a family respected not for its wealth but for its integrity. Village life – for it was truly a village then – revolved slowly about church and family. There were maids in his house to cook and care; there were whole blocks of vacant lots to explore. Just minutes from his front door was the North Prairie and the Des Plaines river. And always there were books to be read to him, and then, quite early, to read for himself. Throughout that world he heard his mother's contralto voice singing: at the Third Congregational Church where she governed the choir and at home on North Kenilworth where she taught the daughters of Oak Park. As counterpoint to her melody stood the solid presence of his father, the Doctor, tall and bearded, stern and loving. It was a world into which Chicago was not allowed to intrude, for the Oak Park founders, like the Hemingways, had built this haven to keep their families safe from the city's vice, filth and hazard of fire. They put in street lights, a sanitary water system to eliminate typhoid fever, and a high school better than any in Chicago. They sent many of their sons and a good many of their daughters to fine eastern colleges. They voted Republican at every chance and always voted to stop Chicago from annexing them. In 1901 they had split off from Cicero, with its battery of saloons and its tawdry people, to form the Village, the largest village in the U.S. as they liked to say. They built fine stone churches with spires that stood as landmarks, and large homes for their large families. On weekday mornings, husbands took the trains into the City to make their money, and at evening they retired to the safety of the Village, where their families were secure. People died in Oak Park, but only half as frequently as in Chicago; they died old and decorously, or young and tragically. No one died in the streets from gun shots. No one was raped. And no one got publicly drunk; it simply was not done in those days. Regularly a father died on the train line when he forgot how fast the engine moved. Oak Parkers were slow to get the hang of it, as if they expected the machinery to behave like a gentleman.

For a boy growing up in those years, life annually quickened at an exciting rate. Horses clopping down dusty streets changed, before his eyes, to automobiles rattling down paved roads. Where once there were family musicals and church functions, clubs began to dominate: the Magazine Club, the Bowling Club, bridge clubs, dance clubs, church clubs; for the wealthy, the Oak Park, the Phoenix and the Colonial clubs; for sportsmen, the Westward Ho Golf Club. The Warrington Opera Company provided a steady flow of drama and Chicago vaudeville, which did not abate the Village's enthusiasm for amateur theatricals. Hardly a week went by without its musical evening, play, public lecture or amateur minstrel show. Oak Parkers delighted in blacking-up for Tambo and Bones to strut their illiterate humor. For a young boy in those pre-war years, Oak Park was a world self-contained and entertained, a world to which its sons returned from the earth's far corners to give magic-lantern lectures on Africa, the Holy Land and China. It was a world about which Hemingway never wrote a single story.

He never wrote about his father's daring attempt to rescue two boys in a runaway wagon. He never wrote about a boy growing up surrounded by sisters in a house brimming with life. He never wrote about his mother's musical accomplishments, his aunt's wit or his uncle's drinking. Nowhere in his fiction did he tell us about the chickens in the back yard, the family horse and buggy, the gas lights in the house, or the winter odors of apple barrels and coal. Not a word was written about Grandfather Hall's funeral or Uncle Willoughby's periodic returns from China laden with strange and rare gifts. When Hemingway invented Nick Adams, he did not give him the vested choir or the cello lessons. Nick never went to church, never listened to his grandfather's war stories, never had an older sister. Nick's parents – the Doctor and the Doctor's wife – never black up for a minstrel show or take Nick to the opera. In Hemingway's fiction, Oak Park remains beneath the surface, invisible and inviolate. It was his first world, the world he lost, not to the war, but to modern times.

Any boy growing up in those days was witness to changes so radical and swift that his children would never be able to understand what he had lost. Oak Park's protective barricades, so carefully constructed, crumbled steadily during the Progressive era. The Villagers, morally and politically conservative to the core, were equally in favor of progress. In those years before the war, nothing was too modern for Oak Park so long as it was tangible enough to be pointed out with civic pride.

In 1899, the year Ernest Hemingway was born, the first automobile entered the Village. By 1904, over thirty automobiles were raising dust in the streets, and someone's maid became the first accident when her skirt got tangled in a wheel, dragging her, unhurt, all of four feet. The next year an old man stepped in front of an auto to become the first motor death, and some complained that the machines were frightening the 491 horses, including the Doctor's lovely black one. In 1907, his tethered horse bolted down Oak Park Avenue until the buggy broke loose and smashed against a tree. The Doctor bought a new buggy, but the new age would not be denied.

Soon Oak Parkers told anyone who would listen that there were more automobiles per capita in the Village than anywhere in the United States. When Wright Elsom opened something called a "garage" no one was certain how to pronounce the word. Elsom did not much care; people could pay their money and take their choice of pronunciations. His best customer was the banker, John Farson, who owned a Franklin, a Packard, two Wintons and a new white Cadillac. In 1911 the Village police got their first auto and the Brooks Laundry converted from horses to trucks. Not everyone changed so quickly. When Ernest Hemingway was twelve, his father was still making his rounds in a black, two-wheeled buggy. Shortly thereafter, the Doctor gave in to progress with a black Ford, which in February of 1914 was stolen from in front of the Municipal Building and recovered the next day in South Side Chicago, empty of gasoline.

Before Ernest was fifteen, the streets were paved and the electric lights turned on. Everywhere phones were ringing as a way of life disappeared. Invading his first world there came silent movies, wind-up Victrolas, safety razors and girls who were not his sisters. The girls had been there all along; he simply did not notice them until he was in high school, where his studied rough edges seldom impressed the real lookers. If they remembered him at all, they recalled his heavy shoes, his scruffy hair and dirty nails. In those days there was nothing remarkable about Ernest Hemingway or particularly promising. Some remembered him as a sometime bully once he had his height about him. One classmate thought him conceited, bumptious and boastful. His family – which included, of course, all living or remembered Hemingways and Halls, even Uncle Leicester Hall mysteriously self-exiled in California – was important but not markedly so, for it was not wealthy. In Oak Park the finest families were wealthy and became finer each year. John Farson, who traveled East frequently to confer with bankers and politicians, was, perhaps, the finest. His goings and doings were a source of local pride; no one knew what the banker might do next but it was always news. He organized the first auto show in Oak Park and then the annual horse show for his daughter to ride in. National Republicans listened to what John Farson said, and the Village basked in his glory, amused when he fought the licensing of autos and proud when he built his mansion, Pleasant Home. When he died in 1910, everyone was certain that he could not be replaced. Then Sears money and meat-packing money moved into Oak Park, and people quickly forgot how rich John Farson had once appeared.

By the time Ernest Hemingway reached puberty, his house on North Kenilworth was electrified, and Oak Park blossomed with washing machines, vacuum cleaners and even hair dryers. By 1913, Villagers, many of whom had grown up on farms, were complaining about smelly chickens and early crowing roosters which they shortly banned. Men, in Vanderbilt collars, still wore dark suits and dark ties, but to the horror of many churchmen they were dancing the Tango, the Maxie, the Fox Trot and even the Lulu Fado. In October 1913 *Oak Leaves* was aghast:

THE SEX DANCE RAMPANT

. . . the germs of disease are not the only evil that reaches the suburban family. The music of the bagnio finds its way to every piano, and our young people habitually sing songs, words and music produced by degenerates.

The demimonde of Paris contributes the popular designs for gowns which grow more and more to emphasize the sex of the wearer and to aggravate tendencies which civilization demands be held in sure control – natural impulses, noble and purposeful, not playthings.

Long ago the music came to Oak Park. It is now "the thing," debauching taste and making the fine things insipid to appetites depraved by constant feeding on the creation of writers of rot.

Next came the gowns from the underworld, and now the

dance has come from the brothel to take its place beside the disease germ, the nasty music and the sex gown.

Ever since the group dance gave way to the waltz, the influence of the dissolute has been growing until now the low life of America is not adequately fecund in immoral tendencies and we must go to South America and bring to Oak Park the tango and the maxie. Everybody is "doing it, doing it," in the words of one of our most popular songs.

The Fox Trot and Tango could be banned at the rare school dances, but still the teenagers would touch. No rules or ordinances could hold back the world. Charging $200 a year for a cigarette license did not stop the sale of smokes to school boys. The new age made no exceptions for Oak Park, When Ernest and his older sister Marcelline were in high school, the last of the horse-drawn fire engines was retired for an engine-driven truck, and local police mounted Harley Davidson motorcycles to run down speeders and scorchers who burned rubber in the streets. During their senior year the last dairy within the Village limits auctioned off its cows, and what had been the North Prairie was filling in with new houses.

By that time the Village was no longer safe from Chicago and Cicero vices, for commuter trains had opened the Village limits to anyone with a nickel fare. Oak Park soon became a lucrative poaching ground for petty thieves, con artists and occasional derelicts. The ten-man police force could not cope with the quick access given thieves by the five train lines making numerous stops throughout the Village. After 1904 it was foolish to leave a house unlocked, day or night. Not a week passed without a house breaker lifting a few valuables. During the winter "panic" of 1910, the Village was literally invaded by desperate, jobless men for whom the wealth of Oak Park was too tempting. During the first week of October, five house burglaries shook the Village. A month later the Sunday evening quiet was broken by gun shots, thieves firing at pursuing citizens. On Christmas Eve, George Moser was attacked and left unconscious in the alley behind his house by armed muggers. Then in June of 1916 police officer

Herman Malow was shot dead on the streets and his fellow officer seriously wounded by automobile bandits, who struck and departed unscathed.

With the rising crime rate came associated vice. *Oak Leaves* railed against the menace:

> We like to fold our hands in complacency and feel that Oak Park is a sort of "Saints' Rest" without any of the vices and snares of other towns. We boast that we have no saloons, no gambling dens and no other resorts of iniquity. But as a matter of fact we have all of these things in a form that makes them vastly more dangerous than if they were flaunted openly in Oak Park territory. . . . Not only are there a half dozen saloons in this corner of Forest Park that live on Oak Park patronage, and that means largely the patronage of Oak Park young men and boys but three of these saloons on our very border maintain the worst sort of gambling joints, in which scores, if not hundreds, of Oak Park school boys are being ruined. And it is rumored at times that the resort keepers of our neighboring village do not always limit the opportunities for debauchery to drinking and gambling.

By 1912, police were arresting school boys Ernest knew for shooting craps in back alleys and gambling in empty box cars. In 1916 when Dr. Hemingway returned from his summer cottage at Lake Walloon, he found the house ransacked and his collection of rare coins stolen. The thieves turned out to be neighborhood children, two of them older boys and the sons of prominent families. What had begun as an outside threat had become an internal problem the Village preferred not to think about: Oak Park boys robbing Oak Park homes.

While the Village tried to isolate itself from Chicago and Cicero, it did not ignore social problems elsewhere. Led by a consortium of well-educated ministers, Oak Parkers rallied to every Progressive cause; the more remote the problem, the greater their enthusiasm. To China and Africa, they sent their missionary sons to heal and save the heathens. No earthquake in

Italy or flood in India was without its Oak Park relief fund. Villagers opposed capital punishment and prison terms for first offenders. "The state is the great mother," they said, "whose duty it is, not to condemn her unfortunate children, but to assist them by kind and wise laws." In the name of Christian charity, they helped derelicts, raised money for destitute mothers and supported a pension plan for working widows with school-age children. The Village funded a local orphanage, winter coal for the poor and an open-air summer camp for the underprivileged. In Oak Park there were few underprivileged children, working widows or destitute mothers, and no one young Hemingway knew was ever sent to prison.

When the sainted Jane Addams of Hull House gave a lecture series at the Scoville Institute in 1907, she played to a packed audience. Pricking the tender collective conscience of Oak Park, she instructed them on the "Relation of Philanthropy to Civic Betterment" and the need for "Industrial Education." She warmed their hearts to the problems of the immigrants, to the horrors of child labor and the sweat shop. In the Village where there were no working girls of the sort she knew, Jane Addams made mothers squirm with her stories of Chicago shop girls facing a brutal working day and preyed upon by every sort of vice. Immediately several of the ladies' organizations began making trips to the City to help poor working girls. Sometimes they even brought them to Oak Park for dinner.

At the forefront of Oak Park reform stood Reverend William E. Barton, rector of the First Congregational Church, Lincoln biographer, and brother of Clara Barton, founder of the Red Cross. When she died, Barton delivered her funeral sermon. To his church all the finest families in Oak Park belonged, and to his words everyone listened. While Ernest Hemingway was growing up, it was not possible in Oak Park to be properly baptized, graduated, married or buried unless Rev. Barton conducted the ceremony. Mixing pragmatism with the New Testament, he was a business man's minister, who saw nothing ironic about his crusade for "clean money." Filthy money, he said, was not only a menace to health but had its influence on the character of those who used it, while clean money, like clean clothes and cleanliness of person, tended to tone up one's morals and self-respect. He could get something of an index of the character of the young man he had married not by the size of the fee but by the quality of the money in which it was paid, its newness and cleanliness. His sermons were frequently published and his common-sense books of piety sold well, as did those of his son Bruce Barton, the advertising man, whose book *The Man Nobody Knows* saw the parables of Jesus as "the most powerful advertisements of all time." Father and son alike found Christ compatible with free enterprise. When his church was struck by lightning and burned, the Village outdid itself pledging funds to rebuild its duplicate, for Rev. Barton was truly the poet of the community, putting well in words what most believed.

When the *Titanic* sank in 1912, Barton's sermon was a monument to the ideals that many of his younger parishioners would carry into the Great War. Barton prayed that:

> we might learn that the men had not proved cowards. I prayed that the fierce, brute terror that comes when death is at hand, might not have seized our men and made them less than gentlemen.
>
> I prayed that they might meet death like gentlemen unafraid, standing in two manly rows beside an open gangway, with women passing down to the boats between them. . . . No race or nation has outlived its heroic age when such an event can occur.

Young Hemingway and other Oak Park youths were only a few years away from their own proving ground to which they would carry the maxim of Roosevelt and Barton: let no man prove a coward in the face of death. Crouching in the trenches of Europe they would discover, as Hemingway's Nick Adams did, that the heroic age was over. But in 1912 with Woodrow Wilson about to become President and the Progressive surge at its high-water mark, Barton reflected the ideals of a country for whom Teddy Roosevelt was still a hero and honor had a sacred meaning.

Whatever the issue, no matter how controversial, Rev. Barton took it to his pulpit with manly, straightforward rhetoric. He supported high-school athletics; opposed cigarettes, alcohol and unclean speech; and faced the racial problem with his usual candor and the unrecognized bias of his age.

I do not plead for social equality. I do not want to marry a negress. I have lived in the south and appreciate the problem of the south. And I can say there is but one solution of the negro problem, which is to let the negro become as much a man as his own ability and character will permit him. He will have a hard enough time trying to change the leopard's spots, some of which are native, some of them painted upon him by ourselves. But if by the grace of God he can bleach them a little, in the name of God help him.

Pulpit issues were frequently complemented with lectures at Scoville Institute which brought in the best professors from the University of Chicago, as well as national figures: Jane Addams, William Howard Taft, Clara Barton, Booker T. Washington – all came to Oak park. Few ideas were condemned out of hand. The Belles-Lettres Society discussed "The Evolution of the Species" and "The Evolution of Society." In 1912, the Village opened its first Montessori school. In 1913, after a heated debate, mandatory sex-education lectures were put into the local high school. But the issue that most stirred the Village was the question of female suffrage.

In 1907, to the amusement of male Oak Parkers, the Illinois Equal Suffrage convention was held at Scoville Institute, where Dr. Anna Blount, a local woman, was the wittiest and most persuasive voice. Two years later a few men were still grinning when seventy-five wives and mothers, most of them members of the Nineteenth Century Club, slogged through a blizzard to campaign for a woman to serve on the high-school board. The next year at the Nakama and the Oak Park Clubs, 400 women attended performances of "How The Vote Was Won." Oak Park women gave speeches, organized committees, raised funds, petitioned legislators and rode in parade floats to rally support for suffrage at the local and state levels. In 1911, eight years before the nation, women in Oak Park won the vote on local issues. In a record turnout for the school board race, women out-voted men two to one, and local politics were never quite the same.

On average, the heart of Oak Park was not engaged in state or national politics. Their Republican votes made little difference to Cook County's Democratic majority. Try as they might, Oak Parkers could not elect a Prohibitionist state representative, nor could they make a dent in the political corruption that surrounded them. With the exception of Teddy Roosevelt's Bull Moose campaign in 1912, national issues seldom surfaced in *Oak Leaves*. The cost, reliability, schedules and danger of rail lines were much more important. The summer before the Great War began, Oak Parkers were not listening for the guns of August; they were too busy arguing about eugenics, the single tax and the Anti-Saloon League.

In mid-July when the forty-five Villagers vacationing in Europe were offered safe passage home on U.S. Navy ships, *Oak Leaves* noted "the bad feature of such an arrangement is that army transports are not as comfortable and hotel-like as are the great passenger ships." It was not going to be their war. They still believed that in 1915 when William Jennings Bryan spoke in Oak Park on "A Causeless War." Perhaps fewer Want ads for servants said, "German girl prefered," but in the main, Oak Park remained aloof from the issue. That fall of 1915, Ernest Hemingway entered his junior year at Oak Park High School. His September expenses totaled $3.25, including 50 cents for a baseball ticket and 50 cents for Caesar's *Gallic Wars*. His inventory of personal property included a box of fish hooks, a jack knife, several books, a chronic case of piles, and knowledge of woodcraft, hunting, fishing, lumbering and farming. As the leaves fell in the glens of neighboring River Forest, a band of gypsies pitched their tents to mend pots, sharpen knvies and tell fortunes. Young Hemingway would hardly have believed his fortune had they accurately foretold his future.

In the spring of 1916, while the Battle of the Somme put out the lights for a generation of Englishmen, Ernest chose for his Junior Debates topic the premise that "the United States government should provide for a citizen army patterned after that of Switzerland." The war would not be an American war. Wilson's campaign slogan reminded voters: "He Kept Us Out of War!" That winter of 1916, with the mud deepening in Picardy and war cemeteries filling up, Hemingway and friends were lecturing at the Community Training School on "good teaching, good leadership, good fathers and a good time." It was his senior year in high school, and for the first time in his life he was gathering attention as the class wit and parodist. In the school paper his Ring Lardner imitations caught everyone's eye, and they laughed when he introduced a mock bill to legalize hunting policemen. None should be killed, he said, during mating season, and no one could kill more policemen in one day than his family could dispose of. When he was elected Senior Class Prophet, *Oak Leaves* expected "something exceptional from Hemingway, as he has shown his ability to write humor many times." That was in April of 1917. American had just entered the war, but in Oak Park High School, the impact had not yet been felt. The school magazine said that in the fall Hemingway was going to the University of Illinois to major in journalism. His class prophecy began with war references in which no classmates were killed or wounded; they had all become quite rich and successful. With more insight and less humor, the class valedictorian, Edward Wagenknecht, told the assembly, "American has entered the world and we must enter it with her. The day has come when no nation and no individual can entertain the monastic conception of life. The new age demands that we live the strenuous life to the full." More than one of those assembled would discover how demanding the strenuous life could be on the western front.

Hemingway did not reach the university that fall of 1917, for by that time boys he knew were volunteering for the war as soon as they turned nineteen. The "strenuous life" was becoming the norm; in the newsreels, papers and magazines, young Hemingway lived with the war day by day. He was still too young by a year to volunteer, and his genetically weak eye could not pass the physical, but he had to get to the front. Going to the university could wait. For years now he had read and imagined the "strenuous life" for himself: exploring the silent places north of Hudson Bay or hunting the African veldt. Now he had the war to imagine. He saw the way the girls turned their heads after uniforms, and he listened to parents puff with pride over their soldier boys. Somehow he was going to get to the war. And return, of course, all decorated to Oak Park. Just now he was eager to be out of the Village with its restraints, customs and decorum. He needed breathing room, some place where the Hemingway name did not weigh so heavily on his shoulders. He did not want to be a doctor nor a missionary. He did not want to sell real estate. He wanted to write. Instinctively he knew he must leave Oak Park to find himself.

In the fall of 1917 Uncle Tyler got his nephew a job on the Kansas City *Star*. Once there, Ernest joined the Missouri Home Guard, delighted with his uniform and weekend maneuvers. During the winter of 1917 when the Red Cross needed drivers for the Italian front, he quickly volunteered, eager for the experience. Two years later he returned to find that the Village had disappeared. Landmarks remained but the quiet moral order, the sense of absolute rightness, the safe haven of home were gone. That world had been disintegrating, barely noticed, beneath his feet since he was twelve. After the war, young Hemingway entered the new age, taking with him the values formed in his first world, the one he had lost, the one he never wrote about.

Chapter One

THE END OF SOMETHING
JANUARY 21, 1919

THIRTEEN days after the burial, New York City and the nation continued to mourn. Across deep water at the Narrows, every thirty minutes shore guns boomed. In grey cold air, flags were still at the half mast, and the flowers at Oyster bay lay unwilted on the grave. The man who reinvented the strenous life was dead. The one who told youth of their need for "rougher, manlier virtues," for physical and moral courage, was dead. The one who said that a boy "must not be a coward or a weakling, a bully, a shirk, or a prig," was dead. Theodore Roosevelt, who knew nothing so low as the man "who shirks his duty, as a soldier," could not see the troop ships returning from the Great War.[1]

Of the six thousand who came home this day, there was one who would later write: "I was always embarrassed by the words sacred, glorious, sacrifice and the expression in vain."[2] But Roosevelt had taught a generation that life was strife. Where better to see the strife than on the killing ground? The young man on the troopship returned to war upon war, writing about them all until finally, in the heart of a much later year, he could go to the war no longer.

From the railing of the *Giuseppe Verdi*, Ernest Hemingway watched gulls wheeling above the welcoming boats. Five hundred navy pilots and ground crewmen were crowded about him.

Ahead, the *De Kalb* and the *George Washington* were jammed with veterans from the western front. As a Red Cross ambulance driver, he was not a soldier, yet he wore the prescribed black arm band of mourning. He was learning fast.

He had been learning that way for some time now. As a cub reporter on the Kansas City *Star*, he learned that the surface of things could be misleading. Beneath the veneer of city politics, he saw graft and corruption. Beneath the jaunty confidence of the tank captain, he sensed the hidden fears of a man shipping out to war. He studied the cool exteriors of emergency room doctors and police captains, men accustomed to violence, wearing cynicism like armour to shield whatever vulnerabilities remained. The world, he learned, was made up of professionals and amateurs who did not fully understand the rules. He knew which side he wanted to be on. Professionals were experts who knew the precise details that gave them credence. He worked at learning details: precise calibers of weapons, various insignia and ribbons, locations of towns and exact distances. Young Hemingway was a quick learner. In Kansas City he learned what it was about a person that caught a reporter's attention. Now he was such a person: six feet tall, alert brown eyes and a quick grin, handsome in his uniform. He watched as the naval aviators trooped down the ship's gang plank, a dark blue wedge entering the crowd. With his weight heavy on his wounded foot, Hemingway hesitated. His brown uniform, well fitted by the Italian tailor, bore his wound stripe on the right sleeve. The Sam Browne belt, which he was not qualified to wear, held him snugly. Hung back over one shoulder, the Italian officer's cape, with its silkish lining, draped forward over his scarred right leg. He leaned against his cane and waited.

The blue stain of Navy pilots back from the Adriatic coast began to spread out into the sea of faces. They all had stories to tell, stories rehearsed and enlarged for seventeen days at sea. They told them at Genoa and at Gibraltar and all through the stormy Atlantic crossing. In reality, it had not been much of a front for Navy pilots. Their flimsy sea planes were short on range, and there were not many targets. Still, they told interesting stories. Hemingway had learned something from listening and from

17

telling. He tried out his stories of Mount Grappa and the Arditi shock troops. He told them about his wounding, showed them the scars. If they thought he had served with the Italian army, Hemingway said nothing to dissuade them.

That had been his first lie. Not a lie exactly. The Red Cross rolling canteen under Jim Gamble was assigned to the Italian army. Well, if not assigned at least that's where thay had been. So it was not exactly a lie to say that he had been with the Italian army, but it was difficult to explain why. If the pilots assumed that he volunteered to go early to the war, it only made the story better. He did not tell them he was a Red Cross man handing out chocolate and cigarettes, blown up in a forward observation post where he had no business to be. He would never see them again anyway.

Below on the pier, Hemingway could see the reporters working their trade, picking a pilot with a medal or two out from the blue crowd. Each Flying Cross, each D.S.C. had a story to tell. The reporter from the *Times* grabbed off the pilot with the most decorations.[3] Hemingway waited, letting the mob rush ahead of him. Then, as he began to hobble down the gang plank, he made sure that his medals and wound stripe were not covered by his cape. The reporter from the *Sun* saw him before he touched the pier.

The first wounded American from the Italian front arrived yesterday by the steamship Giuseppe Verdi of the Transatlantica Line with probably more scars than any other man in or out of uniform, who defied the shrapnel of the Central Powers.

His wounds might have been much less if he had not been constructed by nature on generous proportions, being more than six feet tall and of ample beam.

He is Ernest M. Hemingway, before the war a reporter for the Kansas City *Star*, and hailing from Oak Park, Ill. The surgical chart of his battered person shows 227 marks, indicating where bits of a peculiar kind of Austrian shrapnel, about as thick as a .22 caliber bullet and an inch long, like small cuts from a length of wire, smote him. Some of these bits have been extracted after a dozen or more operations and young Hemingway hopes finally to get them all out, but he still retains a hundred or more.

Hemingway joined the Red Cross in France and was transferred to the Italian front last July. He was distributing cigarettes in the Piave district in the front line trenches when a shell from a trench mortar burst over his head. He said the slugs from the shell felt like the stings of wasps as they bore into him. He crumpled up and two Italian stretcher bearers started over the parapet with him, knowing that he needed swift attention. Austrian machine gunners spotted the party and before they could get over he and the stretcher bearers went down under a storm of machine gun bullets, one of which got Hemingway in the shoulder and another in the right leg. Two other stretcher men took the tall American through the communication trenches to the rear, where he received first aid.[4]

The wound stripe and the medal of valor gave credence to the story, which changed almost every time he told it. When his friend Ted Brumback visited him in the Milan hospital, Hemingway appeared much more heroic. Brumback wrote Hemingway's parents:

The concussion of the explosion knocked him unconscious and buried him in earth. There was an Italian between Ernest and the shell. He was killed instantly, while another, standing a few feet away, had both his legs blown off.

A third Italian was badly wounded and this one Ernest, after he had regained consciousness, picked up on his back and carried to the first aid dugout. He says he did not remember how he got there, nor that he carried the man, until the next day, when an Italian officer told him all about it and said that it had been voted to give him a valor medal for the act.[5]

For Oak Park consumption the story grew more elaborate. In a letter home which his parents immediately turned in to the local newspaper, Hemingway wrote:

The 227 wounds I got from the trench mortar didn't hurt a bit at the time, only my feet felt like I had rubber boots full of water on (hot water) and my knee cap was acting queer. The machine gun bullet just felt like a sharp smack on the leg with an icy snow ball. However it spilled me. But I got up again and got my wounded into the dugout. I kind of collapsed at the dugout.

The Italian I had with me had bled all over me and my coat and pants looked like someone had made currant jelly in them and then punched holes to let the pulp out. Well, my captain who was a great pal of mine (it was his dugout) said, "Poor Hem, he'll be R.I.P. soon." Rest in peace, that is.

You see, they thought I was shot thru my chest, because of my bloody coat. But I made them take my coat and shirt off (I wasn't wearing any undershirt) and the old torso was intact. Then they said that I would probably live. That cheered me up any amount.

I told them in Italian that I wanted to see my legs, tho I was afraid to look at them. So they took off my trousers and the old limbs were still there, but gee, they were a mess. They couldn't figure out how I had walked a hundred and fifty yards with such a load, with both knees shot thru and my right shoe punctured in two big places; also over two hundred flesh wounds.

"Oh," says I, in Italian, "my captain, it is of nothing. In America they all do it. It is thought well not to allow the enemy to perceive that they have captured our goats." The goat speech required some masterful lingual ability, but I got it across and then went to sleep for a couple of minutes.[6]

He had taken the story too far in that letter. In the Milan hospital room in the heat of July, his exaggerations passed for bravery. Staring at his canted leg, heavy in the plaster cast, he could not tell his parents what he really thought when he saw his bloody knee. He could not say how scared he was in another country with surgeons who could not tell him in English if his leg was coming off or not. In the picture he sent home, his lips puckered bravely in a whistle as if it were the easiest thing he had ever done. The shrapnel was real. The machine-gun bullets were real. The story was fiction, but who would ever know? The Italians decorated him with two medals, but they had need of American heroes to honor, for they needed America's support in the war. The first legitimate one – McKey, another rolling-canteen Red Cross man – had unfortunately died when he was blown up. Hemingway was at the right place at the right time. On the western front, he would never have gotten the attention he found in Italy. In the *Sun* interview, he came closest to the truth.[7]

Ten years later, when the fictional Frederic Henry lies wounded in a similar manner in a field hospital, he is asked by his surgeon friend, Rinaldi, if he did nothing brave. Frederic replies that he was eating cheese. Rinaldi asks:

"Didn't you carry anyone on your back? Gordini says you carried several people on your back but the medical major at the first post declares it is impossible. He had to sign the proposition for the citation."
"I didn't carry anybody. I couldn't move."
"That doesn't matter," said Rinaldi.[8]

By 1928, when America was no longer interested in war-heroes or trench adventures, Hemingway modified his experience to fit what the age demanded. Edmund Wilson would call him the "moral barometer" of his time. In 1919, the age demanded heroes, and if his experience did not quite fit the mold, then Hemingway would expand a bit here and there until it did fit. His audience added details, filled in the silences. Sylvia Beach thought he was buried three days beneath the explosion before being rescued. In 1926, Scribner's invented a biography that embarrassed him. It was one thing to tell war stories, quite another to have them memorialized on dust jackets. To this day, the jacket blurb tells us that Hemingway "served as an ambulance driver and infantry man with the Italian army." It is not true, and there is no mention of the Red Cross.

The Y.M.C.A. and the Red Cross, linked in the public mind by their drives for donations and their war work, had begun to smell a little tainted by 1919. Embarrassed by riches, the Y.M.C.A. coffers were filled with one hundred million undistributed dollars when the war ended in November, 1918. Soldiers from the front could not understand why they had been charged money for cigarettes and coffee. Had not the home front donated the money? Was the Y.M.C.A. profiteering from the war? No, it was not, but a lot of doughboys thought it was. Since the Red Cross also distributed postcards, chocolate and cigarettes, the two outfits became linked in the soldiers' minds. Of course, the posters showing Y.M.C.A. men and Red Cross nurses at the forefront of battle soured the collective stomach of veterans who knew better.

The Y.M.C.A. had further alienated many of the troops by its muscular, scrub-faced proselytizing in a war that may have seemed a religious cause back home, but not at the front. The churchy men who supported the war with such deep fervor would find, in the post-war reaction, that they had lost credibility. As the *New York Times* put it, "the American soldier came to France to whip Germans and not to get holy, and consequently he has done considerably better at whipping the Germans than he has at getting religion." Unfortunately, the Y.M.C.A. man:

> looks upon all unchurched soldiers primarily as material to be saved. . . . he will naturally . . . be more or less insistent on matters of faith and conduct in which the average soldier takes but little interest. The typical red-blooded fighting man . . . does not worry about the hereafter or the condition of his soul, certain published abstruse introspections by the exceptional soldier to the contrary notwithstanding, and consequently, does not take over kindly to such admonition,

especially from one who may be relatively safe from the perils of battle.[9]

Back home in Oak Park, every matron of note had her Red Cross uniform, white and starched, to wear to meetings and to pose in for the newspaper. More and more the Red Cross was linked with nursing and benevolent, if somewhat misinformed, home-fronters. One could not tell from the uniform who had been a front-line ambulance driver and who had been a slacker. "Yellow-streaked slacker" was the phrase much in vogue by the end of the war for those able-bodied men who somehow avoided the front lines.

As Roosevelt had told the nation's manhood:

It is at present the duty of every good American to do the best he can with the inadequate or imperfect means provided. Let him, if a man of fighting age, do his utmost to get into the fighting line – Red Cross work, Y.M.C.A. work, driving ambulances, and the like, excellent though it all is, should be left to men not of military age or unfit for military service, and to women; young men of vigorous bodies and sound hearts should be left free to do their proper work in the fighting line.[10]

It is little wonder that Hemingway, along with other Red Cross men, began to invent a different war life for himself. He had gone to the war in search of heroics. If what befell him was an "industrial accident," it would serve. The Red Cross, however, became an embarrassment that he simply eradicated. In Milan he and other Red Cross drivers spent good money on fitted uniforms made to order, which resembled the ones worn by the American Expeditionary Force. Change the uniform, change the story. If he was not a real hero, it was not his fault. Given the proper chance, he was sure he could have been brave. The medals were not a deep lie. Whatever his fears had been, they had not been made public, and most important, he had the wound. That was the real proof, the real division between slackers and front-line soldiers. (At that very moment in Oxford, Mississippi, young William Faulkner was parading about town in a Royal Canadian Air Force uniform complete with pilot's wings which he had not earned, using a cane to ease the limp for a wound he never sustained.)

Raised as he was on the adventure stories of Marryat, Kipling, Alger and Stewart Edward White, young Hemingway tried to make his life fit those fictional models. The man beneath the flowers at Oyster Bay would have understood perfectly. Teddy Roosevelt had never been one to accept the commonplace experience. He had plucked and lucked his way to national heroics: physical fitness, big-game hunting, exploration, ranching, war, local and national politics. He invented himself, continually advocating his own accomplishments as national goals and virtues. Writing about the leisure class of the 1890s, Roosevelt had said:

A man can be freed from the necessity of work only by the fact that he or his fathers before him have worked to good purpose. If the freedom thus purchased is used aright, and the man still does actual work, though of a different kind, whether as a writer or a general, whether in the field of politics or in the field of exploration and adventure, he shows he deserves his good fortune. But if he treats this period of freedom from the need of actual labor as a period . . . of mere enjoyment, he shows that he is simply a cumberer of the earth's surface. . . . A mere life of ease is not in the end a very satisfactory life.[11]

Though he did not belong to it by virtue of his father's work, young Hemingway mixed enough with Oak Park's leisure class to admire its style and resent its smugness. At the Bumstead house he saw the hunting trophies from Idaho and Alaska on the wall. He watched affluent classmates leave Oak Park High School for university training; few of them would ever raise a sweat while earning bread. Hemingway worked enough summer potato fields to know that he did not like manual labor did not care for employers. After 1919, this young man of slender means would work less than four years for wages during the rest of his life. Long before he reached that Jersey pier, he had begun to invent a life for himself, a life which Roosevelt forged and advocated through a shelf of books and articles.

For any boy born at the turn of the century, Theodore Roosevelt was a living legend: western rancher, rough rider, hero of San Juan Hill, the President, African hunter, South American explorer. In popular magazines like *National Geographic, Century* and *Outlook,* his essays regularly detailed his own adventures while preaching the strenuous life. When he went on African safari to gather animals for the Smithsonian, he took cinematographers with him. The skins were not yet stuffed when the movie played in Oak Park. At the dime matinee with all the other school children, Hemingway saw "the most dominant figure since Napoleon, in strenuous stunts peculiarly his own," as the movie was advertised.

Roosevelt may have suggested speaking softly, but he seldom did. A master at publicizing himself, the Colonel lived the adventure and then wrote about it. Whether he was stalking grizzly bears or pursuing outlaws in the Bad Lands, his writing pad was handy. In 1886, as he prepared to chase two horse thieves down the Little Missouri River, he wrote his closest friend, Cabot Lodge, about his preparations for the adventure. He took Matthew Arnold and Tolstoy along to pass the time, and a camera to record the capture. Already, he was planning the illustrated article that soon appeared in *Century* magazine.[12] The legend Roosevelt became was a conscious creation, whose message was simple: a man of moral fiber and physical endurance can do whatever he can imagine himself doing.

Although he did not singlehandedly start the physical fitness craze which swept the nation early in this century, Teddy Roosevelt certainly epitomized it. Every boy knew how the Colonel began as a frail, asthmatic child to build himself into a man. By the time Hemingway was in grade school, physical fitness had become an essential part of education. Jane Addams lectured to Oak Parkers on its benefits and ministers preached it from Oak Park pulpits. By 1910 under Coach Zuppke, the Oak

Park High School football team began to dominate the region. During Hemingway's last three years of grade school, the team went unbeaten, defeating regional champions from both coasts. Players from those years went on to college football; two became all-Americans. Riding the crest, Zuppke left Oak Park to become head coach at Illinois, where he and the great Red Grange became part of football's pantheon. With the frontier gone, with the Indians tamed or buried, American games became the new proving ground. Hemingway's generation came of age with a new definition for manhood: a man must excel in competitive sports. Urban American had arrived, and the problem of what to do with middle clas boys during their turbulent years had found its solution.

In Oak Park, the craze took a number of forms. Cross-country hiking began in 1912 when two high school boys took the train to Milwaukee and walked 150 miles back in three days. *Oak Leaves* praised them for defying the "effete tendencies of modern civilization."[13] The next spring seven boys, all Y.M.C.A. enthusiasts, made the hike. Almost immediately, the Y.M.C.A. began Saturday hikes in the woods, and a concerned parent asked the Village to provide a hike master. In the spring of 1913, as Hemingway was leaving the eighth grade, the first annual cross-country run was established at the high school. Most of the 110 boys who started the four mile course finished. That fall Forest Lowrey, just out of high school, biked 1200 miles to Denver in sixteen days, and then hunted and fished through 250 miles of mountains. He had decided to "take another year of travel and adventure and do some practical work . . . before entering college."[14] Wherever one listened in Oak Park – church, clubs, newspaper – one was told that physical, mental and moral condition correlated: better body, better grades, better boy.

Like so many of his generation, Hemingway, too, was caught up by the lust for physical fitness: long-distance canoe trips during spring break; cross-country hikes in Michigan. Twice he made the high-school cross-country run; twice he finished second to last. But, even in the rain, he did finish. Each fall he battered himself on the football field. Because his growth came late, he spent three years on the 135-pound light-weight team, where he played reserve tackle, guard and center without notable success. During his senior year, a growth spurt allowed him to play second string on the varsity during a mediocre season. That year he also managed the track team, competed with the swimming team – a plunger, or underwater swimmer, he appears not to have placed in any of the meets – and captained the water basketball team. No one from Oak Park would remember him for his athletic ability, but the effort was there; the need was there. To be an American man he had to excel. In Oak Park he had to win, not just play the game. It was never a game with Hemingway: fishing, hunting, tennis, boxing became tests of manhood.

A man, Roosevelt taught, also had to be able to defend himself, relying on physical and moral courage, neither of which could replace the other. "A coward," he said, "who will take a blow without returning it is a contemptible creature."[15] If that seems incompatible with the New Testament, it was not incompatible with a nation that had just fought the Spanish–American War. And young boys in the nation's Sunday schools must have found it invigorating. In his autobiography, Roosevelt recounted learning the lesson:

> I encountered a couple of other boys who were about my own age, but very much more competent and also much mischievous . . . They found that I was a fore-ordained and predestined victim and industriously proceeded to make life miserable for me. The worst feature was that when I finally tried to fight them I discovered that either one singly could . . . handle me with easy contempt.[16]

Immediately the young Roosevelt took up boxing.

At age twelve, Hemingway encountered on an Illinois country road the midwestern equivalents of Roosevelt's rough boys. As he remembered it years later, "And some older boys came along the road when I was carrying the pigeons from the barn to the house and one of them said I didn't shoot those pigeons. I called him a liar and the smaller of the two whipped hell out of me."[17] After that Hemingway, too, took up boxing. Or did he remember it that way after reading Roosevelt? It does not matter. The point is the same: a man must be physically self-reliant – a maxim designed for the young but difficult to maintain. The young ambulance driver with the limp would never quite lose faith, not even when his world made mockery of the self-reliant man. What he saw in the burial pits of Italy, what he experienced in the night wounding raised serious doubts that man, alone, could suffice. Part of him would later understand that there were no winners, that winners take nothing. But there would remain a part of him rooted in Roosevelt's maxim of determination. A man could do whatever he was physically and morally strong enough to do. Self-reliance, as Emerson taught us, is in the American grain.

Directly and indirectly, Hemingway absorbed much of Roosevelt's enthusiasm, determination and interests. Not long after the movie of Roosevelt's African hunt played Oak Park, the Hemingway family-reunion picture shows young Ernest in his safari costume standing at the edge of the smilers. At his side he holds a hat like the one Teddy wore. In *National Geographic*, he devoured Roosevelt's account of the hunt, complete with pictures of dead animals and half-naked native women. Roosevelt's book *African Game Trails* became a permanent part of Hemingway's library. In 1912, when the Bull Moose party splintered the Republican bid to retain the presidency, Roosevelt's nomination came in Chicago. In Oak Park, Anson T. Hemingway–patriarch, Civil War officer, and grandfather whom Hemingway worshipped – Anson Hemingway, it was said, never knowingly sat at the same table with a Democrat. In 1912, Anson Hemingway and Oak Park voted overwhelmingly for Roosevelt and progressive conservatism.

In those days of Hemingway's youth, Roosevelt was in the very air he breathed. His ideas and attitudes had dispersed like pollen, saturating the American scene. "The strenuous life" became a cliché in the mouths of ministers, teachers and fathers of sons. Roosevelt urged parents to "bring up their children not to shirk difficulties, but to meet them and overcome them; not to strive after a life of ignoble ease, but to strive to do their duty . . . and this duty must inevitably take the shape of work in some form or other. . . . the law of work is the fundamental law of our being."[18]

Work and duty, the duty of work – young Hemingway had these maxims by heart from his father early and late. The trick, Ernest learned, was to find work in his pleasure. The last fall before the war, he sweated out his keep at Horton Bay, gathering hay and pulling beans. Whenever he could manage, he fished for pleasure, but sold the fish to his landlady to reduce his rent. In letters to his father, Hemingway emphasized how hard he was working, from early morning to six at evening. It was all hard work – farming and fishing. Only the sale of fish allowed him to show a profit.[19] For the rest of his life, Hemingway would never be able to take "ignoble ease" without feeling his conscience tug. Winter sports in the Alps, bull fights in Spain, hunting in Africa, marlin fishing off Cuba – he could justify them all if he wrote about them. He was not just having fun, he was doing research.

As Roosevelt emphasized, it was not necessary to work menially. The leisured man could become, as he had, a writer, a soldier, a natural historian or an explorer. In 1915, Hemingway made a promise to himself, wrote it out and signed it, making the pledge final:

I desire to do pioneering or exploring work in the 3 last great frontiers Africa, central south America or the country around and north of Hudson Bay. I believe that the Science, English and to a certain extent the Latin that I am now studying in the high school will help me in this object. I intend to specialize in the sciences in college and to join some expedition when I leave college. I believe that any training that I get by hiking in the spring or farm work in the summer or any work in the woods which tends to develope resourcefullness and self reliance is of inestimable value in the work I intend to pursue.

29

I have no desire absolutely to be a millionaire or a rich man but I do intend to do something toward the scientific interests of the world.[20]

Within a year, his goal was modified but not the promise. He wanted to become a writer whose territory was those last frontiers, the proving grounds where Roosevelt's "resourcefullness and self reliance" still mattered. The Doctor had hunted bears in the Smoky Mountains; the Doctor's son would outstrip him, killing dangerous game on the Serengetti Plain and in the western mountains. The habits of marlin, quail, lions and kudus he studied as seriously as a professional naturalist. He never got to college to study science, but languages became his pride: French, Italian, Spanish and a little Swahili. In other countries only amateurs could not speak the language. Eventually the boy who yearned for frontiers understood that man too was an animal whose natural history needed writing. "The Natural History of the Dead" he called it in *Death in the Afternoon*. The grandfather had gone to the Civil War; the grandson went to war upon war, writing about them all.

Hemingway came to his love of natural history from both his grandmother and his father. Adelaide Hemingway, who graduated in botany from Wheaton College, taught sons and grandchildren how to see when they looked at nature. She taught them the parts of flowers with their Latin names. On clear fall nights she taught them the stars. At Oberlin College her son, Clarence, founded a branch of the Agassiz society; in Oak Park he began another branch of the naturalist's club. For twenty years, the Doctor led young boys into the woods to study nature at root source, afterwards gathering to read their essays and observations.

When Roosevelt was nine, he began writing "The Natural History of Insects" and collecting anything that moved. Hemingway, at age ten, was elected assistant curator of the Agassiz Club. In one of his earliest letters, young Hemingway wrote his father from Nantucket that he could buy "an albatross foot here for two dollars for the Agassiz. Is it worth it?"[21] His father's reply assured him that his weasel and kingfisher were fine. About the albatross foot, he said, "It ought to have some sort of history as to *when* and where the specimen was secured and whether it was a *real albatross*. Don't get faked for it is too good a two dollars' worth."[22] The boy learned something valuable: investigate thoroughly and get your money's worth. *Don't get faked* became one of his watchwords. Test every experience for its authenticity. The boy brought home the shiny bill of a swordfish: no doubt that it was real.

From the Italian war he brought back a pistol and a bottle of kummel shaped like a bear: authentic trophies. In his damaged leg he still carried bits of metal, equally authentic. If the war had not been so glorious as advertised, its true experience was still instructional: the whores in the government brothels who teased him for blushing; the taste of grappa; the faces of men bleeding to death; the sound of in-coming artillery; the blue eyes of a nurse; the smell of his own blood; the way dead bodies bloated in the sun. In less than a year he had become a charter member of modern times.

On this day, homeward bound, he was both more and less sure of himself than when he had left. His short war – barely three weeks at the front line – was undigested. The seven months in Italy, most of them in the Milan hospital, exposed him to a life for which he had been unprepared. He had seen and done things impossible in Oak Park. Duty drivers had not needed a father's permission to risk their lives on shell-pocked roads. Thrown in among older men, he was accepted as an equal with the privileges of an officer. In the cafes and clubs of Milan, he drank the wines, the cognacs and beers that Oak Park railed against. It had been good. And an older woman, eight years older, loved him, promised to marry him. She, too, thought him older than nineteen. He let her think so, inventing himself as he went along. They kissed as he had not kissed a girl before, lived a little recklessly, betting on the San Siro races, trying new foods in the Galleria. The world, he now knew, was larger than he had imagined; more various than he had dreamed. The moment his foot touched the Jersey pier, he was caught between two lives – the invented one he had been living and the old one waiting for him in Oak Park. Vaguely he must have known that this was the end of something.

Never again would he be the novice, never again play the innocent. During his three months on the Kansas City *Star* and during his tour in Italy, he learned that only experienced men were respected. A man must seem capable, knowledgeable and self-reliant even if, at his core, he was not. As precisely as he had studied the Chuckwill's Widow and the lake trout, he studied men's voices and their attitudes. Whomever he studied, he could imitate. He could be whomever he imagined himself to be.

But he had not yet learned to be war-weary. That would come later. The excitement of war was still too new on him, and three weeks of battle had not been enough to dull the edge. In Milan he drank with older men, like Chink Dorman-Smith, men so long at the war they had developed hard, protective shells. Almost half a century later, Dorman-Smith still remembered meeting Hemingway on the day of the Armistice. They had both been drinking ale in the Anglo-American Club, strangers to each other.

We said nothing to each other. Then Maria, who looked after the little club . . . rushed in with the news that an Armistice with Austria had been signed that morning. Hem and I looked at each other and then said the same thing simultaneously: "So we are to go on living!" He had his wound on him, I had three wounds on record, lads of our age did not expect long life; this news was a reprieve. We drank a second beer, lunched together, when I discovered that this harmless looking Red Cross youngster had been badly wounded leading Arditi storm troops on Monte Grappa and was now in hospital in Milan, only recently able to get about town on crutches.[23]

Already Hemingway had fictionalized his wounding, transposing its place and circumstance. From men like Dorman-Smith, he learned the trick of understatement and learned to hide his fears from everyone but himself. Roosevelt taught a generation that a man should not allow fear to master him, claiming to have learned the trick from Marryat. Still it was a trick. The fear was real. It was there inside, would not go away. Hemingway was yet too full of home-front propaganda to understand that the fear was human.

On his nineteenth birthday, as he lay wounded in the Milan hospital, his mother wrote him that she rejoiced "to know that in the eyes of humanity my boy is *every inch a man*. . . . God bless you, my darling. . . . It's great to be the mother of a hero."[24] He could not tell her of the pain or the terror; he could not talk about the sleepless nights when he feared losing his leg. He could not say that he sipped at a bottle of brandy to fend off night terrors. He was no hero, but his parent's generation would not understand. Roosevelt had preached national preparedness and personal courage until they believed him. A man, he said, must "be able to suffer punishment without flinching."[25]

The old men who sent America into the war had said a lot of things that were no longer quite believable. President Wilson, now in Europe to forge the lasting peace, was creating more doubts still. The young man on the pier would need time to sort out his experience. Already he knew he could turn it into fiction, which was a way of living with it.

In his rucksack, tucked away between an Italian pistol and his mortar-shredded uniform, Hemingway carried a sheaf of short stories he had written in the hospital and during the voyage back. In one of those stories, Nick Grainger, from Petoskey, Michigan, lies wounded in a Red Cross hospital in Italy. Outside, the crowd is yelling "Viva La Pace!" The war is over. On his bedside table two red, leather boxes, holding his Italian Silver Medal and his War Cross, sit beside a bottle of bichloride of mercury. When his nurse steps out of the room, Nick secretes the antiseptic under the bed clothes.

"I wonder where that bottle of bichloride is. I was certain I left it here. Did Miss Becker take it Mr. Grainger?"
"She must have," said Nick.

Left alone, with only the sounds of the Armistice celebration, Nick reads the citation for the medals:

> Although previously wounded in the left arm and not recommended for active duty, he volunteered for the offensive while the arm was not yet of a complete cure. Wounded twice by the machine guns of the enemy he continued to advance at the head of his platoon with the greatest coolness and valor until struck in the legs by the shell of a trench mortar.

The Silver Medal represents his lost legs, the War Cross his missing left arm. Bitterly, he tells himself, "'I had a rendevous with Death' – but Death broke the date and now it's all over. God double crossed me."[26] Cheated of death and crippled for life, Nick Grainger has chosen his own solution: the bichloride of mercury is a deadly poison.[27] Suicide is preferable to the maimed life he has left to him.

Seven years later he would let his Nick Adams, wounded in Milan, live with his secret fears:

> we all knew that being wounded, after all, was really an accident. I was never ashamed of the ribbons, though, and sometimes, after the cocktail hour, I would imagine myself having done all the things they had done to get their medals; but walking home at night through the empty streets with the cold wind and all the shops closed, trying to keep near the street lights, I knew I would never have done such things, and I was very much afraid to die, and often lay in bed at night by myself, afraid to die and wondering how I would be when I went back to the front again.[28]

Theodore Roosevelt would not have admired Nick Adams any more than he would have admired much of what happened in the American Twenties. Fifty thousand of the Colonel's countrymen, who took his courage into battle, were dead in Europe. The survivors came home with secret fears and doubts about the wages of bravery. The generation that honored Roosevelt's righteousness – the generation of Hemingway's parents – was ill-prepared for what was to come.

In January 1919, that generation was riding a crest of patriotic fervor. American had settled the Great War. Progressive reform had enfranchised women, improved the working conditions of the poor, and taxed the personal income of the rich. Consumer credit was putting the middle class into automobiles, and the country basked in a unity of purpose. It would not last long. Without knowing it, the young man leaving the Jersey City pier was much better prepared than his parents for the twentieth century. He had experienced the quintessential modern experience – the violence of war. There would be no peace in his time. As he waited for his Chicago-bound train, the Russian bolsheviks consolidated gains with heavy artillery. In Berlin, the mob's lynch law made short work of communists. And the Great Powers sat down to carve up the European pie. In the western Pacific, Japan's military men planned for another war. The major conflicts of his time had sprouted, soon to bear bitter fruit. It would be a century for a writer who understood fear and violence. Given a little time, Hemingway would understand them perfectly. Given a little time, he would find the style to match his subject matter.

Just now, however, he did not think about the bolsheviks or the dead man at Oyster Bay. Just now, he had to find his way home. There was just enough time to find a face to meet the faces waiting there.

Chapter Two

HOME AS FOUND
1919

NOTHING in the Village seemed quite the same to him after the war. The houses were as large as he remembered them, the lawns as deep. But the girls, with their bobbed hair and shorter dresses, were better to look at, and now a man could pay his way into dances at the Colonial Club where once it had been rich members and invited guests only. No Hemingway had ever belonged, and only once were he and his sister ever invited. At the dances now there were lots of uniforms, lots of medals. That was different. In the pharmacy window, he saw the collection of war souvenirs: napkin rings made out of star shells; letter knives made out of cartridges; belts and buckles; gas masks and helmets. That, too, was different, but not really different. It was just the sort of display he expected in Oak Park. Soon someone would want to put up a war monument: Oak Park always remembered illustrious sons whose deeds reflected well on the Village.

As usual, the newspaper was beating the drum for the Village's place in national affairs:

Oak Park, it appears, must have representatives prominent in all circles. The community has men in the party of President Wilson, it has citizens who were Hoover's right-hand men . . . it has missionaries on every frontier; a former villager is head of the National Biscuit company, and Oak

Park and River Forest soldiers were leaders in all arms of the service. An Oak Parker is at the center of nearly every important affair.[1]

The sun and the stars still circled about this still point on the Illinois prairie. (When a massive earthquake struck Italy before the war, the *Oak Leaves* headline announced that no Oak Parkers had been killed. When the *Titanic* sank, two recent Oak Park visitors were noted as having gone down with the ship.) Even the *Saturday Evening Post* knew about Oak Park, "a solid mahogany suburb and everybody there is somebody or other. You have to get initiated into the place just as if it were a secret society, it's so exclusive."[2]

Everyone was someone, and someone proposed a "Who's Who" to include all the prominent who had ever lived in the village. If it got written, Anson T. Hemingway would certainly be part of it. Everyone knew Ernest's grandfather, a respected leader in civic affairs. And Uncle George would be in the book: vice president of the bank; dealer in real estate, mortgages and insurance; builder of flats; church deacon; member of every civic club in town and some that he had not yet invented. In Cincinnati, Sinclair Lewis was gathering data on that epitome of boosterism, George Babbitt. When Hemingway read the book two years later, he knew he would never have to write about Uncle George.

Uncle Willoughby might make the book. Oak Park had a passion for missionaries, sending them off to China and Africa to cure and convert the heathen. Doctor Willoughby Hemingway's clinic in China was always a bright spot in the First Congregational annual report. Hemingway had not seen his father's brother for almost seven years. Sometimes he could not remember him clearly. He could remember his cousins speaking Chinese and the exotic Christmas presents, but the faces had started to fade. Willoughby would be in the book, but not Ernest's father, the other Dr. Hemingway.

Except by the patients who never got dunned for their bills, no one would long remember Clarence Edmonds Hemingway. He was neither a missionary on the edge of civilization, nor one of the wealthy doers of Oak Park. He was never a precinct chairman like his brother, George; he never signed a petition for any of the progressive reforms of the village. Neither political nor social, Hemingway's father had only his undistinguished medical practice to recommend him to posterity. Opposed to smoking, drinking, dancing and card playing, he practiced none of the social graces required for the new Oak Park club life. When big money began to invade the Village and posh club houses went up, the Hemingways were not part of the social life that took up a third of the weekly newspaper. Ernest and his older sister, Marcelline, were in high school before they felt the consequences. When their friends – like the Loomis girls or Jack Pentecost – went to the Colonial Club's Christmas party or the Oak Park Club's dances, they were left out. Their father could measure the consequences in terms of income: by not belonging to the social swirl, he cut himself off from the most lucrative medical practice of Oak Park. When the socially prominent sickened and died, Clarence Hemingway was not called in as the attending physician. Doctors did not make much money in those days, but there were several whose families led more comfortable lives than the Hemingways.

Doctor Hemingway worried about money all of his life. He worried when he left his wife at their summer house alone. No unnecessary expenses, he told her. Keep track of every penny in an account book, he said. Recently he had begun investing a bit in Florida land. Brother George, the real-estate genius, had put him on to a good thing, financed with a mortgage on the Oak Park house. Why should he be the only Oak Park Hemingway not making money on land? He dreamed of retiring to a leisurely practice in golden Florida. He never made it. He would die worrying about money.

Sometimes Clarence Hemingway wished he could have been the family missionary. But if he showed none of the financial acumen of his father and brother George, neither had he the zeal of brother Willoughby, nor had his wife, Grace. Willoughby's wife was dedicated to missionary life before she married his brother; Clarence's wife, ever the artist, would not have gone to China unless they promised her an opera of her own. Sometimes, in Oak Park, Clarence Hemingway felt that he was failing himself. But with six children and an independent wife, he did not have much time to think about it in the post-war recession of 1919.

Ernest thought quite a lot about his father, whose prescribed rituals were unchanged by the war. The Doctor still wanted everyone to keep an account book of income and expenditures. As a boy Ernest tried to keep such accounts. Seldom able to do so for more than a month, he at least made the effort whenever his father insisted. His younger sisters, now, did not even make the effort. Yet his father looked much the same as before the war — maybe a little greyer, a little less energetic, a little more nervous, a little more difficult to please. He was not the same father Ernest remembered hunting or exploring with during the Agassiz days. His father no longer had time for anything that gave him much pleasure. Father and son, never ones to share much, had now even less common ground. Ernest Hemingway was home from the war, but he would not be able to stay long. A turning point had passed without his even knowing it.

Each day he put on his uniform, laced the high-topped boots and walked down to the Scoville Institute, whose library shelves had been his chief window on the world before the war. Four years earlier he said that O. Henry, Kipling and Stewart Edward White were his three favorite authors.[3] Now that he was truly trying to write his own stories, he saw how difficult it was to imitate Kipling. So much depended on the setting and the dialect. White was writing kids' stuff — good kids' stuff — and his books on how to camp and hunt were still fine. But he could not write the White stuff. O. Henry, however, would stick with Hemingway for a long time. There was a formula to those stories that he could use. He could see the patterns all right, but he could not yet make them his own any more than he could completely shake off the boy he had been before the war. "Ernie" Hemingway haunted the Village. He could see his former self in the librarian's eyes. If he took off the uniform, he was afraid that his new self might disappear. He walked the streets out of step with the time.

After the winding, narrow streets of Italy, these four-square avenues on a flat plane were less admirable than he remembered them. The grey-stone First Congregational Church, spiritual home of Oak Park's first families, seemed much smaller now that he had seen Milan's massive cathedral. In Milan he had not felt self-conscious in uniform. Here in Oak Park, uniforms were commonplace – over two thousand men had signed up by war's end – but here it felt like a masquerade. Already the newspaper was reminding the vets that they had only three months after demobilization to get into mufti, to store the old uniforms for Memorial Day parades and such. Hemingway's earliest memories of his Grandfather Anson were Memorial Days when the old gentleman broke out his uniform of the Grand Army of the Republic. Sometimes Ernest was allowed to carry the sword. Now he was back from his own war, and already they wanted him to store the uniform. Not yet. He was not ready to become Ernie Hemingway just yet. Agnes Von Kurowsky, his nurse and fiancée in Milan, did not fall in love with Ernie Hemingway, the kid who delivered *Oak Leaves* and wrote funny things for the high-school paper. Agnes, the daughter of an Americanized Polish count, would not have looked twice at him in Oak Park. None of the real lookers ever had, though that was now changing. The young girls noticed him now, and he enjoyed their attention. If he took the uniform off for good, it would be much more difficult to hold on to the Lieutenant he invented in Italy. Four months after he was back, he still wore it. When the village gossips began to talk, Marcelline told them he needed the boots to support his wounded leg.[4] Maybe he did need the boots, but the boots did not require the uniform.

At Scoville Institute library it was good to read about the war. There were some British historians doing a pinpoint job on it, battle by battle. He liked their maps. He liked their precision and detachment. Chink Dorman-Smith had told him about the fighting at Mons. Now he could see it. Later in Paris, when he invented the Big Two-Hearted River, he would have his map of northern Michigan pinned to the wall. The histories were much better than the first-hand accounts of heroes. Guy Empy's *Over the Top* was exciting with its fixed bayonets, but it did not describe what he had seen. There were lots of war stories in the magazines, both real and fictional. He read them carefully. They did not seem to want stories about bitter veterans like Nick Grainger. They wanted clean-cut American heroes: rich kids who turned out to be brave soldiers in spite of being rich, or commoners who did uncommon deeds under pressure. Sometimes there was a beautiful nurse involved. He could do those stories. Maybe he had not seen much action, but what he had seen he had memorized: he knew just how the dead bodies lay in the fields back of the Piave River; he knew exactly how the artillery shells screamed in. Even better, he had listened to survivors from the Caporetto disaster and the bitter alpine fighting. If he could make up believable stories about his own life, stories that older men accepted, then he could write stories for the *Saturday Evening Post*. That's what he had wanted to do for some time now, but he did not tell many people. He did not tell his father. Not yet.

Some of the war histories he took home on his grandmother's library card. Nineteen going on thirty, he still did not own a library card; whenever the Hemingway children wanted books, they had to borrow their parents' cards. During high school, when Ernest was expected to use the Scoville library extensively, it had been a bit embarrassing. By the time he was fourteen, most of his classmates had cards of their own, but his father refused him that privilege. The Doctor wanted to know what his children were reading. Ernest sometimes got around that block by borrowing his grandparents' cards, but that ploy caught up with him when he forgot to return the books on time. (When Marcelline moved out of the Kenilworth Avenue home, she immediately got a library card of her own – a minor declaration of independence.) His father's attitudes and rules were unbending. Ernest and his sisters accepted the restrictions as children, but after the war the Doctor's increasingly erratic moods undermined his authority. Ernest, in the spring of 1919, found it easier to follow the rules than to fight with his father. He lay low and coped. He wrote long letters to Agnes and worried about a job. He talked to his father as little as possible about serious matters.

As with his father, Oak Park was not easy to live with after the war. Ernest had changed rapidly; the Village, at a slower rate. The blacksmith of thirty-eight years was dead; horses were disappearing, but the Village hung on as long as possible. In 1917, horses and cars were still limited to the same speed. Oak Park gave up the annual horse show but it was not ready to surrender completely. With Prohibition less than a year away, the Village's self-imposed prohibition was in conservative agreement with the nation; other strictures were daily irritants to most of the veterans. By charging $100 for a six-month cigarette license, the Village board made it clear they did not favor smoking. The vets, accustomed to cigarettes with their rations or being handed packs by the Y.M.C.A. and Red Cross men, were not going to revert. And the movies, against which the purists continued to rail, were not going to disappear. The Censorship Committee of ministers and club women drew up a movie code so stringent that not one movie in ten could have played in Oak Park. The mechanism, however, proved too cumbersome to enforce. With three movie houses changing bills every two days, the committee would have spent all its waking hours in judgement. Yet in the library, Strindberg, Dostoievsky, Wilde, Flaubert, Zola, Ibsen and Shaw were available. Even Dreiser's *Sister Carrie* was finally on the shelf. Ibsen's *A Doll's House* was a perennial favorite of amateur groups. Oak Park, as Hemingway was beginning to see, was a mass of contradictions.

Sometimes at the library he ran into other veterans. Sometimes they smoked a cigarette in the park and talked about the war, dropping into familiar slang, happy not to have to explain each detail. All their lives in Oak Park they had heard stories about the Civil War their grandfathers fought. Members of the Borrowed Time Club, all men over seventy, and the Phil Sheridan Post of the Grand Army of the Republic retold their war adventures to the point of boredom. *Honor, glory, country* rolled off the tongue as easily as *right* and *wrong*. Everyone was quite

42

sure of their meanings. All their lives these new veterans from the Great War had lived under the aura of past glories, suspecting those days were gone for good. They would never have to prove themselves as their grandfathers had. When the European war started in 1914, few of Hemingway's classmates thought it would be their war, for President Wilson promised neutrality.

In 1916, when a local unit of the National Guard was proposed for Oak Park, fewer than twenty-five citizens attended the meeting.[5] In less than a year the nation's neutrality turned belligerent, and with it was Oak Park. By February of 1917, the club women were rolling bandages and knitting sweaters. The newspaper wondered how many Oak Park men might be drafted if it came to war, calculating that Oak Park's fair share might be 300 men. As more American ships went down in the Atlantic, old men who would never see the trenches took up the war cry. A local poet urged her townspeople to do their duty in a righteous war:

> What is peace worth
> If sinking neutral ships goes on,
> And we just looked upon
> As one who dares not raise her head?
> (We to our war-gains basely wed,
> Who care to be but rich and fed.)
> What could we do so unprepared?
> What did the others do – they dared
> To meet the Hohenzollern hate,
> To arm and mobilize, not wait
> For coldly-calculating plan.
> Three nations rose as one vast clan,
> And still their armies they advance –
> England, Russia, France.
>
> America's glorious name is lost
> If she must ever count the cost
> Of doing right – worse things there are
> Than helping in a righteous war:
> Peace and dishonor.[6]

A few exceptional Oak Parkers volunteered for the war early, enlisting in Canadian or British units. Despite the numerous local lectures and the strident essays in national magazines supporting preparedness, not many Oak Park high-school boys had been anxious for their chance to save western civilization. In March 1917, when a rag-tag Reserver Officer Training Corps unit was formed at the high school, only 100 boys, mostly sophomores and freshmen, volunteered for training. Hemingway wrote a little piece for the school paper making fun of Captain Stevens, who had told them: "This game is a man's game and I know you will all want to play." Hemingway reported a selection of satiric responses from the student body: "I regret we have wasted so much time on mere games." "Hurrah for Tit-tat-toe and Cadet Grey!" "Me for Cadet Grey and pink flowered gaiters." "God save our native land!" "While not entirely against it," Hemingway wrote, "the student body is not carried off its feet by the proposition."[7] Less than a month later, America was in the war: the "game" had begun.

Oak Leaves was certain that Hemingway's generation would not measure up. For years the paper had criticized the softness that suburban ease had fostered in its young men. For years, ministers and lecturers had harangued on the "Boy Problem." The boys of 1917 were pampered; they had too much free time, not enough responsibilities. They smoked too many cigarettes. They watched too many movies. They did not know hard work as their fathers before them: they had no wood to chop, no fields to plow. Nothing heroic could be expected from the class of 1917. One week before President Wilson took his declaration of war to the Congress, an *Oak Leaves* editorial said:

> The idea appears to prevail that war would not affect us here in these suburbs; that some professional soldiers, aided by men enlisted in South Halstead street . . . will go aboard our ships or take the rifles and, like policemen, go out and arrest the enemy. Such is the superficial appearance of this community in the spring of 1917.[8]

When war was declared, Ernest Hemingway and his friends were enjoying spring break on a long canoe trip down the Des

Plaines river. He was seventeen years old, too young until July 21 even to volunteer. He would have one last summer at the lake before he tried to enlist. Even then two barriers stood between Hemingway and the war: his father's permission and his myopic vision. The Doctor did not want his son to volunteer. It was not until after Christmas, 1917, that he relented. Hemingway's weak vision, however, remained. Inherited from his mother, his weak eyes failed the army physical. Finally in January of 1918, while working at the Kansas City *Star,* he was accepted into the Missouri Home Guard. In March, the Home Guard was taken into the National Guard, but by then, Hemingway had volunteered to drive Red Cross ambulances in Italy.[9] So long as it was a foreign war, he was able to joke about the R.O.T.C. Now that it was an American war, his grandfather's example and Roosevelt's rhetoric called him to his duty.

A week into the war, Oak Park held a mass rally and recruiting drive at which the townspeople rose spontaneously to sing "America the Beautiful." Within two weeks 100 Oak Parkers signed up for the duration. The Suburban Club called off its dinner dance, feeling "that it would be inconsistent with the seriousness of the hour to do otherwise." Adelaide Caldwell and George McClary postponed their wedding indefinitely "because of the war." The three Dixon boys, with their parents' permission, dropped out of Harvard, Cornell and Northwestern Universities to volunteer.[10] Oak Park's "blue-eyed pride," as E. E. Cummings would later call the war generation, began to over-run the induction centers. Oak Park had expected 300 men at most to be its quota. Within less than a year, there were 1000 Oak Parkers in uniform. By the time the monument was erected in the park, the bronze tablets named 2500 soldiers from the Village, 56 of whom came home in coffins.

On May 5, a month into the war, the editor of *Oak Leaves* assured his readers:

> Every man who has served in the army is keen for the experience again. The G.A.R. and Spanish war veterans, former regulars and national guardsmen lead in military preparations. . . . those who have been wounded in battle

are more eager than those who merely prepared and never were in touch with the enemy. . . . Old soldiers never tire of talking of their army experience, and boys who now enlist are in the way of having an adventure rich in fellowship. They will find happiness in recalling the army days as long as they live, barring of course mutilation that separates them from their kind or dooms them to incompetence.

Two weeks later, the newspaper which so often fretted about the softness of suburban youth was overjoyed at their response to the war.

OUR WONDERFUL BOYS

A Remarkable Response – No Service
Too Dangerous for Oak Park
and River Forest Lads

Dodging the great German shells in their little ambulances, Oak Park boys already are on the firing line in France.
    . . . Not a branch of the service is too dangerous for the red blooded young men of this, Chicago's most American suburb. Their forefathers fought the British and the Indians, and conquered a wilderness. They, showing the same spirit, have answered the call, and are flocking to the colors. Oak Park mothers, sorrowful but proud, are rejoicing in the strong manhood of their sons. . . . And when the day of battle comes, when ship meets ship amid the crash of guns, or the word goes forth to charge thru shell fire, across no-man's land of death, to the trenches of the foe Oak Park boys will do their duty.

They did their duty, in the Argonne forest and Belleau Wood, at Château Thierry and St. Mihiel. They took their wounds and got their medals. Some died, of course. The paper reported the losses, keeping track of the "game" as if it were another victory banner to be hung. If the war was not exactly what the boys had been promised, they did not write to the newspaper about it. Some things they did not write to anyone. And when they came home – some wounded, some with bad dreams – there were still things they could not talk about except with other veterans. They did not know that all wars were like that; they had only been to one, and it had barely lasted a year. Home-fronters, the returning vets discovered, did not really want to know about the war. They wanted to hear war stories that were funny or scary, but they did not want to hear about the war. *Oak Leaves* told the veterans that it was time to forget the killing, time to return to a productive life. Ernest Hemingway did not think that he would ever forget the killing. He knew he would never forget the sound a trench mortar shell makes just before it explodes.

In the *American Medical Association Journal,* stacked in his father's office, he read about "shell shock," only they called it neurasthesia. Maybe he had neurasthesia. It was a hot item in the magazines. No one really understood it, but some of the vets had it. (Some of the vets had syphilis and gonorrhea, but the magazines did not speak of that. There was a lot about the war of which they did speak.) Even the Oak Park newspaper knew about shell shock. It said that laymen and professionals would be interested in the survey of vets being done by the Epiloptographic Society. It was a safe thing to be interested in. But the more Hemingway read, the less he thought that he had it. If he did, he did not have it bad, except a little maybe in the night. He would not tell his father about that either. Or anyone else just yet. A few years later when he invented Nick Adams, he gave him the shell shock. Nick would lie awake at night listening to the silkworms eat the mulberry leaves. Hemingway had heard the silkworms munch but that was before he was blown up in the night. He too had spent sleepless nights after the wounding, but he did not have it the way Nick would have it, nor as badly.

In the chilly afternoons of early spring he walked slowly down Lake Street toward the high school. It was a place to go, and he needed the exercise. When his sister Ursula got out of school, they walked back to the house together. By that time the mail had arrived. Ernest took the letters from Agnes up to his room to read them in private. She wrote witty and teasing letters, telling him about Torre di Mosto where she was on temporary duty. She had sent him home to find a job. That was what she said, what he promised. Jim Gamble had offered Ernest a year in Italy, expenses paid, just to pal around with him. With the Proctor and Gamble soap money to spend, Jim was good company, but Agnes did not much care for him. She sent Ernest home to get a job, saying she would not marry some loafer on the bum in Europe. So he had come home to Oak Park, knowing he could not work there. In March he wrote Gamble in Italy where, at Gamble's expense, the two of them had spent one delightful week at Taormina on Sicily's rocky coast. Remembering the moonlit water, Mount Etna smoking and the lovely seaside resort, Hemingway told Gamble it had been a mistake to come home. He would die for his country if necessary but he could not live there.[11] His parents were still nagging him about going to college in the fall. He could not imagine himself in college now. He told others that he might go back to the Kansas City *Star* as a reporter, but he knew the *Star* was cutting back on its staff: the market was glutted with demobilized reporters. Besides, Kansas City was a long way from Italy, the only place he had been accepted as a man. If he could sell a few stories to the *Saturday Evening Post* or *Red Book,* maybe he could go back as a writer. He was not sure how writers lived or how much money the *Post* paid. He did not know any writers.

Of the several writers living in Oak Park, he knew only enough about them to suspect that they were not the models he wanted. Oliver Marble Gale wrote historical romances that his mother's friends seemed to read. Charles White did architectural pieces for national magazines and there were some local poets. Edgar Rice Burroughs was making a fortune from *Tarzan* novels, one of which had just been made into a movie. Ernest did not know Burroughs, who made a big splash locally while Hemingway was in Italy. Then there were the ladies who wrote children's books – Mrs. Crummer and Helen Smeeth. Ernest had read children's books and magazines. At the lake house in Michigan, his parents kept bound volumes of *St. Nicholas* for summer reading. It was a magazine he devoured as a boy, indeed all through high school.

Now he began to read *St. Nicholas* seriously, looking for the formula, the trick of the story. From Ben Franklin's *Autobiography,* which he read in high school, he knew that imitation was one way to learn. His first real success had been his Ring Lardner imitations, which he continued in Italy. He wrote a "You Know Me, Al" piece for *Ciao,* the irreverent drivers' broadside which Section Four so enjoyed. Because imitation came easy for him, he practiced it throughout his seven-year apprenticeship. Later in Paris, with the apprenticeship done, he wrote a note to himself:

> Imitating everybody, living and dead, relying on the fact that if you imitate someone obscure enough it will be considered original.

> Education consists in finding sources obscure enough to imitate so that they will be perfectly safe. [12]

As he had learned by then, the emphasis was on *obscure* if you did not want the reviewers to put you down as someone's protégé.

In the spring of 1919, he had not discovered Stein or Anderson. He had not read Conrad, Lawrence or Turgenev. He had not heard of Ezra Pound or James Joyce. His reading was rooted in nineteenth-century British fiction. Other than Jack London's stories and *Call of the Wild,* he had read nothing that could be called modern. Few Americans had. The triumvirate – Twain, Howells and Henry James – that dominated the American scene for more than a generation was only lately dead. Twain died in 1910; James in 1916. Howells continued on alone until 1920. At the Scoville Institute, the Big Three could be found with shelves of their own. The 1890s Naturalists – the truly lost generation – left hardly a ripple on the literary consciousness of Oak Park. Dreiser's *Jenny Gerhardt* and *Sister Carrie* came to the library in 1913. Stephen Crane's *Red Badge of Courage* finally appeared in 1914, the single Crane on the shelf. But no one was recommending the Naturalists to Hemingway. Oak Parkers, as genteel as the best of pre-war America, were thoroughly British and Continental in literary taste, and with them was Hemingway.[13]

Growing up inside that protective shell, Hemingway had no way of knowing what lay beyond the edge of good taste. He did not even know the shape of the shell until he went to the war. If he suspected, that spring after the war, that there was more to writing than he had been taught, no evidence remains. There is nothing to suggest that he had any intention of writing great literature. Writing he regarded as an occupation, a job that produced income. Looking for models, he turned to the popular magazines. Had he stuck to those models, he probably would have become financially successful but he would not have become Ernest Hemingway. It was happenstance and blind fortune that changed his direction, a turn that could only take place beyond the Village limits.

That first spring back from the war he wrote a piece that may have been intended for *St. Nicholas* about two brothers whose family moved from Oak Park to the Hudson Bay area, a place to which Hemingway traveled frequently in his imagination. During high school he read the Stewart Edward White romances set in that far country. In 1916, he wrote in his high-school notebook: "Get to Hudson Bay or Bust." He signed the promise as he habitually did on important matters. To whet his appetite he made lists of provisions, not unlike the lists that White suggested in his how-to-do-it books. Two of the lists are for a "Moose River Hudson Bay Trip," one of which is designed for "4 fellows." The second list is for an "individual outfit." If he could not find three others, he would go it alone. The hero in White's fiction is frequently on his own in the far country. The individual list, aside from the obvious – matches, wool socks, good compass – included a .32 caliber revolver, pipe and tobacco, notebook and two pencils.[14] Hudson Bay men, he knew from his reading, smoked pipes. But in the North country, none of White's heroes took notebook and pencils. At sixteen, Hemingway already knew that he wanted to write. He also knew from White and Roosevelt that writers took notes on their adventures, a lesson reinforced on

Hemingway as a cub reporter on the Kansas City *Star*. One notebook, two pencils – not many notes, just the high points.

The Oak Park children of his story find themselves befriended by a French Canadian trapper who allows them to make the rounds of his trap lines with him. Each trap is discovered sprung but empty, the furred victim ripped away. The trapper, observing the signs, tells the two boys that a wolverine is responsible. Cautiously, they approach the last trap. Empty. When the trapper looks up, the horrible wolverine leaps upon him from the tree above. As they tussle in the snow, the trapper drops his rifle. The beast is ripping him apart when the older brother takes up the rifle and kills the animal, for which the trapper is deeply grateful. Together the three return to town where the father, a mining engineer, is most impressed with his son's courage and resourcefulness.[15]

The story is as juvenile as it sounds, not unlike stories one expected to find in *St. Nicholas*. Yet some of the story's raw elements would be refined in Hemingway's mature writing: the more experienced trapper who instructs the young boys will reappear in different disguises in Hemingway's fiction early and late; the resourceful boy, capable, under pressure, of killing the wolverine, will be tested more than once by Hemingway; the younger brother, who is there to watch, verify and admire his sibling's heroism, will be present in various guises to the very end. In Hemingway's late if not final story – "The Last Good Country" – we find another older brother, Nick Adams, surviving alone in the woods with his sister, Littless, who is his fondest admirer. Equally important in thematic terms is the father to whom the boy relates his adventure and from whom he receives adulation. Hemingway, like many first sons, deeply needed his father's approval. Ernest's conception of how a man should behave, he had learned in school, church, library and home, but mostly it had come from his father, whose growing moodiness and reticence failed the young Hemingway when he most needed support. In many of his early stories we find a son determined to win his father's approval through deeds of bravery. Like Teddy Roosevelt, Hemingway was looking always for his own west, where a self-reliant man could prove himself. To find it at battle fronts, in bull rings, on African plains or the deep blue Gulf stream, he had to leave the Village, but with him he took his father always.

Once famous, Hemingway was remembered somewhat bitterly in Oak Park. A half century after he left, people who never knew him were certain that he hated the Village. In their centennial memorial to Oak Park High School, Villagers could not bring themselves to list either Ernest Hemingway or Frank Lloyd Wright as notable native sons. When Wright deserted his wife and several children for Mamah Borthwick Cheney, wife and mother of three children, the notable event went unmentioned in the newspaper. For years afterwards, Mrs. Anna Lloyd Wright continued to be a social mover in the Village, living as if her husband were simply away on an extended building project. Wife desertion was neither forgivable or mentionable in Oak Park. But while he lived there, Hemingway did nothing to offend the Village code. Sauk Centre had reason to dislike its son, Sinclair Lewis, who satirized the town in *Main Street*. Thomas Wolfe had trouble going home again to Asheville, North Carolina, after his exposé of his townspeople in *Look Homeward, Angel*.

But none of Hemingway's fictional characters grew up in Oak Park. His story of the returning veteran, "Soldier's Home," uses some of his own experience but he moved the locale to Oklahoma. The closest he came to violating the unwritten social code was when he used a local name in "The Short Happy Life of Francis Macomber." Frank Macomber, a local insurance man, sponsored a student essay contest on "The Advantages of Life Insurance," which Ernest was forced to enter by his high-school English teacher. He was barely able to squeeze out the 300 words. But borrowing one name hardly put him in the same league with Lewis and Wolfe. It is hard to imagine Faulkner not writing about Oxford, Mississippi, or Steinbeck leaving the Salinas valley out of his fiction. It is almost axiomatic that American authors write about their home towns, yet Hemingway did not. He may have rejected Oak Park's frequently pompous, sometimes hypocritical Victorian social behavior, but he never fouled the nest.

In 1924, five copies of *In Our Time,* ordered by the Hemingway family, were returned to Paris without explanation. Ernest was deeply hurt. In 1926, he urged Max Perkins, his editor at Scribner's, to push *The Sun Also Rises* in Oak Park where Hemingway was sure the sales would be significant. When the book appeared, his mother wrote him a letter that he kept all his life:

> The critics seem to be full of praise for your style and ability to draw word pictures but the decent ones always regret that you should use such great gifts in perpetuating the lives and habits of so degraded a strata of humanity.
>
> I belong to a current Book Study Class and we have lectures from the literary critics of the various newspapers.
>
> I could not face being present when your last book was to be reviewed, but one of the class told me afterward what was said. That you were prostituting a . . . great ability to the Lowest uses. It is a doubtful honor to produce one of the filthiest books of the year.
>
> What is the matter? Have you ceased to be interested in loyalty, nobility, honor and fineness in life . . . surely you have other words in your vocabulary besides "damn" and "bitch" – Every page fills me with a sick loathing – if I should pick up a book by any other writer with such words in it, I should read no more – but pitch it in the fire.[16]

He should have known better. During his lifetime, the Oak Park he sometimes scorned, sometimes loved as only a native son can scorn and love, that Oak Park did not accept Ernest Hemingway. After the Paris years of the Twenties, he set up Oak Park homes, first in Key West and then in Cuba – large, lawned homes with swimming pools and servants, homes that marked where a personage lived. Such homes, however, did not appear in his fiction. With one exception, the characters he invented would be essentially homeless men, not only without family but without a town to call home.

But his characters were not without those virtues his mother extolled. The *words* may have become obscene to Frederic Henry during the war, but only the words. The values – loyalty, nobility, honor – did not lose their currency. Add love. Add courage. Add self-reliance. And above all else, add duty. Most of his characters make their pilgrimage gravewards accompanied by those good friends. They sustain Robert Jordan at the hour of his death. Colonel Cantwell and Thomas Hudson, in their last good nights, never forget them. And where one finds them most lacking in *The Sun Also Rises*, there life is stale, flat and profitless. Mother Hemingway, like so many readers of our time, missed the point. It was the world that had changed, not her son's values. He, too, was filled much with loathing for a world that no longer honored the old verities. It was life that had become filthy. Like so many of the so-called Moderns, Hemingway remembered throughout his life the lost world in which he grew up. His characters, going down to loneliness or death in other countries, might have no home or family, but many of them could have sat at table with his Grandfather Anson. Between and beneath the lines, many of them were good Oak Parkers.

The Oak Park that nurtured Hemingway pressured its sons to perform at levels above the ordinary, for the boosters could not accept average returns on any of their investments. They demanded winning football teams to the point where a single loss ruined a season. They took pride in owning the most cars, the most phones per capita. Nothing about Oak Park could be ordinary. Seven months into the war, the cover page of *Oak Leaves* urged the citizenry to contribute its million dollar share of the massive Liberty Loan drive. Reminding the readers of the local boys in uniform, the paper said, "We lead the nation in number of men in the armed forces. Why not lead also with our dollars?"[17] Liberty Bonds paid 3%; mortgage money paid 6%. Still Oak Park outdid itself buying bonds; its self-image demanded it.

When the boys came home again that spring of 1919, the same Village enthusiasts demanded bonafide heroes. They were not disappointed. John Cadman came home with broken ribs, fourteen stitches in his side and the Croix de Guerre.

"Wouldn't have missed it for all the money in the world," he puts it; and then he adds with a reminiscent smile: "Every one of those fellows were fine chaps, all high school grads, and I got to see what the size of the world really was."[18]

Baldwin Reich died, bravely of course, meeting death with a smile, *Oak Leaves* reported:

> Early in the morning he was wounded in the arm by a machine gun bullet, but refused to go back. For two hours he worked his automatic rifle and finally was killed. . . . When the final bullet came he dropped with a smile and gave the gun to his loader and urged him on. A little farther on we looked back and he was still waving his hand. At night we went back and found him dead.[19]

Lieutenant Roy Peck came back an air ace, wearing the Distinguished Service Cross – five official kills and four probables. Lieutenant John Gleason got his D.S.C. when he "led his platoon against a strong point defended by machine and anti-tank guns, leaving his tank and leading his command on foot thru a mine field, under heavy rifle fire and machine gun fire. Two days later, in the Montrebeau Woods, he led his platoon against machine gun nests, cleaning them out."[20] Oak Park was not disappointed by its sons. They proved themselves, in the words of Roosevelt, to be made of the right stuff. If the newspaper had questioned their softness before the war began, it now detailed each heroic act.

War stories as well as medals proliferated. It was not enough to have been a myopic Red Cross ambulance driver blown up while distributing chocolate. Pressured by his peers and local expectations, Ernest Hemingway kept right on inventing his fantasy war, the war he would have fought if only he had been given the chance. When the Memorial Committee of Oak Park and River Forest sent out its questionnaire to returning veterans, Hemingway promoted himself to First Lieutenant in the Italian Army. He had served, he said, first in the American Volunteer

Ambulance Service and then in the 690th Infantry Brigatta Ancona. He had fought in three major battles: the Piave Offensive, Monte Grappa between October 26 and November 2, and at Vittorio Veneto.[21] Not a word of it was true.

Wherever one turned in Oak Park, some heroic vet was lecturing on his war experiences. At the Oak Park Club, Marine Lieutenant Curly Brooks "gave an interesting talk, interspersed with clever, amusing anecdotes." Amusing anecdotes were Hemingway's forte. Barely a week back, he got himself invited to speak at the high school:

> The Hanna Club began this year's program on Friday evening, January 31, with a wonderful speech by Ernie Hemingway. He described some of his companions under arms and the fierce way they fight. The attendance was the largest in the history of the club.[22]

"Ernie" told wild stories about Arditi troops who stuffed cigarettes into their bullet wounds and kept on fighting. Throughout his talk, of course, was the implication that he had been one of them. He told of his wounding and how the mortar sounded. The students loved it. The next day, Art Newburn, who had driven ambulances with Hemingway in Red Cross Section Four, returned to Oak Park. He must have been a little surprised to hear of Hemingway's exploits. He had been on Monte Grappa when Hemingway made a short visit while still convalescent. He might have remembered that Ernest was sent back to Milan with a case of jaundice. If he did, it did not stop Hemingway, who knew how to entertain an audience. He gave variations of that talk several times around town – at the First Baptist Church, the Lamar Theater, the Southern Club. At the conclusion of his address to the Longfellow Woman's Club, he told the ladies "to pay no heed to the vicious rumors circulated in regard to various relief organizations."[23] In his "boyish straightforward manner" he did not tell them that he drove for the Red Cross, which remained a sore point, not to be discussed.

Hemingway's lecture circuit concluded with a return engagement at the high school before the entire student body. Warming to his audience, he displayed his war-shredded uniform, adding new details to his heroic deeds under fire. "One man near him whose leg had been shattered was crying openly, calling his mother's name. Lieutenant Hemingway told him with characteristic Yankee repression to 'Shut up with that noise.'" Waiting for the stretcher bearers to arrive, "he threw away his revolver, the temptation to finish the job was so acute." "Then," he said, "I did the only brave thing I did in the whole war – I told them to take the other guys first."[24] Red Cross men, delivering chocolate, were not issued revolvers, but it gave such a authentic note to the story. The pain had been true, real and deep; now the audience knew, from the fictive revolver, just how deep. Here, early in his myth making, suicide was a recurring idea. A decade later in *A Farewell to Arms,* Passini, his life blood draining from where his leg had been blown away, would scream: "Oh mama mia, mama Mia. . . . Oh Jesus shoot me Christ shoot me. . . . Stop it. Stop it. Stop it. Oh Jesus lovely Mary stop it."[25] At Hemingway's own wounding this probably did not happen; it was a fiction from the life he was creating. Pretending to heroism borrowed from trench veterans, seasoned perhaps with a little of Captain Marrayat's fiction, Hemingway enjoyed the local attention. He may have even come to believe parts of his story, at least for the moment. If the Villagers could swallow his tales unsalted, it made a good joke. He told the *Oak Parker* that he had "received thirty-two 45-caliber bullets in his limbs and hands, all of which had been removed except one in the left limb." Twenty-eight of the slugs, he said, were "extracted without taking an anaesthetic."[26] Sometimes it was difficult to keep the jokes separate from the life he was inventing.

The imagined life was not new for young Hemingway. He had been doing it in his stories for some time, inventing lives that he admired. The summer of 1917 – a year before he saw the war – he wrote a piece about Jack Marvin, a much decorated American pilot who returns an ace but still cannot satisfy his father. As the story opens, his father, an ex-champion boxer, is telling Jack, who has just been knocked out in the ring, that he is yellow. The war background came straight out of the magazines and newspapers, including the knowing references to Billy Bishop, a much publicized American fighter pilot.[27] It is a boy's story, a boy trying to please a demanding father. Clichéd and sentimental in treatment, the theme would recur in Hemingway's mature work. Nick Adams' relationship with his father, the doctor, will be strained, lacking some essential ingredient. Nick and his own son will find barriers that they cannot cross.[28]

As he was enjoying the limelight of his invented life, Hemingway wrote several war stories set in Italy. "The Passing of Pickles McCarty" or "The Woppian Way" – a sort of "Horatio Alger goes to war" tale – was another clichéd piece written to a slick magazine model. Nick Neroni, a promising boxer fighting under the name Pickles McCarty, disappears from the ring to join an Italian Arditi battalion. At Asalone he carries on the attack armed only with a knife in each hand. His heroism on the Carso and during the Monte San Gabrielle battles makes returning to the ring pointless. Before Hemingway was finished revising the story in 1919, he achieved the point of view characteristic of his early fiction. The narrator is a forty-two-year-old journalist trying to slip into the besieged Dalmatian city of Fiume, where, in September of 1919, Gabriele d'Annunzio, poet and war hero, led a band of irregulars to claim Dalmatia for Italy. The Peace Conference was determined that the area go to Yugoslavia. Hemingway had never seen Fiume, but he had read and admired d'Annunzio, the last romantic Italian hero. His narrator tells us:

As I smoked I thought of the great amourist who had exhausted the love of women and now was wringing the last drops from love of country onto his white hot soul. Of how he had set the decrees of nations aside by his filibuster. This hero with his occupation gone. A lover who had failed in only one pursuit, that of death in battle. Would he find the death he was looking for at Fiume, or would he be cheated again.[29]

The journalist narrator buys secret passage on a fishing boat where he meets Nick Neroni, also bound for Fiume to fight beside the poet–patriot. He had not seen Nick since he watched him as a boxer before the war. As they sail toward the besieged city, Neroni tells the narrator of his war experiences. This rather elaborate frame for the story allowed Hemingway to have the hero tell his adventure to the passive narrator, who then tells the reader. He would use this detached point of view more than once during his novitiate.

During the following year, the *Saturday Evening Post* and *Red Book* both rejected "The Woppian Way." The last summer before the war, Trumbull White, journalist and editor of *Everybody's Magazine,* told Hemingway to write from personal experience.[30] Almost two years later, he still had not taken the advice. From the slick models, he was imitating the style; the results read like imitations. It would take him three years to find his own voice, and five years before he could treat the Italian experience honestly.

Brash and naive, Hemingway was certain he could convert his real and imaginary life into immediate cash payments, for that was the point. If he could become the writer that he told Agnes he was, she would marry him. Unfortunately, the American reader was a little jaded with the war, for there had been little else to read now for over a year. As the *New York Times* put it:

America mobilized some four million men, most of them young men. It is a mathematical certainty that among them were included thousands of actual and hundreds of thousands of potential playwrights, novelists, and short-story writers. . . . every man who ever wrote fiction or drama before he went to war has seen something that he must hasten to use in a book or a play, and this same urge will have undoubtedly seized on many who were innocent of literary ambition before the war showed them how easy it was to get into print. . . . that practically everything that a novelist or dramatist can say about the war has already been said is beside the point. . . . It is hard to convince any author that he has not something new and essential, which he alone can furnish to a presumably eager world.[31]

If Hemingway had read the editorial, it would not have deterred him. He was on a romantic quest; there was a beautiful woman to be won. He had never been loved by a beautiful woman before. In another part of the country, Scott Fitzgerald had been turned down by an equally beautiful woman, who told him that he did not have enough money. Fitzgerald's hope of winning the lovely Zelda rested on the novel he was writing. Fitzgerald published *This Side of Paradise* and got his reward. Hemingway wrote in vain. Home only a month, he began sending off manuscripts to *Saturday Evening Post*, vowing to bombard that magazine until it gave in.[32]

The *Post* never published a Hemingway story. His imitations returned to him without fail and without comment. Even publication, however, would not have won him Agnes. In March, she wrote him that theirs had not been true love. She was engaged to Duca Domenico Carracciolo, whom she met in the devastated Torre di Mosto. Later she would say that she had not seriously intended to marry Hemingway. She was eight years older, too old to marry him. Her concern had been to get the young man home, away from the older Jim Gamble, whose influence Agnes feared would ruin Ernest. She said:

> Leaving Europe wasn't easy to do because Gamble liked him very much and had money. He wouldn't have had to worry about a thing. I think I felt – more or less – an obligation to look after him a bit. I don't think I was crazy mad about him. He was a very attractive person. He had wit and you could enjoy his company. But I don't think I – I had the feeling that if I shoved him out then, he would start off on that European tour.[33]

Agnes may not have thought theirs a serious affair, but Hemingway certainly did. She was the first mature woman who had loved him. Her rejection, coming as it did with rejections from the *Post,* was an emotional defeat. His invented persona was crumbling apart there in Oak Park, reducing him once more to Ernie Hemingway. He was furious, hurt and much alone. The emotional wreckage sent him to his sick bed at North Kenilworth, where he eased the pain with the bottle of kummel he had smuggled into the house from Italy. It was not just a broken heart; it was a broken mirror. Agnes had believed in the young writer he created. Now, when he most needed her support, she deserted him. Hemingway never forgave her. Although their paths would not cross again, Agnes Von Kurowsky was not forgotten.

That spring of 1919, sulking in his room, he tried to cover his wounds with cynicism. He was already possessive of women — sisters, friends and sweethearts. Reacting almost like a father, he disapproved of his sisters' boyfriends and eventually of their husbands. Later, his several wives would find that divorce did not set them completely free, for he continued to count them in his retinue. He would always need the support of women, need their presence about him. Once he recovered from the hurt of Agnes' rejection, he set about collecting a pride of mostly older women, who found him attractive. In rapid succession over the next sixteen months, he fell in love with any pretty girl in close proximity. To be a man in terms of Oak Park values, he needed a wife. If ever a man was looking to get married, it was Ernest Hemingway in 1919. He was only nineteen, but he continually created the impression that he was several years older. As one of the youngest Red Cross drivers in Italy, he habitually made his age one to three years beyond the truth to fit in more comfortably with the college men who were his peers. From that point on, most people thought him older than his age. He let them. During his brief experience on the Kansas City *Star,* he learned the trick of credibility: a reporter had to appear authoritative, an expert on his subject. He knew that no teenage kid could appear that credible, and he was determined never again to appear unsure of himself. Belief and enthusiasm, Roosevelt said, were the keys: without them there was little chance of doing "a man's work in the world."[34] The rejection by Agnes temporarily blunted his enthusiasm, but not his belief in himself.

Mornings on North Kenilworth, when his father was making his rounds, his mother at club meetings, his sisters in school, Hemingway stayed in his third-floor room writing, He began revising an untitled story begun on the trip home. The story opened in the Galleria of Milan, where an older man tells the young narrator of a poker game he once played. A card shark has, he thinks, set up a "pigeon" for a high stakes kill. The older narrator, seeing the action, folds his hand early. The shark lures his victim into higher and higher bets before the final call. He turns over four kings. The "pigeon" turns over four aces. The remarkable part, the older man tells the young narrator, was that he had folded with two pairs of his own: aces and kings. The shark had cheated and lost at his own game, for his victim was in reality a card sharp as well.[35]

In form the story was not unlike a Kipling "barracks room" piece and, as such, unremarkable. The reversal is an O. Henry touch Hemingway would later use to good effect, but not here. The Galleria story contained little character development or complexity. However, its point of view – older narrator telling young narrator about a game in which he was a witness but not the principal character – was more complex than anything Hemingway had yet attempted. Before he read Joseph Conrad or met Ford Madox Ford, the young Hemingway was learning technique on his own. He was also exploring once more the relationship between an older, more experienced man and a young novice. The old pro's credentials are confirmed by a gold cigarette lighter, engraved with thanks from the Prince of Wales – a gift for winning a horse race that the gamblers were betting to lose.

Gamblers, boxers, veteran soldiers, card players – Hemingway's early subject matter was the life denied in Oak Park, the life beyond the Village limits. He read about it in the Chicago *Tribune*; he and his high-school friends played at it with their secret poker games; he had seen the fringe of it in Italy where he bet on fixed horse races, but nowhere in Oak Park could those kinds of risks be taken. The Village seemed much smaller now and much smaller-minded. He did not show his parents those stories, but steadily he worked at them. That the stories did not noticeably improve was due more to his models than to his writing skills. If Hemingway's subject matter violated the decorum of Oak Park, his basic theme – winning – did not.

Winning was the heart of Village life. Measure it in money or medals or votes, measure it by lots sold or cars owned, but always measure it. The old gambler's engraved lighter was another form of measurement. —

Oak Park measured its war effort in numbers: men enlisted, money raised, bandages rolled. It kept careful count: medals, wounds, deaths, sweaters, socks, hours. They had all been tallied in the weekly paper. The war effort was a mixture of football game and society fund-raiser. The same names that dominated the club dances headed the Patriotic League and the Red Cross Auxiliary. One business man offered a $100 reward for the first Oak Park boy to win a war medal. Another bought, outfitted and donated a patrol boat to the U.S. Navy with the stipulation that his two sons serve on it. Now that the game was won, Oak Park was as eager to "return to normalcy" as the rest of the country.

While Hemingway worked on his penciled manuscripts, his mother listened to Dr. Soares at the Nineteenth Century Club tell the cultural leaders why "It Must Never Happen Again," just as President Wilson's idealistic plans for the peace settlement were beginning to crumble. At the William Beye School in Oak Park, first-graders were demonstrating their skills in marching, tumbling and "going over the top." Uncle George Hemingway got up an Own Your Home Association to push house sales during what was becoming the country's first full-fledged post-war recession. *Oak Leaves* urged all to promote the ideal of home owning, to increase the Village's distinguished record for "the number of home owners, the beauty of their gardens, and the inspiration of domestic and social life."[36] Uncle George was shrewd about money. When it was pricey, he built and promoted rental flats. When rates dropped, he built houses. In bad times he close-hauled, making do with his mortgages and insurance sales. During the two years of war, building had been at a standstill. Now was the time to sell houses to the newly married vets who would settle down to work, if they could find it.

Doctor Hemingway could not have agreed more; the vets, including his son, should settle down to work or go to college as the Hemingways had for two generations. If Ernest did not want to follow his father to Oberlin, a good Congregationalist school, he might go to the state university. What the Doctor could not agree to was the expense for Grace's new cottage. Hemingway's mother spent the spring planning a lake cottage of her own, paid for with her own money. Clarence advised against it: she would be too isolated across the lake, too far from the children; the strain would be too much for her. But it was her money; she could do as she pleased.[37] Grace did, contracting in May with a Horton Bay builder to erect a small cottage on Lake Walloon land she had purchased with an inheritance fourteen years earlier. The Doctor wrote the builder to say that he, Clarence Hemingway, was in no way responsible for his wife's debts. Later Ernest would blame his missing college education on his mother's extravagance, saying she had spent his college money on her Longfield cottage. It was not true. Grace's cottage cost barely $1000, which she could afford from her various inheritances. There was still money left, and the Doctor, who made only $4000 to $5000 dollars a year, was essentially debt-free in 1919. When his oldest son did not go to college that fall, he sent Marcelline to Oberlin. The money was there for Hemingway's college, but four years in school did not fit with the self-image he was creating.

While his mother's cottage turned into a bloody family battle ground, Hemingway tried to ignore the surrounding conflict, the hard words and the tears. He had come back from the war to find his father more snappish, more "nervous," as the family referred to his condition. His mood shifts were less easily dealt with now that Ernest felt himself a man. More and more he and his father argued over matters of little value. "Father and Son" week in February went uncelebrated at North Kenilworth. Without any plan for his future with which he could placate his father, Hemingway fought a holding action. If he lasted until May, he could get away to the lake for a last good summer. He invited Bill Horne, a fellow ambulance driver; Charles Hopkins, who had worked with him on the *Star*; and Bill Smith, who summered at the lake. If he could get enough good people together for the summer, the future could wait.

Chapter Three

SUMMER PEOPLE: PART ONE
1919

I N the summer of every year the Hemingways lived in a house
that looked across the lake to the farm. At the edge of the lake
there was a boat dock, dry and grey in the sun, and the water
shimmered and lapped in the shallows. Summer people went by
the house and down the road to the town. It was the same every
summer. First there was packing and shipping the barrels of food
and supplies, followed by the boat trip up the big lake. Then it
was summer and there was fishing and swimming. Sometimes in
the dark he and his sisters swam naked in the lake, but that was
before the war when they were all much younger.

At first they traveled to the lake together – the Doctor and the
Doctor's wife, Ernest and Marcelline, then later Ursula and
Sunny, and later still Carol and Leicester. Carol was born at the
lake. Ernest remembered that summer quite clearly. They went
to the lake together each July, and each September returned
together. Their coming and going was usually noted by *Oak
Leaves,* partly because the Doctor wanted his patients to know
and partly for another reason. Not all Oak Parkers could afford to
vacation for two summer months.

Friends sometimes came to visit at the lake. One summer
Louis Clarahan spent a month with Ernest, fishing, exploring,
sleeping out in a tent. Relatives almost always came a little,
staying a few days. That sort of visit was usually in the paper,

which in those days printed everyone's name as frequently as possible. The summer of 1911 that Uncle Willoughby visited from China, the cottage and the annex had been jammed with Hemingways.

> This has been Hemingway week at Walloon Lake, Mich., where Dr. and Mrs. Clarence Hemingway and family have been spending the summer at their cottage, according to their custom. They have had as their guests on this occasion Dr. Hemingway's mother, Mrs. A. T. Hemingway of Oak Park, and his brothers, Dr. Willoughby A. Hemingway . . ., George R. Hemingway . . . and Alfred Tyler Hemingway of Kansas City, all of whom were accompanied by all or part of their respective families. The four brothers had not been together for more than eight years.[1]

Sometimes grandfathers came to the lake. Ernest could almost remember Grandfather Hall, who had died in 1905. Sometimes he thought he remembered his visit to the lake, but he might have been remembering the pictures. It was hard to differentiate the summers, so much alike in those days before the war. Each September the paper would print a little notice of their pending return: "We are in receipt of a communication from Dr. C. E. Hemingway, in which he says: "I will be back on duty in Oak Park Thursday, September 11. We have had the best summer of our lives."[2] That is what his father always said – "the best summer of our lives" – said even after he stopped coming to the lake with the family.

Being away from Oak Park all summer, young Hemingway missed out on the social life of the Village, missed picnics and Fourth of July celebrations, missed summer league baseball games. With his myopic eyes, he was a mediocre player, but he missed the friendships that carried over from summer into the school year. No matter: summers on the lake were magic times when he was young. When he was not reading, he was living the life that he read. Ojibway Indians, who lived not far from the cottage through the woods, sometimes came down the road selling handmade baskets. Sometimes his father hired them to saw up beached timber into fire wood. The summer that he was twelve, Dick Boulton and Billy Tabeshaw cut up a beech log that way. His father took a picture.[3] Ernest remembered that scene a long time, the details etched clearly in his mind. Or did he remember the photograph? He was not sure.

It had all changed. Not the lake or Windemere cottage, they were the same after the war. He still woke to the smell of balsam fir and the lapping of water. The sun on the lake glittered as silver as ever, and the low surrounding hills were as dark green as he remembered them. The white clapboard cottage had not changed. The mantel still held its pictures and forget-me-nots from other summers. His mother's piano still needed tuning. But everything else had changed. It had been changing for some time and he had not seen it. As he grew into his teens, there were more duties, more chores expected of him. The stove needed wood; the dock, fixing; across the lake, his mother's land – Longfield Farm – needed a strong back in the potato field. Each summer Ernest saw less of his father. Each summer his father left earlier, coming back alone in the fall to close up the cottage. Each summer his father worried more about the money.

Now it was all changed. Oak Park had grown so large that the paper no longer bothered with the coming and going of Hemingways. In May 1919, as soon as it was warm at the lake, Ernest slipped out of Oak Park, escaping alone to that last good country. He found his mother's new cottage at Longfield almost finished. She would spend at least half her time there with young Carol and Leicester, leaving Ernest and the older girls somewhat alone. His mother would have Ruth Arnold, her live-in voice student, for companionship; Ruth had been with them on North Kenilworth so long that she was part of the family. The plan was fine with Ernest except for being alone with Marcelline. A year older than Ernest, Marcelline was becoming more and more like mother Grace, always taking her side in the arguments just as he usually sided with his father. She and Ernest were fondest of each other when apart. When he was around her, Ernest could see another Oak Park society matron in the making.

Ursula was something else. She wrote to him at the lake:

I'm going to Jackson Park with Marvin. . . . He's loads of fun and has a marvelous car. He's not the same Marvin as the one whose pictures I have – This is a different one. I only met him Monday. Tues. I went to the movies with him in the afternoon and riding with him in his machine in the evening. Wed. he and I and George somebody and Helen went to Lincoln Park in Marvin's car and didn't get back till the folks had had supper. . . . Mother and Dad are peeved with me as usual and Mother says I can't go this afternoon but I'm going just the same because she's going out herself. . . . I'm not coming home after school any day next week any more than I have this week! I'm striking!! I don't know where it will end and I don't care. . . . Don't say anything to the folks about anything that I've told you because I'd jes naturally get hung.[4]

He was not sure that he approved of Ursula's attitude. Certainly he had not openly defied the family rules when he was in high school. There'd been no car to spin about in. His father drove the car always. When he was Ursula's age there were strict rules and time tables, strict accounting. There was football and swimming practice, papers to deliver, a lawn to mow, school work and reading. Whenever he was seriously errant, he wrote his father a note, admitting to his fault and promising to be better.[5] His sisters needed some watching over; he knew exactly what Marvin was after and it was not Ursula's brains.

For a month he had the lake to himself, but he was not alone. Part of the time he stayed with Bill Smith, an older summer friend from St. Louis whose aunt owned a cottage at the Bay. Ernest put in some time helping Bill with garden work.[6] Sometimes he saw Marge and Pudge Bump. Sometimes he went into Horton Bay to eat at the Dilworths or he went over to Joe Bacon's farm which was close to Grace's cottage. But mostly he wrote, fished and thought about what he was going to do when the summer ended. All the while his leg continued to bother him; his right knee sometimes stiffened and ached. That summer to brace it, he wore a tight elastic bandage on his knee cap. Under pressure, the bits of metal left from the wounding were working their way to the surface; in April he'd had a few more pieces of shrapnel removed in the Oak Park hospital. Ernest was learning to live with his rebuilt knee, but he was still having trouble sleeping at night. Once he was worried enough to visit Dr. Guy Conklin in Boyne City. Forty-one years later, Dr. Conklin remembered that "Ernest was badly shell-shocked when he came for treatment in the summer of 1919."[7] In Boyne City, Dr. Conklin had not seen much of the war's aftermath. If he thought Ernest was shell-shocked, it was because Hemingway wanted him to think so.

In June, Grace, Ruth Arnold and his sisters arrived; Ernest helped them move in to both cottages and set up for the summer. They were all very happy then, playing out a familiar ritual. Ruth, quiet as ever, seemed prettier than she had in Oak Park. Always she stuck close by his mother, sharing her delight in the new Grace Cottage, as his mother named it. The children had heard enough of their parents' arguments that spring to know that their father did not approve of the cottage. What surprised them was that their father did not give in, and that she built the cottage over his objections. None of her children really understood how important the cottage was to Grace Hemingway, but they had not read the letter she wrote her husband in a last attempt to get his approval:

It has been my purpose for 14 years ever since I purchased the farm in the face of strong opposition and much abusive language to build a little cottage on this very hill. . . . That it has been steadily thwarted up to the present time has only piled up disappointment – as each year against my advice and desires the farm was leased to the thieving tenants who stole from the place wood, crops, fruit and the very seed sent to them to plant. . . . I have gone faithfully 21 summers to the same place Windemere which was very pleasant and adequate for 8 or 9 years but after my father's death [1905] and two subsequent attacks of typhoid fever which I underwent to say nothing of other causes the place became hateful to me, so much so that I had a nervous breakdown summer after summer when I was forced to spend a summer there, shut in by the hills and lake, no view, no where to go, acting the part of the family drudge, standing at sink and cook stove until the agony in my spinal nerves forced me to lie down and then turn up again and at it, day in and day out. Too exhausted to swim or go anywhere when the opportunity afforded. These have been my summers for many years until the very sight of Windemere brings tears to my eyes and a sob to my throat.

This year . . . I said to my husband, when he was not in a contentious mood, "Would it not be lovely to have a little haven of refuge on our hill, a little shack where we could sleep, and be alone, for a while or have just the little children with us." . . . This was the answer to my prayers for I could do this with my own earnings and be beholden to no one. I could then stay just a mile across the lake – come to and from and help and guide my big children and justify my judgement in their sight by proving to them that the hill top on the farm was a sweet livable place and a joy to them as well as to me. The building of this cottage right now would mean the saving of my nerves for the future and a demonstration in neatness cleanness simplicity and wholesomeness which is sorely needed right now by my four daughters who have an idea that excitement is the only form of happiness worth while.

I pray to God to move your heart to kindness.[8]

After reviewing the letter, she crossed out the phrase *and much abusive language.* Before recopying it, she crossed out the final line as well, not wanting to leave the matter in God's hands. She was going to build the cottage whether or not God moved her husband's heart. God did not and she did.

Clarence Hemingway did not come to Windemere that summer. All the girls agreed with their mother that two months by himself would be soothing for his nerves, which had been strained for some time. His erratic shifts of mood – now gentle, now angry – pained and puzzled his children when they were younger. Now that his older daughters were of age, his unpredictable behavior, while still puzzling, became at times almost impossible to bear. Gradually over the last six years they had seen less and less of him at the lake.

In April 1915, Clarence went to Walloon by himself for a brief vacation, but he was not there at the end of July for Ernest's great blue heron fiasco. When the game warden's son discovered a dead heron in Ernest's boat, Ernest said the dead bird was given to him. A quick lie: he had shot it himself, an impulsive shot with his sister Sunny in the boat watching. The warden's son took the bird for evidence, and Ernest rushed back to Windemere, stopping only long enough to explain the incident. He then went across the lake to Longfield Farm, leaving Grace and the girls to face the game wardens, who soon appeared asking for the Doctor and Ernest. Grace wrote her husband, "I thought them burglars or fiends of some sort, they had such a beastly insinuating sneering way, and would not tell me their business." They said they knew about Ernest's shooting the bird. Grace told them, "If you know so much about my business and that of my family you don't need to give me any further impudence. This tackling a lone woman and her little children . . . and asking impudent questions is not the way to behave yourselves." When the wardens wanted to borrow a boat to cross the lake, Grace refused them. She was less upset about the bird than about Ernest's lying, but "he said he was scared, and said the first thing that came to him. I have not acknowledged anything about the matter, if you don't know, you can't talk." Grace was a large woman and her defense of her son was equal to her size. The wardens did well to leave when they did.[9]

Before he got his wife's letter, Clarence Hemingway had already heard of the incident, probably from his brother, George, in Ironton where Ernest arrived on the run. The Doctor immediately wrote his fugitive son:

Write and tell me the whole of the particulars from "Crackers" trip to date. When was this and were there

witnesses? Who "squealed"? If you have a trial insist on a
jury trial and plead guilty *but innocent* of a legal offense.
Keep *all* guns in window seat until I come. *No hunting!* I
wrote *that* after your rainy hunt early one morning with
Sunny. No guns in a *boat* at *anytime.* Shoot only *vermin* in
emergencies. Remember Daddy loves his big boy and prays
he will keep careful and out of trouble.[10]

The whole incident resolved itself with a $15 fine before a
judge in Boyne City. The heron, however, was not the first
illegal bird Hemingway had killed; on the Evans game farm that
edged Oak Park, he had poached pheasant without getting
caught. His attitude toward the hunting laws was modeled on his
father's. Earlier that summer Ernest wrote his father about a fine
buck he was tracking. His father said he would kill it out of
season when he came up to the lake.[11] In a traditionally religious
home, the Doctor still felt that animals and birds were put on
earth to be hunted. If the law said they were not to be shot, one
simply took care not to be caught. Religious commandments had
nothing to do with game laws. Once in the woods, a man was on
his own, responsible only to himself and the rules of sportsman-
ship. Like his father, Ernest grew to be certain of moral right and
wrong which had little to do with the law, particularly for a boy
raised on the outskirts of corrupt Chicago politics.

When the heron story resurfaced in Hemingway's imagination
almost forty years later, it had become more threatening, more
sinister than it ever was in fact. "The Last Good Country" has
Nick Adams hiding out with his little sister, pursued by game
wardens for an illegal deer kill. In the story it is Nick and his
sister against the world of brutal lawmen, a childish fantasy from
the fiction of Stewart Edward White, a piece of ripe paranoia.
But Ernest was no more paranoid about lawmen than his father.
The law was not to be trusted, for it did not have one's best
interest at heart. As Hemingway aged, his characters became
more and more leery of government agents: Harry Morgan, rum
and illegal immigrant runner in *To Have and Have Not,* loses his
boat to lawmen for whom he has no respect. The white hunter in
"The Short Happy Life of Francis Macomber" pays little attention

to the African hunting laws while being true to his own; Colonel Cantwell in *Across the River and Into the Trees* has lost all respect for bureaucrats and "chickenshit regulations": his ideal is General Patton, who made his own rules. Thomas Hudson, in *Islands in the Stream,* embarks on a suicide mission outside the law, fighting under his own rules of warfare.

And at the very end of his life, Hemingway, traveling westward, was sure that the F.B.I. was following him, sure the Inland Revenue Service was going to take all his money, sure that his bank account was empty. When he checked into St. Mary's hospital for electro-shock therapy for his depression, he worried that taking an assumed name might be a felony.[12] As he aged, he was most happy when outside the three-mile limit – fishing the Gulf stream, or leading irregular troops without authority well ahead of the U.S. Army's push to Paris in World War Two. Had there been any uncharted lands remaining, he would have been a good explorer, providing the team was small and faithful.

His earliest published fiction from high-school years deals with vengeance and bloody murder outside the law. In "Judgement of Manitou," Pierre, who thinks his trapper partner Dick Haywood has stolen his money, sets a snare trap that leaves Dick hanging head downward waiting for wolves to finish him. When Pierre reaches the trap, "Two ravens left off picking at the shapeless something that had once been Dick Haywood." Moments later, the French Canadian steps into Haywood's bear trap. Rather than wait for the wolves, Pierre kills himself with his rifle. The setting, the Far North where it winters at forty-two below zero, is from Stewart Edward White. Dick Haywood "talked to himself as to the travellers of the 'silent places'." White's book *Silent Places* popularized the phrase. The two ravens came directly from a favorite poem, "The Twa Corbies," who pick the bones of the fallen knight. Pierre's suicide is not unlike the one recommended by Kipling to the wounded British soldier on the Afghan plain: "roll to your rifle and blow out your brains." Hemingway's story righted a moral wrong by a somewhat poetic but effective justice outside the law, where, given the proper circumstances, suicide was justified.[13]

In his senior year, Hemingway published "Sepi Jingan," the

story of Indian Billy Tabeshaw's dog who saves Billy from dying at the hands of Paul Black Bird. Billy, telling the story to a nameless but admiring secondary narrator, says that Black Bird could never get drunk, but he always went a little crazy when he drank.

> Paul was Jack-fishing [spearing fish illegally] over on Witch Lake . . . and John Brandar, who was the game warden, went over to pinch him. John always did a job like that alone; so next day, when he didn't show up, his wife sent me over to look for him. I found him, all right. He was lying at the end of the portage, all spread out, face down and a pike-pole stuck through his back.

Because John Brandar was his cousin, Billy takes on the job of tracking down the murderous Black Bird. Ambushed and flat on his back, Billy Tabeshaw is about to go the way of his cousin when his faithful dog, Sepi Jingan, rips out Black Bird's throat. Billy puts the body on the rail line where the "Pere Marquette Resort Limited removed all the traces."[14]

Once more a murderer has met justice without resort to civilization's laws. The theme and the distrust begin early and stay with Hemingway all his life, but they are not abnormal for the times. One need look no further than Owen Wister's *The Virginian* (1902), dedicated to Theodore Roosevelt, to find a similar theme and distrust of the law. When the law is corrupt, rustlers are hanged without benefit of judge or jury. Wister's hero, however, has the good sense to realize that the wild West is past and done; civilization has caught up with the frontier. At the end, the Virginian wisely marries the eastern school marm and buys a small ranch with coal deposits to sell to the coming railroad. For Wister, the country's social and political salvation rode on the marriage of eastern culture and western grit. For Hemingway, the marriage was unconsummated. In his imagination he continued to pursue that lost frontier, searching for the last good country.

The woods and water about Windemere, the Pine Barrens to

the north, the Fox River, the Black — these places were his touchstones. Until the summer of 1918, he had been there every birthday since his first. Lake Walloon was the spawning ground that pulled at his genetic self. Over the years he watched his father lose the lake. The adult world of work, family, bills and responsibilities slowly eroded the pleasure of Windemere. A house full of women did not help. If Hemingway did not seem eager, that summer of 1919, to make plans for the future, perhaps it was because he knew that adults gave up such pleasures. He had put off going to the war for a last summer on the lake only to have it interrupted by the Red Cross orders to sail. This summer might be his last one free. From the Traveler's Insurance payments on his leg wound he still had some money left, but he knew he must take work eventually. He wanted this summer to last as long as possible.

He and Bill Smith, both long-time summer people, gathered friends for extended trout fishing in the Pine Barrens and streams of the upper Michigan peninsula. Red Cross drivers, Kansas City *Star* and high school friends, anyone who loved trout fishing came to the lake that summer. As much as he could, Hemingway stayed away from the cottage and his mother, who continually wanted his help with some domestic task. With his friends, he could drink and smoke, but not around his mother. When possible, he stayed with Bill Smith in Horton Bay at the Charles cottage. Bill's sister, Katy, older than Ernest, attractive and quick-witted, accepted him that summer on equal terms; her slim figure moved nicely under the one-piece bathing suit and her bold, green eyes had a way of fixing a man. Already Carl Edgar was mooning about her like a lovesick puppy, but not young Hemingway. The world had changed and he was through with children's games. He had come back from the war tall, attractive, wounded and in love with Agnes. Agnes was behind him now, not forgotten, just behind him. The world was ripe with good-looking women who, for the first time, stared at him, flirted and kissed. They had been there all the time, but he had not been old enough before the war. Now he was older than he should have been, and the boy–girl game, he found, was played by summer rules much laxer than those of Oak Park. When he was not fishing for trout or working the farm at Longfield, he mastered the rules of summer.

Grace Hemingway had only two children with her at Lake Walloon that summer – Carol, aged eight, and Leicester, four. The rest of her brood were no longer children. Marcelline was twenty-one; Ernest, turning twenty; Ursula, seventeen; Sunny, fifteen. It was well that the Doctor remained in Oak Park, for his nerves would have been strained indeed by the summer men and boys attracted to Windemere. Both Marcelline and Ursula had bloomed into attractive young women, which the summer men did not fail to notice. Even Sunny, less attractive than her older sisters, was beginning to flirt and flaunt. Grace understood. Her girls were in season. She understood, but the game rules had changed since she had been a player: the girls were more forward, the boys less polite. Only Ruth Arnold's presence gave Grace Hemingway the support she needed.

Marcelline, filling out now as plumply as her mother, was in love with Walter, her first serious fellow. The Doctor, at long distance, having been told of the courtship, thought he should give Marce his fatherly advice. Grace could imagine what he would say and how Marce might react. She wrote him:

> I think it will not be best for you to write Marcelline on the special subject for the present. She is wobbly some days and some days perfectly sure of herself – so let time work it out as God wills. Marcelline is not a girl whose heart runs away with her head – she is cool and judicial. I am very patient and think best to keep hands off at this juncture. I feel the utmost confidence in Walter. He is a perfect gentleman.[15]

When Marcelline went into Petoskey with Walter for supplies, Grace sent Ursula with them "as it might cause a sensation in the minds of the rocking chair brigade for Marce and Walter both to leave with suitcases, together."[16] Propriety observed, Grace did her best to monitor her girls and soothe her husband's reactions.

Grace Hemingway found her husband easier to deal with in letters than in person, for she did not tell him everything that happened. Aside from her daughters' suitors and Ernest's cheeky attitude, the summer weeks were pleasant, drifting one into the other. It was easy enough to motorboat back and forth from her new cottage to Windemere, and the older girls took up many of the tedious chores. Gradually, piecemeal, the summer people disbanded, returning to families or jobs. On the first of August, Ruth Arnold returned to Oak Park, leaving Grace a little lonely. By the last week in August, Grace sent Marce, Ursula and Sunny home: Marce to a new job, the younger two to prepare for school's starting. Grace stayed on with Carol and Leicester, waiting for the Doctor to arrive, enjoying a little breathing space. The long summer, which Ernest had done little to shorten, played itself out. When needed at the cottage, he was all too frequently someplace else. Sometimes he helped; mostly he was off fishing, or bringing in friends for supper – more work for Grace, whose arthritis now turned the heavy work into an agony her son did not fully appreciate. Nor had he helped with Marcelline's courtship. Ernest did not like Walter. No sooner had Marce returned to Oak Park than he told his mother that Walter was not a man to be trusted, for he told lies. Having become something of an authority on lying, Hemingway knew exactly how to phrase it. Grace was in a quandary. She did not want to jeopardize Marcelline's prospective engagement to Walter; neither could she abide a liar. The summer lengthened.

Back in Oak Park life was not going at all smoothly. The Doctor had spent the hot months perversely scraping, varnishing and painting Marcelline's room. No sooner was she home than she told him that she intended to move out of the house. The summer heat and his doctoring had done nothing to improve his "nervous condition." The idea of his first-born daughter leaving home only worsened matters. Marcelline wrote her mother that the Doctor was no better than when they had left him for the summer. "He is still excited and exacting but we all try to get along as well as possible."[17] "Dad tries to be nice, but his temperment does not allow him to see things as I do – and tho we get along beautifully on the surface, I feel a thousand miles away from his soul."[18]

Grace understood, having felt the same way herself more than once, but she was certain that Marce would smooth things over with Clarence. If Grace was confident about her oldest daughter with whom she could counsel, about Ursula she was less certain. In Oak Park, Grace had worried about Marvin and his noisy roadster. At the lake Ursula replaced Marvin with Joe, who continued to come by the cottage after Ursula left. Grace worried more about the summer romance with Joe than about Marce's more serious courtship with Walter. Ursula wrote to assure her mother that there was nothing serious between herself and Joe, who had been a "pal" all summer. She pleaded with her mother not to question Joe about their relationship, for he would be offended.[19] With letters flying back and forth between Oak Park and Windemere, Ernest did not want to take sides in the Ursula conflict, for he knew his parents held him guilty of encouraging her behavior. If he knew anything about Marce's plans, he kept it to himself.

The Doctor told Grace how Ursula had behaved since her return, giving his wife more worries. From the Doctor's observation, the situation was serious: his second oldest daughter was boy crazy and bound for disgrace. Grace wrote; Ursula replied: "You seem to have gathered the idea that I must be an unprincipled infant. . . . I have trod the straight and narrow as nearly as anyone could . . . so don't worry yourself. I haven't 'fallen for' anyone. . . . so instead of leading the wildly exciting life you think I'm leading, I am really having a very placid, quiet time."[20] Her father did not believe that for a moment; he told his wife what was going on – boys in automobiles going heaven knew where; phone calls at all hours; coming home hours after school was out. At long distance, Grace must have wondered if her husband's distress was not more imagined than real. His "nerves" seemed no better for his summer rest, which he had managed to make as unpleasant as possible. The worst part, the part Grace truly did not understand, was the fuss he was making over Ruth Arnold.

All that hot summer in Oak Park, the Doctor had treated his patients and written daily, obsessive letters to his wife, numbering each and keeping carbon copies. Each letter battered Grace with details of the heat, the work load, the steady pressures of the house. When he missed a day's letter, he explained how his fingers, numb with fatigue, could not master the typewriter. Two of his letters – both originals and carbons – are missing from the family archives. From the existing evidence, it is clear that the Doctor's missing letters explained why he would no longer allow Ruth Arnold to live with the Hemingways. She could not even visit the house. Ruth, who first came to Grace as a voice student in 1907, had become a permanent fixture at North Kenilworth. The youngest daughter of a River Forest salesman, she was not overly bright, nor had she a promising voice, but she was sincere and hard-working. Dominated at home by her older sisters – one a dress maker, the other a piano teacher – Ruth blossomed at the Hemingways. In 1908, she moved into North Kenilworth as a live-in student and part-time baby sitter and cook. She was thirteen years old, and she loved Grace with daughterly devotion. When Grace was away from Oak Park on her annual mid-winter vacation or summering at Walloon, Ruth wrote her simple, loving letters: "Ever since I've known you, my soul has craved for the luxurious and more beautiful things in life – not so much for bodily comforts as for uplifting surroundings" (1909).[21]

On the Doctor's birthdays, Ruth gave him gifts, and her family once sent him a bouquet of asters. In the Hemingway tradition of nicknames, Ruth was called variously "Boofie" or "Bobs." Her letters to Grace were addressed: "Dearest Muv." Some summers she went to Walloon with the family; always she was one of the family, an older sister to the children and a confidante to Grace. By 1912, her voice was strong enough for a recital in Grace's music room, where she had the day to herself. In 1919, the Oak Park directory listed 600 North Kenilworth Avenue as Ruth's address. She was twenty-three years old, quiet, physically attractive, and Grace's most admiring friend.

When the Hemingway children – first Leicester, then Marcelline and Sunny – wrote autobiographies of their home life, the name of Ruth Arnold did not appear. Oak Parkers all, the children knew better than to rattle the closet bones. Whatever the

Doctor's reasons, the conflict festered beneath the surface during the hot Oak Park summer. Ruth returned to Oak Park on August 2, arriving in the middle of the worst race riot in Chicago history. The trains, she said, were running late. All summer she had given Grace moral support in her decision to build her cottage. Now Ruth was already homesick for Grace. "No distance," she said, "can separate my soul from the one I love so dearly."[22]

On her arrival in Oak Park, Ruth phoned Dr. Hemingway to assure him that Carol's brief sickness at the lake had cleared up and the family doing well. Whatever else she said is lost to us, as is Dr. Hemingway's letter to his wife, written that very day. All we know is Grace's reply:

> Yours of Saturday and Sunday received last evening. Marcelline also had one from you which grieved her as much as mine grieved me because we both realize from those letters that you are no better for the 2 months rest from the family. I have so hoped and prayed that the quiet would help you to readjust your mental attitude and find yourself with God's help in relation to your family. If your mental attitude is really not a thing within your control, then you can count on me to help you all in my power, as long as I live. I will never fail you in trouble. I love you and grieve for you. However, the world is still wholesome and my dear blessed children with all their faults still need me and the dear faithful Ruth, who has given me her youth and her loyal service for these many years, needs me. This is my platform. I shall desert none of you, for fancied wrongs on the part of anyone of the number. You are each one as dear to me as life, and no one in the world can ever take my husband's place unless he abdicates it to play at petty jealousy with his wife's loyal girl friend who has an unhappy and unsympathetic home life.[23]

Her husband's mind was clearly becoming more obsessed and erratic. Twice earlier in their marriage his "nervous condition" had become chronic; each time he had pulled himself together. This time he was pushing Grace right to the edge of her capacity to understand him. When Marcelline wrote from Oak Park at the end of August, nothing she said quieted Grace's fears about her husband's precarious mind. The Doctor obsessively turned any conversation around until he could rant about Ruth Arnold. Marcelline could not bear to hear it. When Ruth called, Marcelline could not tell her why she was banned from the house. When she visited Ruth in the evening, Marce could not tell her father of their long walks together.

No more could Ruth understand the situation. When the girls arrived in Oak Park she immediately called Marcelline to say she would come over, only to be told that she could not be invited. The Doctor would not allow it. Ruth pleaded with Grace: "Oh! dear what is the trouble now? You surely know, please tell me. If only my conscience were guilty I could ask to be forgiven, but I can't feel I am. . . . I have worked for and loved the Hemingway family so long that it seems impossible to cease going there."[24] She thanked God for giving Grace to her as an ideal, and she would have liked nothing better than to be with her that moment, brushing her hair or stroking her aching forehead. The next day Marcelline urged Grace to write Ruth who was lonesome for the family, wanting desperately to visit the children. Marce could not invite her over because her father acted "so insane on the subject."[25]

In the middle of it all, listening and remembering, was Ernest. Years later he would blame his mother for destroying his father and the happy home life he knew as a boy. Some would say that he hated his mother. In 1982, one of his own sons recalled that he was never allowed to visit Grandmother Grace because, Ernest told him, she was androgynous.[26] Allowing for Hemingway's penchant for hyperbole, the judicious reader will remember that love and hate are sometimes indistinguishable. All of Grace Hemingway's children were deeply influenced by her exuberance, which led her unerringly to center stage. The more her husband retreated from the world into his private distress, the more she filled the vacuum. Whether singing, painting or campaigning for local issues, Grace Hall Hemingway was always a public performer during those years when the feminist movement was redefining the roles of women. Later as Ernest continually reworked parts of his fictive life, he put the blame on Grace. By then his father was dead, a suicide. Rather than admit to himself that his father's "nervous" problems might have been a mental disorder, Hemingway found it far more convenient to accuse his mother. Mental problems were frightening and might be hereditary. "Once they've had you certified as nutty," one of his characters would later say, "no one ever has any confidence in you again."[27]

Marcelline had barely been home a week with the Doctor when she used her job in the South Church parish house as an excuse to move into a rented room. The day Clarence Hemingway was packing to join Grace at the lake, Marcelline wrote her mother:

> the tempermental clash that goes on in our house would absolutely ruin my disposition. . . . You and I know how perfect last summer was – How happy *all* of us were – and now we are not [happy] at home. The girls, Urs and Sunny, realize it, and we are very unhappy. I am sure it will be better when you get here. Dad does not *mean* to be irritable and exacting, and he does not even think that he is other than normal in every way, but the facts are that he is not normal at all, in his disposition or attitude toward us or our friends. I know he is tired and has been under a great strain, but . . . it is hard to adjust one's point of view to his outlook on life.[28]

In 1919, Ernest could not have ignored what was obvious to his sisters: their father had mental problems that had gradually over the previous sixteen years become more pronounced and more serious.

When Ernest was four, his father took a week's Thanksgiving vacation to New Orleans – a self-prescribed cure for his depression. He went alone but wrote almost daily notes to the family. Two months later he said that the New Orleans trip had been his salvation.[29] In 1908, Clarence took six weeks off from his fall practice to attend a post-graduate course in obstetrics at the New York Lying-In Hospital. Only Grace and the family knew that he spent the last two weeks of the trip in New Orleans, once more alone. Even Ruth Arnold, in her note to him, hoped that he returned "rested." Grace counseled him: "the way to rest is *not* to read Oak Leaves and get into the old train of thoughts but to give your mind a vacation."[30] She was also concerned that no one in Oak Park should know that he was going to New Orleans. "Do you want me to let the local press know about this vacation? Don't you think it perhaps wiser to let them keep the first idea in their minds that you are taking 'post-grad' work in New York? . . . Try to forget all about us while you are on board ship and rest the worry place in your brain. Just make a business of eating and sleeping and forgetting."[31] Later Ernest would say that his father had been caught in a trap only partially of his own making. What he did not want to discuss was the possibility that the trap had been biological.

Dr. Hemingway's bouts with depression were, to a certain extent, triggered by financial stress: in 1903–04 and again in 1907–09, economic recessions may have been responsible. Between 1917 and 1919, he again exhibited signs of erratic behavior and depression; this time the stress of the war, the murderous flu epidemic and the wounding of his son combined to produce his "nervous" condition. Simultaneously, Grace, who had always earned a considerable income from voice lessons, began to lose pupils to more advanced musical academies then developing in Oak Park. With the Doctor probably making only $4000 a year from his practice, the Hemingway annual income was seriously eroded.

Like any husband with a large family, Clarence Hemingway frequently worried about money: unnecessary household expenses; Grace's cottage; the college education of his children. In 1909, he left a letter to his wife and children listing almost $50,000 of life insurance spread out among eleven different companies and organizations as diverse as the Loyal Americans of Springfield ($1000), the Order of Columbian Knights ($5000), United

States Life Endowment ($5000) and Equitable Life Assurance Society ($10,000). In the text of the letter, he gave Grace explicit advice to follow in the event of his death:

> Understand – the Accident Policy is for Accidental Death or *blood poisoning,* and the Health Policy . . . is not a *life insurance.* . . . All others are for *death benefits.* . . . don't let your grief or sentiment come in between your good dead husband [and] the future provision of and for the necessities, and education of the darling children and your own self – Grace my darling.

With his meticulous list, he left explicit instructions for collecting on the policies: tell one story; write it out; tell all the companies the same story. "And *don't tell all you know* about your own affairs to every one. . . . should there be any doubt at all as to the cause of death . . . make an autopsy and if a Coroner's Inquest is called have Dr. [unreadable] or Dr. Hoektorn [?] present in my interests for you. . . . if *Accident* is Blood Poisoning you can realize on the Aetna Policy."[32]

In 1917, before undergoing surgery to correct a hernia, Dr. Hemingway left a similar list of insurance policies and instructions. In 1928, Dr. A. F. Benson, Coroner's physician, testified that on the sixth day of December, Clarence Hemingway put a bullet into his "right temple 3 centimeters above the external auditory meatus and 3 cm. in front of the ear. The bullet pierced the brain looping under the skin, after shattering the bone of the skull in the left temple 5 cm. above and 7 cm. posterior to the external auditory meatus. There were powder burns at the point of entrance of the bullet. Blood was oozing out of the bullet wound."[33] Six Oak Park men on the Coroner's Jury ruled the death a suicide. Viewed retrospectively, Clarence Hemingway's letter of 1909 reads, perhaps, more ominously than it was intended. There can be no doubt, however, that his "nervous" condition grew progressively more serious after 1904. His compulsive behavior increased steadily. When separated from Grace by their vacations, he wrote a letter each day, and each day expected Grace's letter in the mail, becoming morose if it failed to arrive. The dark brooding over his own death, if not his possible suicide, is there in the 1909 letter. Clarence Hemingway's mind was not well. His wife had known it for some time. For the children, the recognition took longer.

In 1928 the family attributed his suicide to financial worries, the most socially acceptable explanation in Oak Park where men of good breeding took their own lives for only two reasons: money problems and insanity. None of the family wanted to suggest the stigma of insanity, and Clarence's brother George had reason to suppress information on the Doctor's financial affairs. Grace Hemingway, too prostrate with grief she said to appear at the Coroner's Inquest, sent her thirteen-year-old son Leicester to give the bare facts of the suicide. Uncle George testified that his brother had diabetes and a bad heart – a "hopeless case." His mental condition, George said, had been sound and his financial affairs were "in good condition." Neither statement was true. Uncle George apparently wanted the jury to see the suicide as a mercy killing. What George did not say was that Clarence had mortgaged his debt-free house to invest in Florida land that George was touting. He did not say that the Florida land market had peaked; the Doctor was holding lots that were not appreciating.

Clarence Hemingway died at age fifty-seven, suffering from angina and diabetes. The diabetes was treatable with the newly synthesized insulin. A man could live a long time before dying from angina. His Oak Park house was worth more than his debts; his children were mostly grown and three of them were so financially secure that they could have helped in emergency. He had been granted a license to practice medicine in Florida where he was planning to retire. When he closed the bedroom door, sat down on his marriage bed and put the steel barrel to his temple, it was not only the diabetes or the debts that squeezed the trigger. He fell back into a bed that had been a long time making, a bed so wide and deep that it took three of his own children to fill it completely.

Insomnia, erratic blood pressure, blinding headaches and

severe depression were the genetic heritage of Ernest Hemingway, his sisters and brother. They carried it as a legacy from both sides of the family. At age forty-nine, Grace's brother Leicester's insomnia, which bothered him over twenty years, became chronic. Grace herself suffered from mild insomnia, "nerves" and recurrent, blinding headaches that sometimes lasted five days. Her eyes, weakened she claimed by scarlet fever, were in fact genetically weak. Bright light hurt them. Clarence's brother Alfred was also an insomniac, who suffered from "nerves" and low blood pressure.

The genetic union of Hall and Hemingway produced serious problems unto the second generation. Almost all of their children had eye problems, requiring glasses. Ernest, who refused to wear the glasses until after his marriage, had myopic eyes, mildly light-sensitive. Both Marcelline's and Leicester's eyes were markedly weak. Marcelline, Ernest and Ursula all suffered periodically from blinding headaches. Ernest's several severe concussions made worse a situation already serious. The three of them also suffered from insomnia. After being wounded in Italy, Ernest's insomnia grew worse, but Marcelline and Ursula suffered from the same complaint. Marcelline had low blood pressure. Ernest had high blood pressure. Marcelline and Ernest both suffered from diabetes, and both went through periods of severe depression. Eventually three of the Hemingway children took their own lives: Ernest in 1961; Ursula in 1966; Leicester in 1982. Marcelline's death in 1963 was reported to be of natural causes. Leicester suspected suicide. Not Marcelline nor Ernest nor Ursula lived as long as three of their four grandparents. At least one of Marcelline's children suffered from insomnia, hysteria and depression. In high school, the child suffered a partial loss of memory and a nervous breakdown, attributed finally to a low thyroid condition, but the depression recurred even after thyroid treatment.[34]

When Ernest Hemingway put the muzzle of his double-barreled shotgun to his forehead the morning of a much later July, he suffered from all of his father's ills: erratic high blood pressure, insomnia, paranoia, severe depression. Like his father, he kept meticulous lists. Like his father, he saved every totem that touched his hand. Like his father, he wrote letters with fanatic intensity. While courting Hadley Richardson, he wrote to her every day, sometimes twice a day, for almost a year. When he did not receive his daily reply, he was despondent. Like his father, he worried about money when he had no worries. Like his father, he frequently behaved erratically, with rapid mood shifts and sometimes vicious responses. Under stress, real or imagined, the idea of suicide recurred insidiously. Like his father, he was caught in a biological trap not entirely of his own making. The blood line of Clarence Hemingway and Grace Hall has left us several books that will outlast all memory of Oak Park's fine families, but the cost was high.

By the middle of September of that first summer after the war, the lake was beginning to cool. In the clear, chilly night Clarence and Grace built a fire over the hearth stone of Windemere, where, for the first time in many years, they were there in their cabin together, almost alone. Carol and Leicester, asleep, were the ages that Marcelline and Ernest had been those early years at the lake. It must have been a little like time way back, when life was measured from summer's end to summer's end. Gradually the cares washed clean in the lapping of the lake. Their oldest son was back from the war only slightly damaged. Their oldest daughter was close to marrying. Their other four children were apparently healthy. Their Oak Park home was paid for; the Doctor's practice sufficient. Ernest kept away in Horton Bay, leaving them this time to themselves. All of the summer's sharp words and turmoil slowly lost meaning. They did not talk of Ruth Arnold, for Grace knew that Clarence's fits eventually passed. She had gotten her cottage built and survived what might have been called a disastrous summer. Now it was over. Never one to dwell on misfortune, Grace must have told herself that next summer could not possibly be so painful. She had a lot to look forward to.

Chapter Four

STILL LIFE WITH PARENTS
1919–1920

THE cars went on up the road out of sight, around the point at the edge of town. Ernest sat down on the porch with his luggage. He was happy. He had not been unhappy all winter or spring. This was different though. There had been things to prove to himself. Now they were done. There had been a job to do in Toronto. Now that was done. He had done the job. He had made his own way. His stories had sold to the Toronto *Star*. Not the stories of Italy, but newspaper stories. The real stories all came back to him. That did not matter. He had settled the question of who he was. He was a writer. When people asked, that is what he told them. If he stuck to his story, it would become true. Now he was almost home at the lake and it was summer. He was there, in the good place. He was still free. He would try not to let anything spoil the summer.

He had stayed on as long as he could the previous fall. After the summer people had all departed, leaving their addresses, he stayed on at Horton Bay until the waters no longer lapped at empty bottles, cigarette ends and other testimony of summer nights. When it turned too cold to fish, he moved into a rented room in neighboring Petoskey where Marjorie Bump, the cute summer waitress, was in high school. Marjorie, her sister Pudge and Grace Quinlan were like having his sisters with him. Except Marjorie was more than a sister, with her red hair, wide grin and firm little body. She was a nice complication; he could have her if he wanted. Maybe he could have her. There were some in Petoskey who thought he already had. She was two years younger than himself, and together they were special. In a town as small as Petoskey, it was not difficult to seem special. In St. Louis, Bill Smith heard third-hand rumors that worried him: Petoskey people said that Marjorie Bump was engaged to Ernest Hemingway. While he knew that it was not true, he was certain that Marge and Petoskey thought it was. Bill was afraid that Ernest would hurt Marge deeply. [1]

But Ernest had been lonely, needing an audience to play to. The three girls marveled at the stories he was writing when no one else was there to hear them. The stories had been the whole point of the winter. On the typewriter he borrowed from Bill, he stuggled all fall and early winter to break into the popular magazines. When *Saturday Evening Post* flatly rejected his latest version of "The Woppian Way," Ernest wrote on. Edwin Balmer, an older summer person and published short story writer, read some of the manuscripts the previous summer. He encouraged Hemingway, even suggested helping at some vague future date.

No matter how hard he worked at his stories, Hemingway had not yet learned to invent out of his own experience. He used settings that he knew – Kansas City, Chicago, Italy – but the characters remained weak imitations from other men's work. In one untitled story, Punk Alford, a Kansas City newsman who carries a gun, is able to solve the crime that baffles the police. Alford is not, the narrator tells us somewhat awkwardly, the journalist one is accustomed to find in fiction. He does not have wavy black hair; he does not smoke; he does not have a degree in journalism. Punk Alford, after fifteen years on the job, still works late and gardens in his spare time. His winter hobbies are reading seed catalogues and plotting murder mysteries which he never writes. Sent to cover the murder of Henri Barbusse, Alford finds the victim cut almost in two by a missing sword. The police are mystified, but Alford is determined to play "Arsenic Lupin" and catch the killer, which he does of course. Simple logic leads him to Richard Marsden, a world traveler in British East Africa,

Afghanistan and Tibet, who collects old weapons. Alford finds him holding a two-handed sword that once belonged to Richard Coeur de Lion, a sword that Marsden loves like a woman and also fears for its strange power. "I was afraid that sometime I would use her," he tells Alford. To get the sword out óf his life, he sold the weapon to Barbusse, but then Marsden, regretting the sale, went to buy it back. Barbusse would not sell. In a rage, Marsden killed him with the sword. Alford understands, remembering in Homer how the sight of weapons can excite a warrior to violence. Alford and Marsden walk down to the river, where Alford throws the sword into the black water. Marsden hesitates and then follows the sword, choosing suicide rather than jail.[2]

As with much of his juvenilia, Hemingway filled this story with slang phrases and newly acquired interests. Alford, for instance, prefers François Villon's poetry to that of Robert W. Service. Henri Barbusse's name was lifted intact from the French author, whose realistic war novel *Under Fire* Hemingway read in Milan. As with his half-fictional fishing stories for the Toronto *Star*, Hemingway slipped a familiar name into the plot: "Mussey," who runs the city desk, is taken from Morris Musselman with whom Hemingway was collaborating on a play. The Punk Alford character, later to proliferate in the B movies, is from Ring Lardner; the plot is from *Black Cat* mystery magazine; the style is out of *St. Nicholas* magazine for children. Dying with his sword rather than on it, Marsden's stoic suicide is a barely motivated but convenient ending in a disturbing pattern. Both Marsden and Nick Grainger, when trapped by circumstance, choose suicide rather than let fate grind them out. Only the Kansas City streets bear the least semblance to Hemingway's own experience. Not a word of the dialogue rings true. The story went unsold.

Imitating the market place – the slick magazines like *Saturday Evening Post*, *Century*, and *Red Book* – Hemingway was not confused by theories of literary art. The point of writing fiction was to make money. Before 1920, he never read the "little magazines," and even after he did, he seldom published in them: they did not pay. His goal from the start was to make a respectable living from his fiction. Whatever that required he would do, but he expected payment in return. Two years later, in his nastiest bill-collector's voice, he would dun John McClure, editor of the *Double Dealer,* for a paltry sum. Payment, however small, legitimized the work. That he had learned all his early life in Oak Park, where his only unearned money had been birthday windfalls and a meager allowance. Before Hemingway went to the war, his weekly allowance was 17 cents – a penny for each of his years – barely enough for tram fare to Chicago's Loop and back.

It took him five years to find his true métier, and seven to find the market place. First his narrative voice had to lose the worldly-wise tone he picked up around the city desk of the Kansas City *Star.* That Petoskey fall he wrote a piece he called "The Ash Heels Tendon," the beginning of which illustrates how much he had yet to learn:

> In a former unenlightened time there was a saying "In vino veritas" which meant roughly that under the influence of the cup that queers, a man sloughed off his dross of reserve and conventionality and showed the true metal of his self. The true self might be happy, might be poetic, might be morbid, or might be pugnacious. In the rude nomen-clature of our forefathers these revealed conditions were denominated in order – laughing, sloppy, crying and fighting jag.
>
> A man with his shell removed by the corrosive action of alcohol might present as unattractive an appearance as the shrunken, misshapen nudity of an unprotected hermit crab. Another with a rock-like exterior might prove to be genial, generous and companionable under the influence. But there were men in those days on whose inner personality alcohol had no more effect than a sluicing of the pyramids with vinegar would have on the caskets within.[3]

Trying to sound like an experienced observer of low life, here is the young Hemingway doing Kipling in south-side Chicago. He is using that slightly condescending but knowledgeable narrator that Kipling used about every third story, a narrator detached from the natives and to whom it is given to witness strange or comic events. Compare Hemingway's beginning with the following from his master:

> Shakespeare says something about worms, or it may be giants or beetles, turning if you tread on them too severely. The safest plan is never to tread on a worm – not even on the last new subaltern from Home, with buttons hardly out of their tissue paper, and the red of sappy English beef in his cheeks. This is a story of a worm that turned. ("His Wedded Wife")

Both writers, master and apprentice, are going to tell us moral tales to illustrate their opening adage. Kipling can get away with it; Hemingway cannot, for he over-writes the opening, trying too hard to be a man of experience. Moreover, as Hemingway's story reveals, he simply does not know enough about Chicago gangsters and police detectives to carry the story off.

Jack Farrel, the Irish police detective in "The Ash Heels Tendon", sets out to capture a hardened assassin, Hand Evans, who is known to frequent a local bar. Evans has turned up to kill one Pinky Miller, who is told: "Somebody's due for a one way trip to that land out of which's bourn no travellers return. You ain't afraid to die, are you, Pinky?" But the detective knows the gunman's weakness, his "ash heels tendon" as Farrel calls it. The young Hemingway could not resist mixing Ring Lardner in with his Kipling and Shakespeare. Evans, we discover, is really an Italian – Guardalabene. At the crisis a Caruso record plays and Guardalabene is so emotionally overcome by the Italian tenor that he is easily captured by Farrel. The Italian gunman may have been able to drink without showing ill effects, but he was vulnerable to opera.

Most of the action takes place in a bar, where the bartender provides a good deal of flashback information. Knowledgeable bartenders would be part of the Hemingway stable for the rest of his writing life. The significant consumption of alcohol, for which he would be later criticized by a generation that did not understand the effect of Prohibition much less the effect of Oak Park's abstemious gentry, would always be a part of Hemingway. And because he drank, some would assume that he rebelled against all of Oak Park's mores. Not true and not the point. The "dry" vote in Oak Park, rallied by churches and supported by drinkers and non-drinkers, was to prevent saloons and riff-raff from encroaching on the Village. Unlike the Hemingway house, most of the affluent families had their liquor cabinets, from which Hemingway and his high-school friends occasionally nipped. What irritated Hemingway was the hypocrisy that would vote dry and drink at home. In the 1919–20 stories, Hemingway's characters frequently drink or hang about bars, as does many other fictional character during those days of Prohibition.

His earliest characters are frequently winners – boxing champions, fighter pilots, ace reporters, tough war veterans – usually young and audacious. Like Horatio Alger's heroes, these men are the masters of their own lives; nothing is impossible for them once they have put their minds to it. Unlike Alger's and more like Kipling's characters, these men live outside of normal or respectable society: they are men without homes and without women. It is a little like an Alger character living on the underside of American life, Ragged Dick before he got out of the Bowery. Hemingway, who very early read all the Alger he could find, was himself operating in a familiar Alger mode: pluck and luck. As he later said, anyone could become a writer if he worked at it hard enough. He had worked at it hard for over a year now without much luck.

Among the several rejected manuscripts in his suitcase, there was a series of unfinished sketches begun the previous November of 1919 and unlike anything else he had tried. He called it "Cross Roads." He and Bill Smith almost simultaneously saw that the local inhabitants of Horton Bay might become amusing fiction. Bill's response to Hemingway's suggestion kicked off the project:

Isn't it odd, but I was just thinking myself of sketches anent
the Bayites. Together we could tear 'em off easy. I don't
know about alone. You try it at least. I will myself. One
trouble is I can't tell the form in which to put 'em. I spent
about a 1/2 an hour on what I enclose. It's 250 words but
don't you think an introduction is necessary? I can't see how
you'd handle the first one in a paragraph. After that it
would be fairly easy. I can do the dialogue like Babe Ruth
connecting for a triple but I can't tell about the other part of
it. . . . Perhaps you can work it over in some way or suggest
a proper method of writage. If you want to, toss in a
description of Bert or begin the thing down on the point as
it really took place. I didn't do it because it would make it
too long.[4]

What Bill enclosed was a sketch of Bert, a local farmer, talking
in local dialect about Bob White, the only man from Horton Bay
to serve in the Great War. In less than a week, Smith was reading
five similar sketches that Hemingway had typed out on Pauline
Snow, Ed Paige, Bob White, Old Man Hurd and Billy Gilbert,
an Ojibway Indian war veteran. Smith read them carefully,
replying with astute observations.

Billy Gilbert is a whang – a pearl of the primal hydrazation
and the others are fair but not so good as I know you can do.
To me, Bird, they aren't quite human enuf. I believe I'd
toss in a little more dialogue. That's the salient feature of
the Bayite aside from his character which can be well
divulged thru the medium of conversation.[5]

Hemingway's sketch of Billy Gilbert shows the young Indian
returning to the Bay after his enlistment in the Black Watch. No
one at the Bay pays much attention to his three would stripes or
his impressive decorations, because they don't know what they
mean. Besides, all the boys came back with ribbons, some of
which they purchased after their discharge. The Bayites are much
amused by Billy's kilt, making it the butt of jokes. When he

reaches his shack, he discovers that his wife has sold their meager property, taken up with Simon Green's boy and moved down state. Billy, without comment, shoulders his pack and marches down the road into the dark whistling "It's a long way to Tipperary."[6] Billy Gilbert is much like the other young men who populate Hemingway's early fiction: a war veteran with wounds and decorations, self-sufficient, and an outsider. His restraint under social pressure is new, as is Hemingway's ironic depiction of the unappreciated veteran. Six years later Billy would reappear in Hemingway's satire, *Torrents of Spring*.

More daring and much more prophetic was Hemingway's sketch of the waitress, Pauline Snow. We are told by a detached and invisible narrator that Pauline is the only beautiful girl ever to grow up at the Bay. "She was like an Easter lily coming up straight and lithe and beautiful out of a dung heap." Shades of Stephen Crane's *Maggie,* which it seems impossible that Hemingway had read in 1919. When Art Simmons, her lover, tells her, "We didn't come down here to talk about sunsets, kiddo!", he sounds a lot like Maggie's lover, Pete. Pauline, lovely and frightened, goes on long evening walks with the rough-handed Simmons until the neighbors begin to complain. The sketch ends with Pauline being sent off to the correction school at Coldwater, and Art, after a little while, marrying one of the Jenkins girls. It is a bucolic *Maggie* done in two hundred and fifty words.

These sketches represent Hemingway's earliest use of Horton Bay and its people. When he published his first Nick Adams stories five years later, the Bay is their setting. Pauline becomes Liz Coates, and the story becomes "Up In Michigan," probably the earliest story in Hemingway's published canon. The concept of an understated, ironic sketch to reveal attitude, character or situation matured eventually into the brilliant paragraphs of Hemingway's *in our time* (1924). When Bill Smith told Hemingway to let the characters reveal themselves through their own words, he could not have given better advice. Dialogue would, of course, become his hallmark.

Encouraged by Smith, Hemingway wrote three more sketches:

old man Horton, Hank Erforth and Warren Sumner – all real people from the Bay area. The Horton sketch brings in local folk belief when Horton's sick wife refuses to die until the feather bed is removed from the house. Hank Erforth and his burning house receive no aid from some summer people who think he is simply moving furniture. The Warren Sumner sketch is almost as brutal as the Pauline Snow one. Mrs. Sumner, who spent her youth as a camp follower to the lumberjacks, has bequeathed one of her daughters a nose caving in, possibly from syphilis. Warren won't have it treated but he is having her teeth straightened, for they still have possibilities.[7] Speaking in their own distinctive dialect, the Bay characters are the first indication of Hemingway's potential. Here his gift for satire combines with the detached, ironic understatement that eventually will serve him well. Here, also, is that vicious side of Hemingway that served him less well: all the characters were real people living around the Bay.

Later the critics would find innumerable influences on Hemingway's early work. Gertrude Stein and Sherwood Anderson, quite rightly, would get most of the credit. But in the fall of 1919, he had not yet read Anderson (*Winesburg, Ohio* had just been published), and he was two years away from Stein and Paris. Their influence on his early publications is important, but they were not the first influences. The idea for the sketches came from his model for fiction – *Saturday Evening Post*. As soon as Bill Smith read the first sketches, he wrote Hemingway that "Any of your stuff tho has this 'Anthology of Another Town' in current Sat. Post beat."[8] What both Hemingway and Smith had read that fall was the beginning of a long serial by E. W. Howe: "Anthology of Another Town," a nostalgic collection of small-town characters whose otherwise dull lives were sometimes punctuated by a remarkable experience. If that sounds like *Winesburg, Ohio,* we should not be surprised. Small-town life in rural America was becoming the subject matter for several writers. Hamlin Garland's stories in the 1890s had depicted the joys, frustrations and minor tragedies of the farm community. In 1916, Edgar Lee Masters exposed small town lives with his *Spoon River Anthology,* to which Howe's title alluded. The tragedy and comedy beneath the dull lives of rural characters became popular with urban readers who had themselves escaped such settings no more than a generation or two earlier. Grandfather Anson T. Hemingway, after long years as a city man, fondly recalled his early life on the farm, and the Hemingways still had rural relatives living in Dyersville, Iowa.

Howe's sketches, like the Hemingway and Smith imitations, are quite short, some no more than a few words:

Hon. Martin Holbrook

Ten years ago Martin Holbrook was a member of Congress and has been proud of it ever since. But people do not remember his efforts in their behalf. About all they say of his experience at the Capital is:

"You wouldn't think that man had been in Congress, would you?"[9]

Others run to two and three hundred words. None is much longer than a single column in print. The point of view is always that of a detached narrator relating what he has overheard or observed, and usually making some comment on the character.

Sandy McPherson

Sandy McPherson, the barber, says he charges five dollars for shaving a dead man because he is compelled to throw away the razor he uses. But how do we know he throws the razor away?[10]

Just as Bill Smith urged Hemingway to do, Howe frequently lets the characters' own words make his point. As for models, Hemingway could have done worse than Howe, a veteran journalist and realist from the preceding literary generation and author of the well-known *Story of a Country Town* (1883).

When a shortage of funds drove Hemingway to a Toronto job in January 1920, he had finished eight of the Horton Bay sketches. Their terse form had to be taken to Gertrude Stein's school in Paris before he could hone it to the cutting edge of *in our time*. The detached and slightly ironic point of view that he tried out in "Cross Roads" eventually became his own, but that 1919 winter in Petoskey, he did not fully realize the possibilities. The sketches went no further.

Just as the Traveler's Insurance money for his wounding played out, Hemingway fell into the softest job of his life: paid companion to young Ralph Connable, son of the Canadian head of the Woolworth stores. Mrs. Harriet Connable heard Ernest give his bloody Italian War lecture at the Ladies' Aid Society in Petoskey. Like most older people (with the exception of Hemingway's parents) Mrs. Connable was most impressed with the young man just a year older than her lame son. Her husband offered Hemingway the run of their impressive Toronto house, with its cook and maids, library, tennis court, skating rink and billiard room; in return, Ernest would spend the winter as young Ralph's companion while the Connables and daughter Dorothy sunned in Florida. Ernest would have his days free, for Ralph had a tutor in the mornings and worked at the Woolworth warehouse in the afternoons. Hemingway's main duty would be to accompany the boy to evening entertainments and weekend events, "sports and pleasures that would be sane and sensible," like the boxing matches. Ernest's days were to be his own to use for his writing. The Connables would pick up all of his expenses and pay him $50 a month. With two million veterans out of work, the job was a gift from heaven. Hemingway immediately accepted.[11]

It was stop-gap work, something to do to get through the year to another summer at the lake, a reprieve from making a decision, a little more time to write. His parents still wanted him to go to college; he was playing with the idea, but not too seriously, In April 1920, Ted Brumback wrote Ernest of his visit to North Kenilworth. The two old friends from Kansas City and Red Cross days were vaguely planning on going to the west coast and working their way to the Orient as seamen. Because such an adventure meant forgoing college, Hemingway's mother was particularly opposed to the idea. As Ted explained,

I talked eloquently about the inestimatable opportunity such a trip would give you in the writing game. Your mother is against it as she wants you to go to college. I told her that it's life that a budding young author must see for himself. Musty books will never make one able to write. I cited O. Henry, the greatest short story writer of all and he had had practically no education. . . . the same with Stevenson, Kipling, Conrad and others. . . . Your mother was convinced it would be a fine thing, but still she deplores your lack of "college background" whatever that means. I told her "college background" had never done much for me. Of course she's fundamentally right but there's no reason in the world a man shouldn't educate himself. [12]

After the war, it was his mother who continually brought up his college education. Ernest went so far as to visit friends at Michigan and Illinois, but never committed himself, for at some point during his senior year in high school he had decided to become a writer. Since the end of the Civil War, the portal to the profession had been newspaper work, not the university. London, Norris, Dreiser, Crane, Howe, Lardner, Ade and Twain all had their roots in journalism. As Carl Edgar, a summer person and Kansas City *Star* friend, told him: college was "of damn little practical value" for the novice writer. Writing, he said, "takes one hell of a lot of effort and moreover continuous effort to get anything you want. If you get anywhere in five years you'll be doing good". [13] Five years after Edgar's advice, Hemingway published *In Our Time*.

As Ernest rested on the cottage porch contemplating the summer before him, college remained a problem deferred. Soon enough the Hemingway brood would arrive at Windemere; soon enough he would have to deal with his mother's nagging. Still, he had a lot to feel good about: the stack of manuscripts in his suitcase; the girls who would be back for the summer – Marge Bump, Katy Smith, Irene Goldstein. Bonnie Bonnell wrote him from Toronto:

We, the undersigned, solemnly affirm and declare, that you are a poor prune, a drinker of your own bathwater and eater of your young; given to low African games and Dago drinks; a wine-bibber, a frequenter of dives, whose god is the belly.[14]

He was not certain he would ever go back to Toronto, but as long as there was a chance, Bonnie was a nice bit to have in reserve. It was good to have women now that their legs were showing. It was good to have the saved money in his pocket and the stories he sold to the Toronto *Star*. The *Star* was that unexpected bit of luck that every boy with pluck is supposed to get. Ernest made his own luck, hanging about the *Star* office so much that eventually they offered him piece work. He had strung out his credentials from the Kansas City *Star* without quite saying that he had been only a cub reporter, and he told wild stories about his Italian war and wilder stories about his youth – a runaway who had been riding the rails.[15]

Some of the features he sold to Cranston, the editor, were almost as interesting as the fictive life he had fashioned. He wrote stories on the prize fights, bootleggers, dice games and trout fishing – mostly feature writing on topics that would reappear in his fiction. Quite proud of his publications, he clipped them and sent them back to Oak Park both for his father's adulation and as proof of his professional ability. His father wrote: "Send me frequent papers with your work. I am so very pleased you have made good in your chosen profession."[16]

Although Dr. Hemingway encouraged his son's desire to write fiction, it seemed to him a chancy way to make a living. Journalism at least provided a regularly paying job. For Ernest, however, newspaper work was merely a support system that would give him the time for his fiction. Had he wanted a full-time job with the *Star*, he might have had it that spring, but he did not want to give up the summer at the lake. In the adult world of work, a man could not take the summer off to fish. This, the summer of his twenty-first birthday, might be the last good summer. He had thought that in the summer of '17 and again last summer. Summers at the lake you held on to as long as possible. His father had hung on until Ernest was about twelve; then the two months disappeared for him. That's what happened to you in the adult world. Ernest did not want to think about that prospect.

Since the previous summer he had been twice to Oak Park for all of two weeks. Neither visit went particularly well. At Christmas, he could not understand his father's Christian martyr role, nor did he have much sympathy with his mother's ever present physical problems. Now she was taking a wood working course at the high school. His father told him it was for her "nervous" condition. It was more likely physical therapy for her aches and pains, which were called rheumatism but were really arthritis. If anyone needed therapy for "nervousness," it was Dr. Hemingway, who would be the last to admit it. Clarence Hemingway could never accept physical ailments in his own body; for the doctor to be sick was an admission of defeat. His thwarted missionary dream got its only solace when he himself was ministering unto the sick. If he neglected collecting bills from his poorer patients, it gave him the pleasure of Christian charity. Ernest, in his affluent phase, would always collect his due, but he also gave money generously to friends in need. His father was with him always: in his blood and beneath the surface of his public life.

In the house of the Doctor, where six children and a talented wife vied for affection, sickness was the certain way to the father's attention. Ernest, for all his real physical problems, learned this lesson early and practiced it late, long after his father was dead. When he was a boy, Ernest responded to all of his father's passions: natural history, fishing, hiking, hunting. But after 1912, when young Hemingway most needed his father's strong male image, the Doctor seemed to lose interest in their common pursuits. Clarence Hemingway still loved the woods and the lake, but more and more he loved them alone; more and more Ernest had been shut out. He still remembered when his father, after twenty years, gave up the Agassiz Club just when Ernest became seriously involved in it. After his twelfth birthday,

Ernest spent less and less time with his father on the lake or in the hunting fields – a loss he could not understand. As his father became increasingly withdrawn, demanding, sometimes morose, Ernest tried ever harder to gain his affection. A sore throat, he discovered, could always get his father's attention. Ernest developed a lot of sore throats over the next several years. If his father had a hernia, Ernest developed a hernia. When his father suspected he had angina, Ernest immediately developed angina, or so he told friends.

The Christmas visit had not ended well. With the Doctor playing his long-suffering role, Ernest spent much of his week away from the house. When it was over, Clarence took his son's overdue books back to the Scoville Institute and returned Grandmother Adelaide's library card that Ernest had borrowed once more. He even cleaned up the room that Ernest left in such a mess. "Try to develope more responsibility and neatness and Order," he wrote his son. [17] From Ernest's point of view, it was not order that was needed in that house. He wanted his father to assert himself under his own roof, but could not tell him that. Later Hemingway would look back on North Kenilworth as a battleground on which his father lost the engagement.

> There is only one thing to do if a man is married to a woman with whom he has nothing in common, with whom there can be no question of justice but only a gross fact of utter selfishness and hysterical emotionalism and that is to get rid of her. He might try to whip her first but it would probably be no good. Whoever, in a marriage of that sort, wins the first encounter is in command and, having lost, to continue to appeal to reason, to write letters at night, hysterical logical letters explaining your position, to have it out before the children – then the inevitable making up, loser received by victor with some magnanimity, every thing that had been told the children cancelled, the home full of love, and mother carried you darling, over her heart all those months and her heart beat in your heart. Oh yes and what about his heart and when did it beat and who beats it now and what a

hollow sound it makes. I've seen him when we used to row in the boat in the evening, trolling, the lake quiet, the sun down behind the hills. [18]

In fragments and published fiction Hemingway tried afterwards to recapture the man, his father, as he was in the boy's early years.

His father came back to him in the fall of the year, or in the early spring when there had been jacksnipe on the prairie, or when he saw shocks of corn, or when he saw a lake, or if he ever saw a horse and buggy, or when he saw, or heard, wild geese, or in a duck blind. . . . His father was with him, suddenly, in deserted orchards and in new-plowed fields, in thickets, on small hills, or when going through dead grass, whenever splitting wood or hauling water, by grist mills, cider mills and dams and always with open fires. The towns he lived in were not towns his father knew. After he was fifteen he had shared nothing with him. [19]

American fathers so frequently disappoint their writing sons, leaving them heavy baggage to carry home.

That Hemingway did not see his parents clearly, that he blamed his mother whom he so resembled in temperament, that he carried his parents' conflicts with him forever makes clearer the crucial summer of 1920. If his father would not assert himself as the dominant male in the Hemingway family, then Ernest would be his surrogate. The summer of his majority became his declaration of independence in the war with his mother. He did not plan it that way, but that is how it worked out. If Grace thought the 1919 summer a constant skirmish with Ernest, she would remember the 1920 summer as a bloody battle fought largely across the kitchen table at Windemere.

The letter Grace Hemingway wrote Ernest in March did little to oil the waters that those two had troubled over Christmas:

Some day, dear boy, you will really come to *know* your mother. . . . You are always in my heart and prayers and I know that you will be a great hearted noble man because I have faith in God and confidence in you. Not for nothing are you the great great grandson of that noble Christian Rev. William Edward Miller and the grandson of the finest, purest, noblest man I have ever known, *Ernest Hall*.[20]

Grace's emphasis on the Hall side of the family, without any mention of the Hemingways, did nothing but focus Ernest's anger. He saw his father and his father's family as the victims of his mother's ego. He had only to look at the children's names to confirm his analysis. He had been named for his maternal grandfather and his middle name – Miller – came from his mother's uncle and great grandfather. Carol was named for Grace's mother Caroline Hancock Hall. Leicester bore the name of Grace's brother. Of the six children, only Leicester's middle name – Clarence – memorialized the Doctor and the Doctor's family.

Grace Hemingway never let her children or Oak Park forget her father or the Hall family. Soon after her father's death, the following story appeared in *Oak Leaves*:

In memory of her father, Ernest Hall, whose death occurred May 10, 1905, Mrs. Grace Hall Hemingway has presented to the Third Congregational Church a copy of Holman Hunt's "The Light of the World." The gift recalls a visit of Mrs. Hemingway and her father to Oxford in 1896 and a pilgrimage to Liddon Memorial chapel in Keble College, where the original painting hangs.

The artist has represented Christ standing in the dead of night before a door. The hinges are rusted and the doorway is overgrown with ivy. Before the threshold is a tangle of weeds. A bat driven from the shadows is circling about. The Savior bears a lantern in His left hand. His right is raised in the act of knocking. Upon his head is a crown of thorns.

The copy is more than half life size and framed in rosewood. It will hang in the auditorium of the church. A more beautiful memorial could hardly be conceived than such a subjet with such personal associations placed in the setting of a church. It will speak eloquently to a generation of the Christian character of the one in whose memory it is given.[21]

Every Sunday morning, young Hemingway saw the wandering Jesus with his sad, suffering face outside the closed door. And every Sunday he was reminded of his departed Grandfather Hall, whom his mother was forever holding up to him as a standard of excellence. It could not have escaped him that his mother's memorial gift was tinged with personal vanity: Ernest Hall was never a member of the Congregational Church in Oak Park. But then Grace Hall Hemingway was always one who let her little light shine. If the painting reflected well on her while it memorialized her sainted father, so much the better.

In 1932–33, Hemingway wrote a story called "The Light of the World," which was set not far from Lake Walloon. Nick Adams, coming in the night to the door of, not a cottage, but a railroad depot, opens it to discover five whores and a homosexual cook – not exactly what middle-class Christians expected Christ to find behind the closed door. The story, ironically, is still about Christian charity, but not in a form that Grace Hemingway would appreciate. Hemingway always said the story was a favorite of his. He also said, "It is about many things and you would be ill-advised to think it is a simple tale."[22] Given his mother's associations with the painting, this brutal little story became a private memorial to Grace's preoccupation with the Hall family.

His mother kept a detailed genealogy of that family, tracing it back to John Hancock and still more distinguished English roots. Although the Hemingway line also came from England, Grace gave them short shrift. When she died in June of 1951, Ruth Arnold, who had lived with her for years as a companion, found among her remains a cloying family history of the Halls, which Grace composed that her children might always feel pride for their heritage. In July, Ruth sent a copy to Ernest with the note, "Would like to hear from you." She signed it: "Love, Bobby."[23]

Grace Ernestine Hall was always her father's child. His love of music and opera led her to voice training in New York and a debut on the opera stage. When his wife died in 1895, Ernest Hall took his only daughter on an extended visit to England just before her marriage to Clarence Hemingway. She never forgot the trip, which was almost like the wedding trip that she and Clarence could not afford. After their marriage, they moved into Ernest Hall's house down the block from Anson Hemingway. There Marcelline, Ernest and Ursula were all born. When Ernest Hall died in 1905, Grace's inheritance, including the sale of the Hall house, allowed her to pay for the large house she built for her Hemingway family on North Kenilworth. The three-story stucco home had a small front office for the Doctor and an enormous music room for Grace's voice pupils and recitals. While Ernest was growing up, his mother's income was usually more than his father's. Marcelline remembers that her mother, at her peak, was earning $1000 a month. This figure is probably exaggerated, but it was larger than Dr. Hemingway's income which between 1900 and 1920 grew from about $2000 a year to perhaps $5000 a year. If Grace Hemingway had a large voice in the family's affairs, it was proportionate to her contribution.

Those were the days of the suffragist movement; those were the days before women could vote. In Oak Park, where the conservative majority was also progressive and where women had time, education and money enough to think for themselves, the feminists got a modicum of their voting rights as early as 1902, when, for the first time, they could vote for university trustees. Only twenty women exercised that privilege; Grace Hall Hemingway was one of the twenty.[24] Not long afterwards the Suburban Civics and Equal Suffrage Club was formed with Grandmother Hemingway as a director and her daughter-in-law Grace a member. One of Ernest's early memories from a trip to Nantucket was going with Grace to a suffragist meeting, through which he says he slept.[25] He would have done well to have listened.

In those days in Oak Park, wives were known in the newspaper by their husbands' names: Mrs. John Farson, Mrs. William

Barton. In contrast, Hemingway's mother always appeared as Mrs. Grace Hall Hemingway. Only two other women appeared in such fashion: Dr. Anna Blount, who led the suffragist movement in Oak Park and Illinois, and made contributions at the national level in the fight for the vote; and Belle Watson-Melville, a performer on the national Chautauqua circuit. Grace Hall-Hemingway – always hyphenated when she wrote the copy, unhyphenated otherwise – was a woman in advance of her time. She absolutely refused to submerge her talents beneath the waters of a male-dominated society. She may have given up a career in opera to marry Clarence Hemingway, but she never imagined that she was giving up her identity.

In Oak Park Grace was not only a leading voice teacher, whose students gave numerous recitals, she was also a composer. She wrote music and lyrics for such songs as "If I Could Know," "Madonna's Prayer," "Serenade," "God Laid Me Aside to Rest Me" and "Lovely Walloona." Although these titles may sound less than exciting today, in their time they pleased Oak Parkers well enough. They also pleased two publishing houses – Oliver Ditson Co. in Chicago, and Summy Co. in New York – pleased them well enough to publish the sheet music. Grace's royalties never amounted to any great figure, but in the years after the turn of the century, she quite rightly thought of herself as a professional musician.

Wherever Oak Parkers gathered in the name of progress or culture, Grace was there to perform her music: Woman's Christian Temperance Union meetings, Fine Arts Society, P.T.A., Congregational Church, suffrage meetings, or the Nineteenth Century Club. In a town filled with trained voices, Grace Hall Hemingway's contralto was in demand. In 1904 she and Belle Watson-Melville played to a packed house at the Third Congregational Church. The local newspaper account – never, to be sure, critical – shows us Grace at her prime.

Mrs. Hemingway was received with great enthusiasm and her artistic rendering of her entire portion of the program was of a decided excellence which few ever attain. The pathos of her first love song still rings in our ears. This was followed by the "Serenade," of Mrs. Hemingway's own composition, a brilliant number and brilliantly sung. Mrs. Hemingway's last song, "If No One Ever Marries Me," displayed her wonderful versatility. She became suddenly piquant, saucy and full of childish enthusiasm. We appreciate Mrs. Hemingway here in Oak Park and wish we might hear her more frequently.[26]

When first married, Grace sang with some regularity at Oak Park's most preferred church – the First Congregational. But when Mrs. Furbeck, wife of an Oak Park leader, got a stranglehold on the choir, the Hemingways in 1904 moved to the Third Congregational. There Grace quickly became chairman of the music committee and director of the vested choir, in which both Ernest and Marcelline sang in their time. Music in Oak Park was also politics.

Grace Hall Hemingway never cherished, accepted or resigned herself to the role of housewife and mother. For most of Ernest's home years, she employed two girls living in: a maid/cook who periodically came and went, and Ruth Arnold, baby sitter and confidante. Some have said that the Hemingways could not retain their hired help because Grace was impossible to work for. *Oak Leaves* belies the rumor. In seventeen years, ten new maids worked at the Hemingways; for the first ten years, they frequently hired a new maid when they returned from Walloon, indicating their previous girl had not wanted to be unemployed for two months of the summer. Compared with other North Kenilworth families, the Hemingways kept their maids for an average time span. Paying a dollar a week above the going rate, they had no difficulty in finding recruits for their ad which somehow always ran at the top of the Help Wanted column. It invariably read:

WANTED – General housekeeper with experience; highest wages paid; modern skylight kitchen; no washing; German preferred; apply at once; phone Oak Park 181; Dr. C. E. Hemingway, 600 N. Kenilworth av.

Almost every other such ad listed the wife's name, if a name were listed, but not at North Kenilworth. Dr. Hemingway did the hiring of maids, and given his penchant for order and neatness, he probably saw to their firing as well. In the family correspondence, only the Doctor refers to the maids. Grace was, no doubt, interested, but it was the Doctor who was home in his office more than his wife. Grace had meetings to attend: Nineteenth Century Club meetings, W.C.T.U. meetings, Daughters of the American Revolution meetings, church and choir meetings. When the Fine Arts Society was formed in Oak Park, Grace chaired the music committee. When the P.T.A. met, Grace pleaded for the display of loaned art in the local schools. When the Y.M.C.A. opened its facilities to women in Oak Park, Grace was among the first seventy to sign up. When her oldest son was assigned Jack London's *Call of the Wild* as required reading his freshman year, Grace went before the School Board to complain that no Christian gentleman should read such a book. Grace Hall Hemingway was a busy woman. She had music pupils to instruct, recitals to plan. If she was uninterested in household management, her income allowed her to pay others to clean and cook.

There were those in Oak Park who would say that poor Dr. Hemingway had to do all the cooking and house keeping at North Kenilworth because his wife, who had such a high opinion of herself, could not be bothered. Clarence did, in fact, enjoy baking pies, putting up preserves and canning vegetables. Grace, in fact, did not. Poor Dr. Hemingway very likely had exactly the sort of wife that his soul needed to suffer with. Grace bore him the large family that emulated his own. She washed, cooked and cleaned for that family two months every summer under primitive conditions: a wood stove, an out-house, no electricity, no hot water. In return, Grace annually got her separate vacation – sometimes Nantucket, sometimes California – and she got her own life in Oak Park.

For the first ten years of their marriage, the Doctor and the Doctor's wife were equally prominent in the social/professional doings of Oak Park. She sang and he gave lectures. She instructed, and he led the Agassiz. They took pride in not belonging to the purely social clubs like the Colonial and the Oak Park Clubs. He did not approve of the smoking, drinking, card playing or dancing that went on there. She thought herself a cultural cut above most of such club's membership. After 1906, it was Grace whose name was more prominent in the village. From 1913 on, Clarence Hemingway became more and more reclusive, more and more "nervous." When Ernest was between six and seventeen, his mother became the driving social force in the family. His father retreated into his practice and the enforcement of the strict rules that governed his children.

A 1913 newspaper account of Dr. Hemingway's views on raising children opens a window into the house at North Kenilworth. His topic was "The Conservation of Youth."

> He spoke of the young manhood period in which character is formed which either makes or breaks the life, and of dangers encountered and evils resulting from lack of self-control, self-indulgence, recklessness and unwisely choosing companions.
>
> He placed stress upon the necessity for not alone building up physical strength, but also choosing active Christian associates, developing the mind and stimulating moral growth as well, thru resisting temptations, since each step in self-control lends additional strength and beauty to the character. He quoted Oliver Wendell Holmes' advice that "each select his own ancestors," but did not enter into details of the method, altho apparently endorsing its wisdom. [27]

Self-control, self-denial, caution, Christian precepts, moral growth – these are the watchwords young Hemingway heard all too often at home. As for selecting "his own ancestors," Ernest had little opportunity; his mother took care of that, forever holding up the Hall–Hancock line as the ideal. When Ernest needed a strong male role model, his mother dominated the household. He had only his Civil War grandfather, Anson Hemingway, and his missionary uncle, Willoughby, to idolize. The grandfather had gone to war, the uncle into far countries. In time the boy would outstrip these models. Modifying his father's advice to "select his own ancestors," he created himself anew, arranging and modifying his life to become the person he saw in his private mirror. For whatever had gone wrong in the house of his youth, Ernest blamed his mother. At an age when most young men rebel against their father's control, Ernest rebelled against his mother's.

That he did was ironic. That he never saw how much he resembled Grace was a little sad. Certainly Grace thought well of herself – too well, some Villagers would later say. Certainly Grace was pretentious and something of a snob. But just as certainly, Grace was a public performer, whether accompanied by music or simply walking down the street. To this day, old hands in Oak Park remember Grace Hall Hemingway quite clearly. They remember how she looked on the sidewalk. They remember her singing. They remember the painting she took up when her voice aged. About the Doctor, they have little to say. No clear images remain. Grace, however, left her mark, and her children she marked forever. Marcelline, after acting in some amateur theatrics and publishing a one-act play, became a public lecturer who told midwestern audiences what was current on the New York stage and led theater tours to Broadway. Ursula became a noted ceramicist in Hawaii. Sunny worked seriously at her harp, hoping to achieve concert quality. Leicester became a writer. And her elder son became Ernest Hemingway.

Fathers and sons, a title Hemingway would later use ironically, were not always close in turn of the century Oak Park. The "boy problem," which ministers so loved to resolve, centered on the work ethic and role models. In Ernest's earliest years, his father had needed no public lecturing to excite his sense of responsibility. During summers at the lake, Agassiz outings, winter bird hunts, Clarence Hemingway cultivated a close relationship with his son. In those years the Doctor was a progressive father, one who tried to be friend and mentor to his son. At the annual "address to fathers" at the First Congregational Church, he listened with self-approval when the Professor said:

The heart of every father yearns for the love and respect of his boy. As a rule we are at our best when with our children.

They expect the best of us and we are unwilling that they be disappointed. From them we hide our foibles and for them we bring forth the best we have in character. If this is true .... the safest companion for a boy is his father. . . . the boy is on the safe road to the making of a good man as long as he is a close companion of his father.[28]

A 1910 newspaper photograph shows the family gathered on the porch at North Kenilworth, a reunion of the 1890 high-school class grouped about them. In the center are Clarence and Grace Hemingway – large, expansive, smiling in the arms of friends. Off at one side, a little shy, a little diffident in his Roosevelt safari costume, stands the Doctor's son. Listen to the reporter's description:

> There are houses and there are homes; they are not nec-essarily synonymous. It was one of the latter that was opened for a reunion of the class of 1890 Oak Park High School. Dr. Clarence Edmund Hemingway and Grace Hall, his wife, were members of that class, and ten years ago celebrated the event in like manner. . . . There were thirty-four at the mid-day dinner. The table was spread in the great music room. . . .
> . . . Dr. and Mrs. Hemingway are both professional. At least one of Dr. "Ed's" inventions is in common surgical use, and Grace Hall's pupils show the highest vocal train-ing. Their children, brought up to a normal, rational view of life, a happy childhood, merging into lives of service, and the fullest development of the higher as well as the lower faculties, promise much.[29]

The year is 1910. Shortly thereafter Dr. Hemingway gave up the Agassiz Club, donating the collection of stuffed birds and ani-mals to the high school. Whatever father and son had shared was fixed in memory. What was left to share was embedded quite literally in Ernest's blood.

While Ernest was preparing to leave Petoskey for Toronto, Dr.

Hemingway wrote nostalgic letters in which he promised his son time to "chum together" at Christmas. Maybe they could take in a play or two. But Christmas ended badly. Ernest tried to make it up at Easter, sending his mother an enormous lily. Grace, Clarence and Ursula wrote separately to tell him how much it had meant to her. Once more the Doctor was looking forward to seeing his elder son for the summer. He signed his letters, "your old Scout Chum." It all sounded plausible in Toronto, but after a one week home at the end of May, anger and harsh words once again wedged Hemingway apart from both parents. He stayed in Oak Park only long enough to march in the Honor Guard on Memorial Day when they dedicated the war monument.[30] Among the several hundred names on the bronze tablet was Ernest M. Hemingway. Oak Park had tied up its war effort which was now officially closed. It was the last time he wore his uniform. When Ted Brumback, his old friend from Kansas City and Red Cross Section Four, finally got his car repaired, Ernest was out of the house so quickly that he forgot to pack his treasured Italian pistol. He was bound for the lake a jump ahead of his mother and the children.

His father tried to reach him in Chicago before he left, but Ernest was too quick for him. Instead the Doctor wrote him at Horton Bay a letter filled with distance. The "old Scout Chum" was once again "Father," the rule-maker who, when forced, sided with Grace. In his most Christian voice, he told Ernest that he should

think more of what others have done for you and try to be charitable and kind and gentle. Do not doubt but that I am proud of your ability and independence but try and soften your temper and never threaten your Father and Mother. We have both tried many trying years of your life to help you and I trust you will live to see the joy of a family of your own, with some of the cares and anxieties and responsibilities that go with the experience. I want you to represent all that is good and noble and brave and courteous in Mankind, and fear God and respect Woman.[31]

Ernest sat on the porch of the cottage reading the letter. He would respect Woman all right, the best looker close to hand. He lit a cigarette and watched the sun glitter silver off the lake, which remained unchanged after all the summers. The pines stood dark green as ever. Nothing was different, he told himself. Nothing but the Point. Mrs. Dilsworth had sold the Point, the place where the summer people always fished, sold the Point to two Jews who wanted to build a club house.[32] That changed everything about the lake for him. He would go to Petoskey when his mother arrived with the young children. He would help muscle the baggage, the crates and barrels shipped by Montgomery Ward out to the cottages. He would try to be noble and courteous, but the summer was not beginning as he had planned. He had walked away from a good job in Toronto to spend one more summer, the summer of his majority, on the lake. Already the long-range forecast was less than promising.

Chapter Five

SUMMER PEOPLE: PART TWO
1920

IT was the summer that Warren G. Harding slipped into the Republican nomination in Chicago, on the tenth ballot. "Filled up on a pair of eights," he said. It was the summer after the White Sox lost the World Series to the Cincinnati Reds. Rumors said the Series was fixed; an investigation was beginning. It was the summer they arrested former heavyweight champion Jack Johnson on the Mann Act for transporting an unmarried woman across a state line. Good bye, Black Jack. It was the summer that everyone was reading *This Side of Paradise* by a new writer, Scott Fitzgerald, and a generation of young girls woke up to find that they were flappers. It was the summer that the Palmer Acts deported alien radicals and the bootleggers began to thrive on Prohibition, while the rest of the country twitched in the post-war recession. It was the first summer of the Twenties and Hemingway's last summer on the lake, the last of the summer people.

By the third week in June the cast was assembled: Bill Smith and his pretty sister, Katy; Carl Edgar and Ted Brumback, friends since Kansas City; Irene Goldstein and Marjorie Bump, and Ernest. Five years later, Hemingway's Nick Adams remembered that summer nostalgically:

the long trips in the car, fishing in the bay, reading in the hammock on hot days, swimming off the dock, playing baseball in Charlevoix and Petoskey, living at the Bay, the Madame's cooking, the way she had with servants, eating in the dining room looking out the window across the long fields and the point to the lake, talking with her, drinking with Bill's old man, fishing trips away from the farm, just lying around. [1]

The fictional summer was the best part; Nick Adams did not have a mother to fight with, did not have chores to nag at him as Hemingway did. Nick did not have any sisters to create problems. Hemingway had Ursula and Sunny, but no Marcelline that summer. Her job in Chicago kept her away. For Ernest it was just as well. Since the previous summer, a distance had wedged between himself and Marcelline. She held her brother responsible for their parents' reaction against her summer suitor, her first serious affair. Although Ernest tried in his best jocular way to make amends, the distance between them remained unbridged. The two were never again close and seldom corresponded.

At Windemere, Grace began the long summer in reduced circumstances. She was forty-eight years old, florid of face and overweight. Arthritis plagued her arms and shoulders; heavy lifting, washing and ironing left her in pain. Her congenitally weak eyes still gave her headaches in bright sunlight, and she was no longer able to cope easily with the emotional stresses her brood inevitably produced. From Oak Park the Doctor sent her permanganate, salicylates, throat tabs and Seiler's tablets. "Please take at least five grains of the Sodium Salicalate . . . dissolved in a half cup of hot water two or three times a day." [2] (Three aspirin and call me in the morning.) For her constipation, he advised Cream of Tartar once or twice a day. To worsen matters, her menstrual period was becoming erratic, even stopping under stress. Quite possibly she was beginning her change of life. Without Marcelline for assistance and comfort, without Ruth Arnold for friendship, with less money than in previous summers and with two teenage daughters attracting male attention, Grace Hall Hemingway did not need any crises with her son Ernest.

116

What she needed was her husband as he had been in the early years at Windemere. In those summers Dr. Hemingway truly enjoyed the physical demands of their somewhat primitive summer cottage. He had enjoyed working up a sweat chopping wood or hoeing the garden. Killing chickens, mending and painting, burying garbage had all given him pleasure. Windemere had been his escape from the civilized routine of Oak Park, a vestige of the pioneer life for which he longed. It was not missionary work in China, but it was demanding and wholesome. None of his children took the same pleasure in hard manual labor, least of all Ernest. Clarence could make a game of washing laundry in the lake; without Clarence, it was no game. Like his father, Ernest sweated easily and profusely, but he seldom enjoyed sweating at anything he considered work. Chores at Windemere were a lot of work.

The demands of summer did not change over the years, and Grace was no longer a young woman. In her twenties she had been able to cook, wash, clean and care for the children and still have the strength to row her father and father-in-law across the lake for a picnic. At forty-eight, she rightly expected her oldest son to take up his father's chores. Had there been less temperamental conflict between them, Ernest might have done what Grace considered his duty. As things were in the summer of 1920, he spent as little time at Windemere as possible. When present, he did the chores but made it clear to his mother they were chores. The boat dock got repaired but Grace was losing the war of words. Their conflict was as unrelenting as it can be between two strong wills. Knowing how his mother opposed smoking, drinking, gambling and cursing, Ernest made almost a fetish of all four. From Chicago he had a friend send up rank-smelling Russian cigarettes rolled in brown paper. After his feature stories for the *Star* on gambling and bootlegging, he made no secret about his own drinking. Grace fought back. She reminded him that he had been home for eighteen months and still had no steady job, In her letters to the Doctor, she reported their son's abusive and insulting language. "I think Ernest is trying to irritate us in some way," the Doctor said.[3]

As was his way, Hemingway could be perfectly charming, perfectly ingratiating across other kitchen tables. At Bill Smith's cottage he was witty and boyish around the aunt, Mrs. Charles, or "the Madame" as she was called. In their apple orchard he worked without complaint. To their table he brought gifts of fresh trout. Everyone loved Ernest. They loved his sense of humor and his tall tales. They loved the confident way he handled himself. It was only at Windemere that his mother brought out the vicious, bitchy side of him. Many of those who loved him were later to discover it for themselves, but that summer he convinced his friends that the root problem was his mother.

There was much about Hemingway in those days that made him good company. Riveting his attention to whomever he spoke, he gave special meaning to conversations. He could generate intensity just listening, which he did well, trapping dialogue in his mind for future use. The men delighted in his infectious humor, which could exaggerate anything into a tall tale or a mock heroic adventure. With his keen eye for parody, Ernest amused them with imitations of local bumpkins and city tourists. He was always kidding someone: Bill Smith about his new mustache; Carl Edgar about his hopelessly shy love for Katy Smith. And he could joke about himself – "the great Hemingstein," boy war-hero, savior of civilization, master woodsman, drinker extraordinary and the poorest boy on the block. It was all great fun that last summer at the lake – the drinking, the jokes, the long fishing trips. He joked about everything but fishing, which was his religion. No one knew more about the trout that he, or took their capture more seriously. Fishing with Ernest was a competitive sport at which he did not like to lose. His drive to excel could turn a simple hike into a contested race, an afternoon's swim into a test of endurance. No one could drink more, stay under water longer or remember better than Ernest. That competitive edge sometimes grated on the summer men, but only a little.

Most of all he charmed the ladies, young and old. The summer of his majority, he was remarkably handsome. Women who met him after the war never forgot him. Compensating for his conflict with his mother, he was particularly drawn to older women. Mrs. Charles was delighted with him. With equal magnetism, he charmed much younger girls, so much so that his mother called him a "menace to youth." Grace Quinlan, barely a teenager the summer before, fell obviously in love with Ernest. Some of Hemingway's tenderest letters were written to her, whom he fondly called "little sister," as, in his prime, he would call pretty young girls, who fell within range of his magnetism, "daughter."

Young Hemingway was rapidly developing a powerful sexual sense of himself, a sense that women recognized and responded to. In Italy, Agnes Von Kurowsky, eight years his senior, had been charmed by it. After his twentieth birthday, he was seldom without a woman, and he understood perfectly his attraction. Six years later he wrote:

It was liking, and liking the body, and introducing the body, and persuading, and taking chances, and never frightening, and assuming about the other person, and always taking never asking, and gentleness and liking, and making liking and happiness, and joking and making people not afraid. And making it all right afterwards. It wasn't loving. Loving was frightening. He, Nicholas Adams, could have what he wanted because of something in him.[4]

During Hemingway's high-school years, sex education was the center of national debate. Oak Park, conservative in behavior but usually progressive in education, accepted sex education as having some merit. Boys could learn a healthy Christian approach to their bodies at the Y.M.C.A. The First Congregational Church sponsored lectures for separate classes of boys and girls in their teens. In 1915, Dr. Hemingway gave "a short sex talk" to fifty members of the Boy's High School club.[5] According to Hemingway's fictional Nick Adams, "His father had summed up the whole matter by stating that masturbation produced blindness, insanity, and death, while a man who went with prostitutes would contract hideous venereal diseases and that the thing to do was to keep your hands off of people."[6]

Whether or not this Victorian advice is representative of Dr. Hemingway's "short sex talk," it certainly was not the limit of Ernest's early sexual education. Growing up as he did in a house full of women and with his father's medical library on the shelves, he was fully aware of female anatomy. His four younger siblings were all born in the home; in fact, Carol was born at Windemere the summer that Ernest was twelve. If anything, Ernest had more theoretical knowledge about sexual relations than most boys growing up in Oak Park.

By the summer of 1920, Ernest had little hands-on experience, but he had detailed knowledge of sexual anatomy and techniques. What he learned in the army brothels in Italy and listening to soldiers talk, he supplemented with reading. During his Toronto winter, he bought and read the Havelock Ellis book, *Erotic Symbolism*. In 1920, Ellis' frank discussion of sex shocked the conventional middle class reader, but not the young Hemingway. Ellis confirmed what Ernest suspected: women enjoyed sex as much as he did. In *Erotic Symbolism* he found detailed explanations of the female orgasm as well as copious analysis and examples of the Krafft-Ebing fetishes, including the erotic nature of hair, a fetish present in his fiction and in his private life. He found the book so fascinating that he sent his copy to Bill Smith as evidence to support Hemingway's theory of the sexual appetite in women.

Smith, four years older than Ernest, could not read Ellis with Hemingway's appreciation, and returned the book almost immediately:

My summary return of Havelock – after an impartial perusal – was due in part to lack of any genoowind interest in the volume and also to the fact that it ain't a parlor ornament. To state it sans any embellishments the writer was in no wise impressed. When a guy seems to deal chiefly, in fact almost entirely, with a bunch of degenerates I begin to grow weary, unless they are frightfully novel rates and the birds

Ellis picked out weren't. Also when a male comes at me on a more or less scientific basis and then quotes Boccaccio I feel like turning to the detective story or Police Gazette. Maybe the enditer missed the highlights in Havelock or hasn't got the dome to appreciate it, but if all his books are like Erotic Symbolism, don't hold him up as an advocate of your beezage theory. Incidentally I couldn't find any confirmation of the theory in Hav[elock].[7]

Had Smith read Ellis more carefully, he would have found an interesting description of the sexually active woman: short stature, small breasts, wide hips, dark hair, brilliant eyes. Had Bill Smith thought about it, he would have seen a mirror image of his sister Katherine. Certainly Ernest thought about her quite a lot that summer. Katy Smith was eight years older than Ernest, attractive, independent and a free spirit. Her bright green eyes held a man's attention with implied promises just out of reach. All that summer of 1920, she and Ernest were close companions; Marjorie Bump could not compete with the older woman. Ernest kept Marge in reserve, but he saw more of Katy. When the men were not off on fishing trips, Katy was with them at the lake swimming, or in Petoskey playing tennis, or at the Charles cottage eating a meal. Between herself and Ernest there was a strong sexual attraction which they both understood without having to put it into words. It was not love. And they understood that too. A man did not need to read Havelock Ellis to know when the sexual magnetism was working. As Ernest would later write, "all the equipment you will ever have is provided and each man learns all there is for him to know about it without advice."[8]

Earlier in April, Ted Brumback suggested to Hemingway a course of self-study he thought would "be invaluable to you in your writing. That's psychology. It's so damn interesting. . . . you learn how other people think, what they do when certain things happen, and how you are like or unlike them. . . . You can learn how to assign motives for every action."[9] Brumback urged him to read an elementary book or two from the Toronto library; then he advised Hemingway to read William James and

Sigmund Freud. There is no hard evidence that he did either. Freud, of course, would have been impossible to avoid in the Twenties; his idiom and his complexes were so much a part of the cultural atmosphere that Hemingway absorbed them without ever opening a book. William James' text, *Psychology*, did not become part of Hemingway's library until he reached Paris, where Gertrude Stein also held him up as mentor.

No one was recommending Havelock Ellis to Hemingway in 1920, but how like the writer he became that he should have read Ellis so studiously. Freud might explain the psychology of sexual behavior, but Ellis gave his reader a potpourri of Krafft-Ebing, case histories, clinical descriptions and classical references. The psychologists were interested in the *why* of behavior; Ellis, like Hemingway, was interested in the *what*. Later when Hemingway tried to explain Brett Ashley's hypersexual behavior in *The Sun Also Rises,* he found he could not tell *why*. In a deleted portion of the first draft, the narrator tells us that he does not understand the lady; he simply reports *what* she does, leaving it to the reader to figure out the *why* for himself. Hemingway was not uninterested in the psychological motivations of his characters. Many of his women would bear deep psychic scars: Catherine Barkley in *A Farewell to Arms* is "a little crazy" from the loss of her fiancé; Maria in *For Whom the Bell Tolls* is mentally scarred from the gang rape she endured. But Hemingway's central concern in his mature fiction would be with how his characters spoke and acted, not why they behaved as they did. We had to figure that out for ourselves.

Among the other descriptions Hemingway read in Ellis, there were fairly explicit observations on the basic positions for sexual congress. While such information would hardly be news to any contemporary teenager, in 1920 discussion of sexual positions in print, even the primary "missionary" position, was taboo. In Oak Park, where it was illegal to "indecently exhibit any stallion or bull," illegal to "write or draw, cut, make or exhibit any lewd or indecent word, sentence, design or figure," sophisticated sexual information was nearly impossible to come by. Village Ordinance no. 1916 spelled out the prohibition:

No person or persons shall sell or offer to sell, give away, distribute or have in his or her possession with intent to give away, sell or distribute within the Village of Oak Park, any book, pamphlet, circular, hand bill, advertisement or notice of any kind purporting to treat of, or treating of, diseases known as "venereal diseases," describing or explaining the genital organs, giving or purporting to give the nature and remedies of diseases peculiar to females or the nature or causes of nervous debility, sterility or barrenness, gonorrhea, gleet, stricture, syphilis, affection of the prostate gland or the remedies therefor, or the cause or remedies for abortion or miscarriage, or articles or means of preventing conception, under a penalty of not less than twenty dollars nor more than two hundred dollars.

Nor could anyone give "information from whom or where medicine or anything whatever may be obtained for the cure, prevention or treatment of uterine diseases, or diseases peculiar to females; venereal diseases or diseases of the genital organs."[10] For a group so determined to prevent understanding of sexual matters, the framers of this ordinance seem particularly well informed of the possibilities.

When Hemingway wrote "Summer People" in 1926, his Nick Adams meets the fictional Kate at a night rendezvous beneath a hemlock tree. There, in frank and tender nakedness, they make love atop blankets that Kate has brought for that purpose. It is not their first such meeting. Nick, as explicitly as Hemingway could write at that time, shows a sophisticated technique to which Kate responds beautifully. Nick enters Kate from the rear, her buttocks pressed into his groin, his expert hands free to caress her.

"Is it good this way?" he said.

"I love it. I love it. Oh come, Wemedge. Please come. Come, come. Please, Wemedge. Please, please, Wemedge."[11]

If Hemingway was not having intercourse with Katy Smith that summer of 1920, he certainly wanted to, and in Paris he gave her to Nick Adams as a gift.[12]

Nicholas Adams and Kate, making love beneath the stars, join a long list of Hemingway lovers whom necessity or choice put to bed upon the good earth. Nick's earliest sexual memory is of Trudy Gilby, the Indian girl who "did first what no one has done better" beneath another hemlock tree. Liz Coates loses her virginity to the blacksmith, Jim Gilmore, at night beside the Horton Bay warehouse. "The hemlock planks of the dock were hard and splintery and cold." Beneath or upon the hemlock tree, his lovers find life. In the midst of the Spanish Civil War, Robert Jordan and Maria make love in a mountain meadow of heather, "and he felt the earth move out and away from under him." Later Maria comes to his sleeping bag laid out on a bower of fresh-cut spruce, "making an alliance against death with him." What our first parents found in that farthest Garden, Hemingway's lovers rediscover: sex and death.[13]

In Toronto Hemingway not only discovered Ellis, whom he would continue to read as late as 1939, but he began to read another writer who would become more important to the development of his fiction: Joseph Conrad. By April 1920, Hemingway was recommending the exiled Pole's *Victory* to Ted Brumback, who agreed absolutely that Joseph Conrad was "king of them all."[14] Unfortunately, in *Victory* (1915) Conrad was not writing with the depth or complexity of his monumental works – *Nostromo, Lord Jim, Heart of Darkness* – nor was his style so admirable as it had been in "Youth," *Typhoon* or *The Nigger of the Narcissus*. Given Hemingway's penchant for Captain Marryat, Kipling, Alger and the incurable romantic d'Annunzio, perhaps it was better that his first Conrad was *Victory,* an exciting, if not well imagined, adventure story. Axel Heyst on a remote island with the subservient Lena was the stuff of mildly erotic adolescent daydreams, just the book for a young man beginning his serious literary education.[15]

Influences, however, are absorbed unconsciously and slowly. Nothing that Hemingway was writing in 1920 bore much resemblance to Conrad. He continued to look for models in the popular market place, and his stories continued to be clichéd and stilted. Among the now dog-eared typescripts he brought to the lake that summer were several that he had sent earlier to Edwin Balmer for advice, stories rejected by the popular market and for good reason. Hemingway had learned almost nothing from his "Cross Roads" experiment.

He had not yet found the distance or the technique for fictionalizing his own experience honestly. "The Mercenaries," which he had finished the previous January, was another tall tale that he had first retailed in Petoskey as his own adventure. Set in the backroom of Cambrinus, a Chicago bar frequented by veterans, the story is heavily influenced by Ring Lardner. Only the point of view shows any growing awareness of technique: the narrator, Rinaldi Rinaldo, tells the reader a war story told to him in the bar by Perry Graves, an American mercenary on his way to Peru to sell his military skills in the war with Chile. This detached narrator may be related to Conrad's Marlow, whose habit of telling other men's stories Hemingway had discovered, but more likely it was the result of Hemingway's newspaper experience: in interviews the reporter is always the detached secondary narrator. "The Mercenaries" takes place in Taormina, Sicily, late in the war. Graves, an American sergeant, has a passionate love affair with the wife or mistress of a famous Italian air ace, Il Lupo, whose picture decorated numerous magazine covers. Caught in compromising conditions, Graves faces a duel with Il Lupo. The courageous Graves, who fears death not at all, takes the challenge stoically. Facing each other with drawn pistols, their left hands touching across the table, the two soldiers wait as a servant counts to three. Il Lupo, under pressure to maintain his reputation, falters. At the count of two he tries to fire, but Graves is too quick for him, shooting the pistol out of his hand. American courage, sexual prowess and a casual attitude toward death — nothing could have been further removed from Hemingway's own experience, or anyone else's for that matter.[16] A barracks-room tale, "The Mercenaries" betrays none of the fear or the horror that Hemingway discovered in Italy.

The story's roots went back to the winter of 1918, when Jim Gamble, who was taking leave at Taormina, invited Ernest to visit him where there was "lots of atmosphere and I should think plenty to write about."[17] With Agnes on temporary assignment away from Milan, Hemingway left for Sicily, but on his return told Eric Dorman-Smith that he had seen nothing of the island "except from a bedroom window because his hostess in the first small hotel he stopped in had hiden his clothes and kept him to herself for a week."[18] Actually he and Gamble spent a pleasant, relaxed week in the fishing village, a week that Hemingway never mentioned except in his limited correspondence with Gamble. In March 1919, Gamble said that after Hemingway left "there was not a day in which I did not think of you and how the only thing lacking was a congenial spirit like yourself to sample a nearly perfect situation." He then invited Ernest to visit him at his family's summer home near Elkin Park, Pennsylvania.[19] Hemingway turned down Gamble's invitation but two months later invited Gamble to Walloon for the summer. He also told his friend about the end of the Agnes affair. Gamble said, "I'm glad to see that you had more sense than to pity yourself. It after all is much better. . . . Don't get caught on the rebound."[20] Whatever it was about Jim Gamble that had bothered Agnes in Milan did not bother Ernest, and Oak Parker that he was, Hemingway did not see Gamble's money as an impediment to friendship.

By the fall of 1919, Hemingway had embroidered on the Taormina story until, in the version he told Dutch Pailthorp in Petoskey, it was Ernest himself who seduced the older Italian lovely and faced her irate warrior husband. He was saved from a duel, he said, when the woman distracted her husband long enough for Ernest to escape. The entire fantasy carries overtones of the aging, Italian poet/war-hero Gabriele d'Annunzio, whose rhetoric had nudged Italy into the war and whose air exploits had thrilled that nation. D'Annunzio was everything Hemingway wanted to be: a famous writer, a warrior beloved by his country. The poet had immortalized his affair with the actress Elenora Duse in *Il Fuoco*, a histrionic and romantic idyl that Ernest

126

obviously admired. He gave translations of the novel – *The Flame* – to several women he dated after the war.

Over the next quarter century Hemingway's fiction would cycle back to Italy time and again. In the last case – *Across the River and Into the Trees* – another aging warrior, Colonel Cantwell, indulges his failing heart in an idyllic affair with the young, lovely and Italian Renata. On the Venetian canals where d'Annunzio's poet and actress played out their romantic tryst in *The Flame,* Cantwell and Renata romance in a gondola. The bawdy story of Perry Graves and his older Italian paramour comes half circle to an aging soldier and an Italian teenage wonder. The fantasies of young men, like Lear's eels, are difficult to keep down; from the bubbling pot they rise up in various guises. The only overt vestige of "The Mercenaries" retained in Hemingway's mature work was the name of Rinaldi Rinaldo. When he began the terse sketches for *in our time,* Rinaldo became the Italian soldier who lay wounded with Nick Adams against the wall of the ravaged town. And in 1928, Hemingway would use the name Rinaldi once again for the Italian doctor in *A Farewell to Arms.*

In Toronto he had written about Italy. In Paris he would write about Horton Bay. The best part, he later insisted, was making it up, inventing the country and living in it day by day. His most complex and perhaps his most interesting creation was himself. His early war fantasies of courageous, experienced men in dangerous situations were experimental drafts for the self that he was inventing. Like Tom Sawyer, young Hemingway was a middle-class, urban boy who longed for adventures. Eventually he became what he pretended to be.

All that winter and into the spring, Ernest had been making up places to go: South America, the Far East, New Mexico – any place different and strange. He had not forgotten his high school promise to become an explorer, nor had he lost his dream of travel. The Italian war had whetted his appetite for farther fields. He was sure he could not live in Oak Park. By the end of the summer his parents were certain they did not want him in Oak Park, although from a distance his letters were less hostile than he frequently was in their home. It was his twenty-first summer; the letting go was bloody surgery without even local anesthetic.

Dr. Hemingway tried to be supportive, but, for reasons Ernest did not understand, his father's tone remained distant no matter how lovingly he signed his letters. The more his nerves deteriorated, the more rigid the Doctor's discipline became. He worried continually about Ernest's friends: were they good Christians? From Kansas City in 1917, Ernest had assured his father of the Christian devotion of Carl Edgar and Charles Hopkins, men Dr. Hemingway doubted before ever meeting them. When Ernest sailed to the war in Italy, his father urged him to associate with the Y.M.C.A. men, strong Christians all. Ernest found it more and more difficult to speak honestly with his father, whose stern morality would not bend and whose Christian forgiveness Ernest found self-serving and difficult to accept.

The Doctor and his son parted hurriedly in June, leaving everything unsaid. Clarence could not say his fears; Ernest could not speak his needs. The Doctor's letters that summer frequently contained some plaintive part, some little thing that betrayed his growing paranoia and left Ernest feeling guilty, angry or both. Misunderstanding grew out of the smallest events. "I am sorry you forget to ask for the little Wop automatic," his father wrote. "I forgot about it entirely. I have given it wrapped to mother exactly as you handed it to me. All the shells I know anything of for it are herewith as you handed them to me. Wish when I went upstairs to bid you good bye you had thought of it."[21] The simplest gesture could raise a barrier between them. Father and son were failing each other, and neither knew why.

In Oak Park the Doctor got Grace's side of the story through the mail and wrote regularly supporting her position. At Windemere, Ernest chaffed under his mother's moralizing proverbs. So long as he remained at Horton Bay, he was a young man among slightly older men who accepted him as their equal, for they had shared experiences: newspaper days in Kansas City, war days in Italy. As soon as he walked through the cottage door, Grace expected him to be partly the boy of earlier summers and partly the handy man of Windemere, performing the work once done by his father. The disparity between the role that Hemingway had invented for himself and the roles his mother expected of him would, in the best of circumstances, produce conflict. The summer of 1920 was not the best of circumstances.

Without either Marcelline or Ruth Arnold for support, Mother Grace was more alone at the lake than in all the previous summers. Her middle daughters – Ursula and Sunny – enjoyed the work at Windemere no more than Ernest did. Both were teenagers (eighteen and sixteen) more interested in boys than in helping their mother. Where Marcelline accepted Grace's view, Ursula and Sunny were rebellious. They kept secrets and broke rules; given the chance they would side with Ernest. When Grace was not nagging the girls to work, she had to supervise Sunny, whose poor final grades made the Doctor demand a read-aloud program for the summer. All summer Grace listened to Sunny's voice droning away at the required books. From her point of view, Grace was single-handedly fighting a war with disorder. "Hope Ernest has been over to help you," Clarence wrote from the Village.

Though Grace intended to spend most of her summer in her new cottage at Longfield, she found herself tied more tightly than ever to Windemere. It was not safe to let the girls out of her sight for long, and the daily drudgery of washing and cooking bound her to the lee shore. Ruth Arnold sent magazines and chat, planning her mid-summer visit.

> I suppose the Dr. will be going North soon. I haven't seen him at all. When he comes, have him stay as long as he will. I don't want him to think he must leave a certain time on account of my coming up. If he stays all summer all right. I would be broken hearted not to get up but would far rather be, Dearest, than have any talk. So remember he comes first.[22]

Clarence wrote wearily of Oak Park's heat and Marcelline's endless dances; his disapproval went unsaid but understood. Had it not been for Grace, none of his children would have gone to dancing school. Tentatively, he was planning to visit Windemere the first week in July, staying perhaps until Ernest's twenty-first birthday. "Take a day off," he told Grace. "You are working too hard, my darling. I want to find you rested."[23]

Little chance of that, not for Grace, who neither loved the work nor could shirk the responsibility of it. There were evenings when her upper arms and shoulders so ached from heavy lifting that she sat stupid at the kitchen table, unable to get the coffee cup to her lips without it shaking and spilling. But if Clarence's "nerves" improved from his summer without children, perhaps it would be worth it. From his letters, she was not sure. This summer he was once more typing and numbering each of them. By June 25, she had been gone nineteen days from North Kenilworth, and his letter was numbered nineteen. By lantern light at the end of each day, Grace wrote the letter she knew her husband expected. Two days without mail did grievous harm to his nerves. What she needed from the Doctor was emotional support and understanding. What she got were lectures on how to discipline the children and directives for keeping a strict account of all her summer expenditures. By August she was furious, refusing to keep such accounts. She had spent no money on movies, candy, sundaes or fruit. She bought ice cream only on birthdays. There were no luxuries at Windemere, only necessities.[24]

With Marcelline wrapped up in dances, a new boy friend, wedding parties and a trip to Massachusetts, Grace had no outlet for her emotions other than letters to Ruth Arnold, who was still not welcome at North Kenilworth. Ruth, responsive as always, sympathized: "By the sound of your letter Muv I'm afraid you're lonesome. . . . When I get up, I won't let you be lonesome. . . . Dearest when I choose to send a little love gift up, please don't mention it to Dr. It seems so silly to make this request but will explain later."[25] When Doctor Hemingway arrived at Windemere, Ruth continued to write cheery letters, not knowing how long he would stay. She told Grace about Fourth of July in the Village and her date for the dance there. There was also a new friend: "I have met the most charming girl, not at all beautiful, but I think the charm which lasts and the charm which appeals to the heart is a thing independent of beautiful. I don't think it best to write Beth yet. There are so few that know about it. Will tell you all about it later."[26]

"There are so few that know about *it*." The indefinite pronoun dangles there, encouraging a jaded age to speculations that would likely have reduced Ruth to tears. Throughout Grace's middle years she received similar letters from young girls whose voices she had coached, letters filled with love and admiration. *It* may have involved the streak of spiritualism that ran deep in Grace, a spiritualism touched with Christian mysticism. Music was not merely her art, music was a window opening on to spiritual knowing. As a young girl on her trip to England, Grace had drawn for herself an elaborate horoscope which she kept all her life. At least once she thought she had a mystic insight: a death foretold. Occasionally, no doubt, her music lessons brought to her a young girl given to intuitive flashes and religious fervor. To this type of girl Grace was bound, for no one in her own home, least of all the Doctor, had any sympathy for her mysticism. In her later years, she received letters from this circle of initiates that spoke of "fleeting glimpses into the 'holy of holies'" and of finding "the meaning of God and myself, which really is one and the same thing."[27] The touching letters continued to come when Grace was into her sixties, letters that called "our association a spiritual gift, the blessing of which I shall always hold priceless."[28] In 1940, when Marcelline faced an operation for her partially paralyzed upper intestine, she told her mother: "Please don't write me any spiritualism. It isn't what I need now."[29] In 1941, Grace sent Carol a subscription to the *Spiritualist Monthly*. In 1942, a letter to Grace from Blanche Fletcher speaks of reading *The Psychic Observer* and being somewhat disappointed by the play *Blithe Spirit*. Blanche remembers "Annie" who could foresee the future and cure pain. "In the new age," she writes, "we will all demonstrate as the Christian Scientists now try to do – they are just a *little* ahead of their time!"[30] While the Doctor was alive, Grace could not fully indulge the spiritualist bent, for which he had little sympathy. His 1928 suicide removed all restraints.

When Hemingway wrote "The Doctor and the Doctor's Wife"

in 1924, he left much of the marital conflict beneath the surface of his prose. Looking for a shorthand way of emphasizing the marriage's incompatibility, he made Mrs. Adams a Christian Scientist. Readers of the story have pointed out that Grace was not a Christian Scientist, and the story was, therefore, not meant to be read as biography. What none of us have suspected and what none of the children ever told us was that Grace was a spiritualist. Grace did not believe medicine or doctors wrong, but she was, all her life, inclined to the mystic. This inclination, of no great importance early in her marriage, grew in fervor as she aged, raising another barrier between herself and her husband. It was the age of the Ouija board and Harry Houdini's passionate debunking of table-rappers. It was the age of Eliot's Madame Sosostris and her "wicked pack of cards," the age of Madame Blavatsky and the Theosophists. In Oak Park the caravan of gypsies still came each year to petty thieve, mend pots and tell outrageous fortunes.

Between themselves, Grace and Ruth Arnold shared these spiritualist beliefs. The Doctor, man of science and skeptic, found himself alienated in his own home, or so his paranoia told him. Ruth, who virtually raised Carol and Leicester as a surrogate mother, became to his mind a threat to the family, an unwholesome influence, a divisive presence. In 1919 he had sent her home. In 1920, he was speaking to her, but she was still unwelcome at North Kenilworth. However, at Anson Hemingway's house where she picked up magazines to send Grace, Ruth met no hostility. Had there been the least palpable scandal, Grandmother Adelaide with her keen sensors would have been first to know and first to bar Ruth completely from family contact.

But rumors and gossip in Oak Park were like snakes: chop them in pieces and still the pieces writhe. In the 1930s, when Grace sold the family house and moved into smaller quarters in River Forest, Ruth Arnold sometimes lived with her as a friend and nurse to Grace's infirmities. A few tongues still wagged. Grace felt compelled to write two such gossips a testy note:

> Ruth tells me that you have been misinformed by the repetition of an old malicious story. In the first place, Ruth

never had such a thought; and in the second place, Dr. Hemingway and his wife were never separated. They were loving and sympathetic every day of their lives. No more understanding people would live together 32 years, thru sunshine and shadow. . . . As for Ruth, I have known and loved her for nearly 30 years, and she has always been loyal and true to the Hemingway family. Every one of my children come to see her and are grateful for all her many kindnesses. I trust you will hasten to make amends for hurting her feelings with the repetition of an old untrue story.[31]

Whatever the truth was, Grace kept it to herself. When Clarence arrived that summer of 1920 at Windemere, he knew that Ruth Arnold waited patiently in Oak Park for his departure so she might come to the lake. This secret sharing that bound Ruth to his wife did nothing to improve his frame of mind. His son Ernest did even less. Seeing firsthand how little help Ernest had provided at the cottage brought out the Doctor's disciplinarian side. His son, wisely, spent as little time as he could at Windemere those two weeks of July. The way Ursula and Sunny took Ernest's part only increased the Doctor's anger in a cottage divided. The Doctor stood firmly on Grace's side, reminding his son how his mother's failing health required physical help. Ernest, who knew that the only way to father's attention and sympathy was through physical illness, thought his mother was playing the same game he played so well. If sons cannot believe in their parents' youth, they find it equally difficult to accept their aging bodies. Angry words passed from father to son; insulting words were returned. The Doctor's "nervousness" increased. He had intended to be at Windemere to celebrate his son's majority on July 21, but returned to Oak Park almost a week early. With his oldest son beyond his control, he left his wife to deal with the problem. Before departing, he advised Ernest to find work somewhere away from Windemere and Horton Bay.

Back in Oak Park he immediately wrote Grace about their recalcitrant son.

I contend that no gentleman need use common vulgar words in any ordinary conversation. It shows a degraded type of ... superficial mind. ... I advised him to ... work at good wages and at least cut down his living expenses. I also sincerely hoped that now he had attained the legal age he would be more considerate of others and use less vitrolistic words.[32]

Still Ernest did not leave Windemere. Not yet.

Most parents and sons reach a breaking point, a point of departure necessary for sons to become men. Perhaps unconsciously, but with growing intensity, Hemingway that summer was forcing his parents to make the break. On his own, he could easily have put a distance so wide between parents and himself that there would have been no question about his filial duties. But he did not do it. At similar breaking points in his later life, he would force others to initiate the change. In 1923, when he wanted to quit journalism, he did his best to force his Toronto editor to fire him. When he wanted out of his 1924 contract with Boni and Liveright, he wrote a satire of Sherwood Anderson, *Torrents of Spring,* that forced Horace Liveright, his and Anderson's publisher, to terminate their agreement. At the end of his first marriage, he left it to his wife to raise the issue of divorce. When World War Two began in Europe, it took a challenge from his third wife, Martha Gellhorn, to prod Hemingway out of Cuba and into the war zone. She made it onto the beachhead before him. In the summer of 1920, consciously or not, he was forcing his parents to make the break. So, with his father departed, Ernest stayed on at the lake, angry, chafing, but still playing the game.

For his twenty-first birthday, Grace prepared an appropriate feast for her son and Ted Brumback. His father, to whom he had not written, sent him a five-dollar check for a present. Out of pique, Ernest did not cash it. On July 22, the second day of Ernest's majority, his father wrote him:

Try not to be a sponger. . . . It is best for you [and Ted] to change camps and go to new fields to conquer, it is altogether too hard on your mother to entertain you and your friends, when she is not having help and you are so hard to please and are so insulting to your dear mother. So please pack up and try elsewhere until you are again invited . . . to Windemere. . . . Try and look this matter square in the face as an honest boy and be as kind and considerate to your mother and sisters as you are to Madame Charles and Bill Smith.[33]

Twice now his father had told him to leave Windemere, but he did not pack. The break had to be with his mother.

On July 25, Ruth Arnold arrived at the lake.

The next evening Ernest came in at 9:00 p.m. hungry. Grace fixed a late supper for herself and her son. As they ate, Ernest accused her of reading "moron literature" in the *American* magazine and asked if she read the *Atlantic* just so that someone would see her reading it. Grace's response is unrecorded. As they sat there at the kitchen table, both held secrets. For three days Grace had been drafting and correcting a letter to Ernest that was to be the breaking-off that he had spent the summer provoking. Ernest's secret was the late-night picnic at Ryan's Point that Ursula and Sunny had arranged with their neighboring friends, Elizabeth and Bob Loomis, and two young visitors at the Loomis cottage. Ted and Ernest were also going. Ruth Arnold knew, but said nothing. At midnight, when Grace was soundly sleeping, the group sneaked out of Windemere to their rendezvous.

At three in the morning of July 27, Grace was awakened by Mrs. Loomis banging at the door. Her Oak Park neighbor had wakened to find her children and guests missing from their beds. She immediately suspected Hemingway collusion, for the thirteen year-old Jean Reynolds had been flirting with Ernest. By lantern light Grace and Mrs. Loomis searched for their charges. Finally Ruth Arnold, in tears, told them where the children had gone. When the harmless cookout and sing-song at the Point broke up at 3:00 a.m., the Hemingway contingent returned to an armed camp. Much ado and harsh words followed. The furious Mrs. Loomis would not speak to the Hemingway group.

At 10:00 a.m. the next morning, Grace told Ernest and Ted to pack and leave Windemere. As she wrote the Doctor, "Ernest called me every name he could think of, and said everything vile about me; but I kept my tongue and did not get hysterical." Grace realized that the night party had not been "wicked." What she objected to was the deceit "and the general lawlessness that Ernest instills into all young boys and girls." The stress had caused Grace's period to stop abruptly, leaving her face "congested almost to purple."[34] The escapade of itself was not terribly significant, but it pushed Grace beyond the edge of tolerance. She handed Ernest the letter she had so carefully drafted. Six weeks later she sent a second copy to Clarence.

My Dear Son Ernest,

For three years, since you decided, at the age of eighteen years, that you did not need any further advice or guidance from your parents, I have tried to keep silence and let you work out your own salvation; by that I mean, your own philosophy of life – your code of ethics in dealing with men, women, and children. Now, at the age of twenty-one, and being, according to some of your best friends and well-wishers, so sadly in need of good guidance, I shall brave your anger, and speak this once more to you.

A mother's love seems to me like a bank. Each child that is born to her, enters the world with a large and prosperous bank account, seemingly inexhaustible. For the first five years he draws, and draws – physical labor and pain – loss of sleep – watching and soothing, waiting upon, bathing, dressing, amusing. The Mother is practically a body slave to his every whim.

There are no deposits in the bank account during all the early years. "Cheery-o," thinks the mother, "some day he will be a comfort to me and return all I am doing for him," and she is content.

Then, for the next ten years, or so, up to adolescence, while the bank is heavily drawn on, for love and sympathy, championship in time of trouble or injustice, nursing thru illnesses, teaching and guiding, developing the young body and mind and soul, at all and any expense to the often exhausted parents during this time – there are a few deposits of pennies, in the way of services willingly done, some thoughtfulness and "thank yous."

Truly, the bank account is perilously low, for there is nothing coming in, no deposits, unless occasional spells of regret for past conduct make him come to her with an "I'm sorry and will truly try to do better."

But now, adolescence is past – full manhood is here. The bank is still paying out love, sympathy with wrongs, and enthusiasm for all ventures; courtesies and entertainment of friends who have nothing in common with mother, who, unless they are well bred, scarcely notice her existence.

The bank goes on handing out understanding and interest in budding love affairs, joy in plans of every sort. The account needs some deposits, by this time, some good sized ones in the way of gratitude and appreciation, interest in Mother's ideas and affairs. Little comforts provided for the home; a desire to favor any of Mother's peculiar prejudices, on no account to outrage her ideals – Flowers, fruit, candy, or something pretty to wear, brought home to mother, with a kiss and a squeeze – The unfailing desire to make much of her feeble efforts, to praise her cooking, back up her little schemes; a real interest in hearing her sing, or play the piano, or tell the stories that she loves to tell – A surreptitious paying of bills, just to get them off Mother's mind; Thoughtful remembrances and celebration of her birthday and Mother's day (the sweet letter accompanying the gift of flowers, she treasures most of all). These are merely a few of the deposits which keep the account in good standing.

Many mothers I know are receiving these, and much more substantial gifts and returns from sons of less abilities than my son. Unless you, my son, Ernest, come to yourself, cease your lazy loafing, and pleasure seeking – borrowing with no thought of returning – stop trying to graft a living off anybody and everybody – spending all your earnings lavishly and wastefully on luxuries for yourself – stop trading on your handsome face, to fool little gullible girls, and neglecting your duties to God and your Savior Jesus Christ – unless, in other words, you come into your manhood – there is nothing before you but bankruptcy: *You have over drawn.*

This world, which is your world, is crying out for men, real men, with brawn and muscle, moral as well as physical – men whose mothers can look up to them, instead of hanging their heads in shame at having borne them. Purity of speech and life, have been taught you from earliest childhood. You are born of a race of gentlemen – men who would scorn to accept anything from anybody without rendering a just equivalent, men who were clean mouthed, chivalrous to all women, grateful and generous. You were named for the two finest and noblest gentlemen I have ever known. See to it that you do not disgrace their memories.

Do not come back until your tongue has learned not to insult and shame your mother.

When you have changed your ideas and aims in life, you will find your mother waiting to welcome you, whether it be in this world or the next – loving you and longing for your love.

The Lord watch between me and thee while we are absent, one from the other.

> Your still hoping and praying mother,
> Grace Hall Hemingway[35]

Ernest moved out of the cottage.

Grace won the battle but the war between mother and son continued at long range through the rest of the summer. To his father Ernest wrote his side of the story. The Doctor stood firmly behind his wife. When he got the copy of her letter to Ernest, he called it "a masterpiece," a letter he would prize "as the right conception of the Mother's part of the game of family life."[36] When Ursula and Sunny returned to Oak Park for the beginning of school, Clarence thought he could see Ernest's influence in their rebellious behavior. He assured Grace, who remained at her own cottage with Ruth Arnold and the two yougest Hemingways, that he was up to the task of discipline. He urged her to stay as long as possible at the Longfield cottage, but he was beginning to have some doubts about his prodigal son's dismissal. Ursula and Sunny said that the problem was Grace, not Ernest. The Doctor wrote:

> I want so much for you to regain the love and affection of all of your daughters, and it will only be possible when all are rested and in reasonable frames of mind. I am doing the unselfish thing to stay here and protect and guide the girls. . . . I continue to pray for Ernest and believe that God will soften his heart and that we all shall again be united in love. If you falsely accused him, be sure to beg his pardon, even if he had made mistakes. For false accusations grow more sore all the time and separate many dear friends and relatives.[37]

By the middle of September, the Doctor was writing Ernest conciliatory letters, urging him to help Grace with the closing of the cottage. He was sure that the "few misunderstandings" between mother and son could be made right.[38] And to Grace he wrote that she should love Ernest. "He is our boy and we must always love and forgive each other."[39]

Grace stayed on at Longfield while the Doctor did his "duty" in Oak Park. September came and went. The apples in the Charles orchard ripened in the cooling fall air, and Ernest could be seen working at the harvest. In October Grace finally returned to Oak Park, having stayed longer at the lake than ever before. The rift with Ernest was gradually closing over. She returned his library books and sympathized with one of his periodic injuries – a belly bruised badly on a boat cleat. "I hope your internal injury is giving you no more trouble," she wrote. "I could not sleep the night after you told me about it (sympathetic nervous pain) so sorry you should have to suffer so much torture."[40]

By Christmas it was as if the summer wars had never happened. On the surface, at least, the family appeared whole once more. But Ernest never again lived at 600 North Kenilworth, and he never forgot the summer's conflict. Nor did he ever remember it quite right. Nor did he ever complete the break with his mother. Years later he would call her an "all-American bitch," but when she was in need, he did his duty. After his father's suicide in 1928, he borrowed $30,000 dollars from his publisher against future royalties to set up a trust fund that weathered Grace through to her death in 1951. Her July 24 letter came truer than she could have foreseen: he literally made the bank deposits she laid claim to, "a surreptitious paying of bills."

The summer's events, hardly catastrophic in retrospect, loomed large in Hemingway's imagination. In the fictional versions he told friends, he gave the impression that he had been thrown out of his home young and spent much of his early life on the road. In his printed fiction, the characters seldom have a home. We find them living in hotels or at battle fronts, a little rootless. If they have parents, lovers promise each other they will not have to meet them. At the very end, Thomas Hudson in *Islands in the Stream* has a house but no wife; his children are lost. And none of the characters lives in a place like Oak Park.

Hemingway broke the binding ties that summer. At twenty-one, he was free to create himself in his own fictive image. The longest and last summer at the lake was over. He returned to Windemere but twice more, and then but for a few days. Long before her death, his mother gave the cottage to Ernest as his inheritance, hoping that he would summer there once again, hoping that his children would fish and swim where for twenty-one years her oldest boy had summered. The seasons passed, taking their toll on paint and shingle. The rowboat's caulking rotted out. Ernest paid the taxes but never opened the doors, not for himself, not for any of his siblings. On his forty-fourth birthday, Ursula wrote reminding him of the good summers at the lake. He replied that Windemere was still the clearest part of his life, and for that reason he could not go back.[41]

As long as she was physically able, Grace continued to spend summers in Grace Cottage across the lake at Longfield. On his birthday in 1946 she wrote one of her last letters to her son.

> I walked over to Windemere, and thought of all the happy days we spent there. I grieved to realize that you cared nothing for the place and had never been even to see it in the past eleven years. . . . For some time it was broken into almost every winter by marauders. . . . the mice have gnawed holes into the house . . . the front porch floor and roof are fast disappearing. The steps . . . have rotted away. The neighbors call it the haunted house. . . . The yard is littered with broken down trees. . . . The woodshed and boathouse have lost their roofs.[42]

Mother and son, misunderstanding each other to the end. He never went back and he never left. Windemere haunted his fiction always. After his mother's death in 1951, Hemingway began but did not finish "The Last Good Country," a fictional version of the great heron incident. Nick Adams, pursued by two murderous game wardens, escapes into the woods with his precocious little sister, who is there to witness and admire her stalwart brother. Her wise child's preoccupation with incest amuses Nick who dismisses the idea as impractical. Self-reliant, Nick survives by his wits and his woodsman's skills. His absent father is unmentioned. His mother, when faced with the game wardens, takes to her sick bed with a headache. In the woods Nick and his sister make their "browse bed" of balsam on hemlock: the children of Dr. Adams returned to the fallen Garden.

Chapter Six

CHICAGO
1920

IN the fall of the year his father came to close the cottage, but Ernest did not go there anymore. The apples in the Charles orchard were all picked; the summer people departed. Marge Bump was in St. Louis, a Washington University freshman; Irene Goldstein, departed. Ernest drove back as far as Chicago with Bill Smith and Mrs. Charles. A man of no fortune, he traveled light: a few clothes, a box of manuscripts and several letters of rejection. He spoke bravely of jobs awaiting him, imaginary jobs on the Kansas City *Star* and New Mexican dude ranches. But there was nothing waiting for Ernest in Chicago, nothing, at least, that he had imagined.

At Bill Horne's apartment, he was promised a free room until a job came through, and he was always welcome at Kenley Smith's where a literate bunch of men frequently gathered and Katy was sometimes in residence. With the little money he had managed to save, he was excited about moving in with the crowd of slightly older men at Kenley's. Ernest still wore his Italian officer's cape for warmth and flair; he still had his enormous energy. Whatever was pulsating, whatever was alive interested him: boxing, opera, gangsters, movies, vaudeville, drinking, dancing. Although he knew parts of Chicago well, he had never lived at the heart of it. From Oak Park, a nickel ride got a boy to the Loop, but Oak Park boys could seldom stay long in the city.

Either they were going to the Field Museum or the Art Institute, to a play or a White Sox game, but their parents expected them home for supper. When they did sneak into the city to catch a bit of low life, they felt very daring. So much was forbidden an Oak Park boy, it was easy to be bad, and the invisible walls around Oak Park made the city all the more attractive to a young man. Hemingway entered Chicago that fall with no prospects but high expectations. Something, he was certain, would turn up. Katy would be there; he counted on her. What he did not expect was Hadley Richardson.

It was the time when skirts got shorter and the last legal whiskey was disappearing. It was the time of the silent movies; it was the time when Chaplin was king. And all the white girls were humming, "*You're on my mind the whole night long. I'm for you right or wrong.*" You could hear it at *George White's Scandals of 1920* or buy the Victor record to play on the new Victrola. *Right or wrong, the whole night long.* We were right when we went to the war, but now the war was not so right. Had it all been wrong? The Senate would not join the League of Nations. Woodrow Wilson lay dying in the White House, his settlement with Japan in the Pacific was called a disaster. All fall in Chicago the papers ran the story: the next war would be in the Pacific, probably centering on Hawaii. In Russia the war had not stopped: Reds and Whites; factions splitting, falling; frozen bodies piling up like cord wood at railway stops. Elsewhere the endless Irish Question blazed brighter than ever: I.R.A., Black and Tans; Dublin and Cork burned, Liverpool burned. In Fiume, Italy, the aging romantic, Gabriele d'Annunzio, and his rag-tag army continued to contest the socialist takeover. Right or wrong, the war was not over. Senator Harding from Ohio promised to settle up the European debts, return the country to normalcy, and keep us out of foreign tangles. Ernest was not involved in the first election in which he could vote, for there were other concerns much closer home.

Cicotte, Williams and Shoeless Joe Jackson – stars of the White Sox ball club that lost the 1919 World Series – confessed that they had fixed the outcome, thrown the series for money.

Other confessions followed. The boys of summer had sold their birthright to east coast gamblers. Suckered once more, Ernest had lost money betting on the Sox. Wrong or right, the bottom line was the money. There was nothing that could not be bought or sold, given the right connections. Ernest understood about money. Money was the benchmark for all measurements in Oak Park, and the White Sox affirmed the profit motive: the players made more money losing the Series than they would have made winning it. Every day the *Tribune* bannered corruption. Police and judges were on the take; the whiskey ring of Mike "da Pike" Heitler had fifty cops in league with it.

30 POLICE ACCUSED IN RUM SCANDAL

The politicians were not far behind. "Bath House" John knew how to grease a wheel and deliver the vote. Every day in the *Tribune* the bodies piled up.

3 DIE, 2 DYING, 4 SHOT
IN DAY OF GUN FIGHTS

FIND TWO GIRLS SLAIN IN PARK

The girls, always game for a party, died from alcoholic poisoning. Almost 200 Chicagoans were murdered that year. Another 550 died violently in automobiles. "Vampire" cars hit and ran, leaving no forwarding address. Frank Campione the first member of the Cardinella gang to drop through the trap door on the end of a rope, went down beside a Negro wife-killer. Ernest took it all in, saving bits and pieces for later use.

Down in the "blind pigs" and "speakeasies," the jazz drummer kept the beat up tempo, and the black girl with the throaty voice sang, "*Aggravatin' papa, don't you try to two time me. . . . Aggravatin' papa, treat me kind or let me be. . . . I mean just let me be. Listen while I get you told. Stop messin' 'round, sweet jelly roll.*" You could not buy that on Victor records, but the words still stuck. Five years later they would pop up as a riff in *The Sun Also Rises.*[1] And the black girl said, "*Once you were true, but papa, now sweet mama can't depend on you.*" But the girls could depend upon Ernest to write interesting letters. Grace Quinlan in Petoskey, Marge in St. Louis, got their letters filled with gossip, inventions and partial truths. Ernest liked to write the girls. He liked to get letters. The girls wrote letters back filled with amusing mush. Sometimes he showed the letters to Katy Smith, whom he still pursued.

Katy was there at Kenley's apartment when the last of the summer people arrived. Before Ernest could set his duffle bag down, she was telling him about her friend from St. Louis. Ernest should be nice to her, Katy said. Sure, sure. Ernest was always nice to the girls. Just then Bill came down from upstairs to say that Hadley was there. Mrs. Charles, who had known Hadley for years, was most surprised. They all trooped up to the bedroom where a tall girl with bobbed red hair waited, a little flustered by so much attention. It ws the first time Ernest saw Hadley Richardson, and she was the new country.

The men smoked cigarettes and talked with their hands. Some of the women were smoking. They all talked at once. On the table two wine bottles were almost empty. She listened. It was all very different, not at all like St. Louis. Here everyone talked loudly about art and writers and fishing, and everyone had strange names – Fever and Horney and Wemedge and Boid. Even Katy Smith was called Butstein or Stut. Hadley did not understand and it did not matter. No one explained anything. Where was the lake? She did not ask. The Victrola trumpeted the new jazz records, giving an insistent urgency to the words that swirled about her. With her bobbed hair and her new blue dress, the hemline raised, she was almost a part of that crowd. They called her Hash. She had come a long way from St. Louis, where her grand piano played no jazz, and where Fonnie, her older sister, never tired of telling her how fragile she was.

In Chicago she did not feel fragile. She felt saved. Kenley and Katy took her to piano concerts, literary parties and silent movies. She met interesting people like Sherwood Anderson, whose books she now must read. God bless Katherine Foster Smith, who rescued her from the rites of mourning and lawyers' jargon. She had known Katy Smith all her life. At Mary Institute they shared eight years of classes together, and during the ten years since graduation they had remained close. Kenley, the oldest Smith, she did not know well, but she grew up with Katy and her younger brother, Bill. Now she felt that Katy had kept growing where she had stopped. The last ten years were dusty years suspended out of time, years so quiet that all she could now hear were the piano notes echoing through the house where her fierce mother had finally died. In that cool evening in Chicago her life, quite of its own accord, began to revive. There in Kenley Smith's rented rooms the sadness began to lift, the dust to slough away.

In the talk of Italian war days and trout fishing at the Bay, she was a little left out, listening and watching. The men talked and with them was Ernest, taller, younger, more handsome than any man there. He was eight years younger than she, but in all that smoky talk he had eyes for her only. A fool for red hair or blonde, he was drawn to Hadley Richardson as if to a magnet. Before the wine was gone, she was laughing. Before the evening ended she was playing Kenley's piano. Be nice to her, Katy told Ernest. She watched amused as Ernest's intensity charmed her friend. He had that ability to fix his brown eyes on a woman's face until the world disappeared. For that evening Hadley forgot her mother's funeral, forgot the responsibilities of executing the will. No man had ever looked at her that way.

In early November, after Harding's election, she returned to St. Louis in love. Every day she had been with Ernest. Every day there were more revelations. He told her about the lake, about his parents, about the summer débâcle. He told her about his Italian war and all about his writing. Some of what he told her was true, and most of what he told her he believed. At least when he said it he believed it. She told him about her life in St. Louis, about her mother's recent death, about her father's suicide when she was fourteen. But she did not say a word about her substantial trust fund. Hadley Richardson had led a protected life, but she was no fool.

Their needs made a perfect match. She had lost her mother,

the controlling force in her life; he had broken with his mother's dominance. Both needed support, but of different kinds. Hadley gave Ernest the female attention and unqualified admiration he would need all his years. Ernest gave her his unbounded sense of his own destiny; he gave her his enthusiasm for life and returned to her the gift of laughter. For seventeen years Hadley had been without strong male affection. She listened to Ernest's dreams for a literary life and approved. She read his clichéd fiction and found the stories wonderful. Together they roamed the Chicago streets, ate in the Italian restaurants, and talked alone at night on Kenley's roof, away from the crowd. With Hadley as his perfect audience, Ernest performed eagerly, acting out the role of young writer almost as he was inventing it.

That first October when he met her. Hadley was twenty-nine years old, well on her way to becoming a spinster aunt. Ernest was twenty-one and looking for someone to marry. In spite of his boasting, there is little evidence that he was sexually promiscuous. Between the desire and the deed there fell the mores of Oak Park. In the pre-war era that formed his values, sexual congress with a proper woman betokened matrimony, an attitude found in most of his fictional characters. Frederic Henry, in *A Farewell to Arms*, feels obliged to marry Catherine Barkley as soon as he has bedded her. For practical reasons she resists. Without benefit of clergy, he thinks of them as married nonetheless. In *For Whom the Bell Tolls*, Maria is no sooner in Robert Jordan's sleeping bag than he thinks of her as his wife. Hemingway gave us men who enjoy their women without marriage but not without a sense of responsibility: sex, love, marriage – the oldest triple play is affirmed in principle. In his fiction, death usually intervenes to remove the obligation. Sex was important to Hemingway, but not without responsibility. There was the rub. In Oak Park a man married the woman he lay with. In his fiction he might escape that unwritten rule, but in his own life Hemingway was a native son. He was capable of one night stands and casual beddings, but he could not sustain an affair without marrying the woman or at least asking.

When Hadley met him, she was older but less experienced

than he, dependent, hesitant, starved for affection, emotionally distraught by her mother's death, and unaccustomed to making decisions. She was pretty but not beautiful: solidly built, almost chunky. With her red hair and freckles, she looked like a taller version of Marge Bump. When Ernest put her on the St. Louis train, he had no intention of marrying Hadley Richardson. Later he would say that the moment he saw her he wanted her for wife, but that fall there were too many available women. From Toronto, Bonnie Bonnell, tall and attractive, sent Morse coded messages in her letters: "I Love You." Irene Goldstein, who danced so well and loved to party, was in Chicago, as was Katy Smith. Hadley was good to be with but so were a lot of girls. It was a game, as he later wrote, a lot like bridge "in which you said things instead of playing cards."

For an amateur, Hadley played the game rather well. No sooner had she returned to St. Louis than she wrote Hemingway: "Why did you say to me . . . on the car last night when I said I didn't know anything that I knew *too* much?"[2] She was fishing long distance, not knowing that writers never throw away a good line. Four years later, Hemingway would write:

> "I know it," Marjorie said happily.
>
> "You know everything," Nick said.
>
> "Oh, Nick, please cut it out! Please, please don't be that way."
>
> "I can't help it," Nick said. "You do. You know everything. That's the trouble. You know you do."[3]

More than one of Hadley's good lines showed up in his fiction, but then she wrote a lot of letters during their eleven month courtship. Together for less than three weeks of that year, their relationship grew more on paper than in the flesh. During the first two months Hadley's tone was cheery but cautious, certainly not over-eager. Their age difference bothered her; it also bothered her sister, Fonnie, who, married and mothered, felt she must protect her fragile younger sister now that their mother was dead. For years Hadley had been treated like a semi-invalid. In her youth a fall from a balcony had put her in bed for some months with a strained back. Ever since, she had been told how delicate her health was, how fragile her bones. Fonnie, that is Mrs. Roland Usher and mother of two, was all too eager to take her mother's place in protecting Hadley, who would live past ninety. Hadley, who came to believe in her fictional fragility, returned from Chicago noticeably changed, happier than she should have been, more color to her cheeks, a little less submissive.

For the next month Hadley answered the letters that bombarded her from Chicago. Her tone was friendly but not infatuated; however, she always asked questions that encouraged answers. Particularly she asked about Ernest's writing. That was the best bait. Better educated and better read – sometimes almost too well read – Hadley had the good sense not to flaunt her education. She gathered that Hemingway was sensitive about not having gone to college. She had finished her freshman year at Bryn Mawr in 1911 but had gone no farther. Her eight years at Mary Institute, a private girls' school founded by T. S. Eliot's grandfather, had been somewhat more demanding than Hemingway's public-school education. Graduating with honors, Hadley's 88.5 grade point average placed her fourteenth in a class of fifty-four. She took eight years of French and Latin, compared to Hemingway's three years of Latin.[4] She did not have his facility for picking up a language from the streets and the newspapers, but her textbook French was excellent. Later Hemingway would say that he taught himself French from reading sports coverage of events he had seen.[5] He did not say that Hadley also taught him about the language. That was the nice thing about words on paper: he could create his life exactly as he wished it to be, and eventually come to believe it.

Like Hemingway's high-school reading, Hadley's education concentrated on classic British writers: Chaucer, Bunyan, Spenser, Shakespeare and Milton. Both knew Chaucer's General Prologue and Knight's Tale well enough to allude to them. But in her senior year Hadley read for two semesters in the British authors of the eighteenth and nineteenth centuries, whereas Ernest knew only a few of the classic British novels.[6] She also studied art history and upon graduation toured Europe with her mother. Hemingway toured only in the Chicago Art Institute; his European sojourn did not include museums or edifices. From 1920 on, he learned quickly about classical art, and Hadley was one of his teachers.

As well-schooled as Hemingway was in classical music at his mother's knee, Hadley's musical abilities outstripped his. Not only was she fluent in the classics, she was also a pianist of concert ability. There were two baby grand pianos in her grandfather's house, one in her own. After her year at Bryn Mawr, she threw herself into rigorous study and practice, for it was her only visible accomplishment and her only source of pride. For several years she imagined a life on the concert stage not unlike the operatic career that Grace Hemingway once longed for. After Hemingway met Hadley, his somewhat dormant interest in pianists began to bloom. In January, he wrote his mother that he

> went to hear Benny Moiseiwitsch play at orchestra hall in the afternoon. Moiseiwitsch is the best pianist there is now I think. He's infinitely superior to Levitski or Jeosh Hoffman and I think he has it on Rachmaninoff or Gabrilowitch – he's in the first four anyway.
>
> He played a much better program that he did the last time I heard him, Chopin's B. Minor Concerto and the sunken cathedral, Cathedral Engloutie or something like that by Debussy and then two of Liszt with the Campanella and some modern stuff that I forget the names of. I'm quoting from memory or I'd be more accurate. [7]

As a boy, Hemingway was no stranger to classical music. As her father had taken her, Grace took Ernest to Chicago opera during his early years, and the Chicago Symphony played an annual benefit series in Oak Park, where a high percentage of the middle-class gentry were not only musically conversant but actually skilled musicians. But until he met Hadley, Hemingway never wrote letters about listening to classical pianists. Now he was not only listening, he was also judging their quality, without

1 Ernest Hall with his son, Leicester, and his daughter, Grace. (John F. Kennedy Library)

2 Clarence Edmonds
Hemingway, c. 1900.
(John F. Kennedy Library)

3 Anson Tyler
Hemingway, Ernest's
beloved grandfather.
(John F. Kennedy Library)

4 Ernest, Grace, Clarence and Marcelline on the beach at Lake Walloon, c. 1902. (John F. Kennedy Library)

5 Clarence and Grace Hemingway with their children Ursula, Ernest and Marcelline, c. 1903. Ernest and Marcelline are dressed alike, as they frequently were for formal occasions. (John F. Kennedy Library)

6   Ernest in his fringed shirt and pants with his sisters, Ursula and Marcelline, admiring their mother's pike. Summer of 1904. (John F. Kennedy Library)

7   Hemingway family c. 1910: Ernest, the Doctor, Grace, Ursula, Sunny, Marcelline. (John F. Kennedy Library)

8 Ernest, fishing in Michigan in the summer of 1913. (John F. Kennedy Library)

9 Ernest in the Michigan woods during the summer of 1916. (John F. Kennedy Library)

10   Ernest and a highschool classmate cross-country hiking when physical fitness became a national passion (1916). (John F. Kennedy Library)

11 As soon as he got the wound stripes and medals sewn on to his tailored uniform, Hemingway went to the Milan photographer. Note the U.S. insignia which he did not rate – and the absence of any Red Cross insignia. (John F. Kennedy Library)

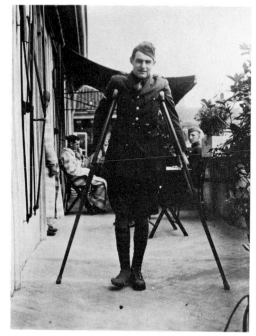

12 At the Milan hospital in the fall of 1918, Hemingway posing on his new crutches. His right leg is not yet fully healed from his operation. (Library of Congress)

13 Agnes Von Kurowsky, in
black hat, 1918 *(left)*; in
nurse's uniform, 1920 *(below)*.
(Red Cross Archives)

14 January, 1919. Ernest, home from the wars, continued to wear his uniform, boots and Italian officer's cape as long as possible. (John F. Kennedy Library)

15 Summer 1919 in the lake at Windemere: Grace in her dark glasses, holding Leicester; standing at the back is Grace's faithful companion, Ruth Arnold. (John F. Kennedy Library)

16 Marjorie Bump during the winter of 1919–20, at Petoskey, Michigan. (John F. Kennedy Library)

17 The "Summer People" in 1920: Carl Edgar, Katy Smith, Marcelline with her hair newly bobbed, Bill Horne, Ernest with his Italian pistol, and Bill Smith with his new mustache. (John F. Kennedy Library)

18 Bill Smith, Ernest, Carl Edgar (standing), ?, Marcelline, Katy Smith, and Lucille Dick in the summer of 1920. (John F. Kennedy Library)

19 Marcelline Hemingway with her "bobbed" hair, c. 1921.
(John F. Kennedy Library)

20   Hadley Richardson in 1910, on graduating from Mary Institute
in St. Louis. (Mary Institute, St. Louis, Mo.)

21   Ernest and Hadley during his brief visit to St. Louis in March 1921.
(John F. Kennedy Library)

22   Hadley Richardson on her wedding day in Michigan, September 3rd,
1921. (John F. Kennedy Library)

23 Ernest and Bill Smith (fifth and sixth from left) on Ernest's wedding day, September 3rd, 1921. (John F. Kennedy Library)

24 Ernest with his new bride, Hadley Richardson, on his arm. To their left: Grace, Carol, Marcelline; to their right: Sunny, Leicester and the Doctor. Fall, 1921. (John F. Kennedy Library)

telling his mother that is renewed interest came from Hadley. All his life he had a way of using the experience and knowledge of others as if it were his own. He learned quickly, making his tutors feel important as he focused his intensity on their field of knowledge. Whether it was boxing or painting, military tactics or politics, Hemingway, once interested, had the knack of picking up information quickly and making it his own. More than one tutor would find himself surpassed by this student who did not always give credit where due.

In St. Louis Hadley spent the month of November dealing with the complexities of her mother's will. She and Fonnie were both named as the executors, but Fonnie had signed her responsibility over to a lawyer. Hadley dealt with the unpaid bills: grocer, druggist, milkman and undertaker. There were stocks and bonds to be evaluated; notes to be collected; property assessed. With little experience in money management, she still realized that every nickel counted, for from the residue would come her trust fund. The estate was not vast, but Florence Wyman Richardson had rather improved the fallen fortune she inherited from her hopelessly incompetent and somewhat alcoholic husband.

Hadley's grandfather, James Richardson Sr., had been one of St. Louis' movers and shapers. Before the Civil War he founded the Richardson Drug Company which by 1883 occupied six lots on North Main St., three warehouses on the levee, and four more lots on North Second St. It was the largest drug company west of the Mississippi, with stock on hand worth a half million dollars. For years he served as director of several St. Louis banks as well as on the Board of Education. He was also responsible for building the public library system into a civic asset. His two sons, Clifford and James Jr., gradually took over the drug business: Clifford to Omaha to manage the branch office; Hadley's father, James Jr., in St. Louis as Secretary Treasurer of the corporation. No one could have been less suited to the job, for her father hated the drug business. In 1889, three years before Hadley's birth, the St. Louis warehouse burned down, never to be rebuilt. James used the fire as an excuse to resign from active management, but retained his half interest in the lucrative business.[8] In 1893, the founding father, James Sr., died. His will, dated just after the company fire in 1889, left an estate of $300,000, none of which went to Clifford or James Jr., for he had already given them their fair share of the estate – the Richardson Drug Co. For the children of James Jr. he set up a $50,000 trust to be shared equally.[9]

In 1893, half interest in the Richardson Drug Company was worth at least $150,000. Within ten years Hadley's father reduced that figure to $50,000 with precious little to show for his spending. Of course he supported his civic-minded wife, Florence, in her various good works, provided private education for his children, and generally contributed to the public welfare of St. Louis. But this was $150,000 before the advent of personal income taxes. By today's inflated values, James Richardson went through at least $400,000 in twelve years. Drinking became a hobby, but liquor was cheap. He did not buy land. He did not invest much in St. Louis business ventures. What he did, apparently, was gamble on the stock market. The two crashes of 1893 and 1897 must have put a considerable dent in the fortune. By 1904 he was desperate and despondent, a founding father's youngest son who had slipped further and further down the social register. His house on Cates Ave. was something less grand than the parental home on Cabanne. He was still respected but mainly now for his Richardson name, not his money.

In 1904 something snapped in James Richardson. During the first eleven months of that year he borrowed $20,000 in twelve separate loans from the Richardson Drug Co., using his patrimonial stock as collateral. During the last month of 1904, he floated four more loans at St. Louis banks for another $9500, using the same stock as collateral. A month after the last loan, he had nothing to show for the $29,500 but a $500 bill outstanding with a stockbroker. Throughout January 1905 he gambled heavily in the commodities market, buying and selling May wheat futures in ten and twenty thousand bushel orders. But wheat futures had peaked; farmers had overplanted for May. By the end of January, Richardson owed his broker $500, more than some employees earned in an entire year. During January he also ran up a $150 bill with one Ivan Skobal, who called himself a doctor, but who really ran a water-cure treatment, a glorified bath. Since October, Richardson had been spending $5 a day at Skobol's baths, when $5 could hire a maid for a week. On February 8, 1905, James Richardson Jr. put a pistol to his temple and pulled the trigger. When his will was probated all that remained of the $29,500 were the signed letters of debt.[10]

The only testimony at the Medical Examiner's hearing was given by his wife, Florence.

He has been in poor health for some time, catarrhal trouble, suffered from insomnia and worried very much, and has business troubles. Otherwise was cheerful and had never spoken of suicide. About 5:30 a.m. . . . I heard a shot in his bedchamber. I waited two or three minutes, did not realize it was a pistol shot at first. I got up, went to his room, found him on the floor, bleeding from wound in right side of head.[11]

Four hours later he was dead. At fourteen Hadley lost the father who doted on her, the father whom she, more than any of the children, resembled. As she watched him dying that Sunday morning, she could not understand his act, but there was no doubt about her pain of loss. No man filled that loss until she met Ernest Hemingway fifteen years later.

The St. Louis *Globe* did not mention Richardson's suicide. The family may have fallen financially but the name still commanded respect. Florence Wyman Richardson, accustomed to better times, began the task of salvaging what fortune was left. Like Grace Hall Hemingway, she was a tough, intelligent lady who frequently got her own way. As executor, she liquidated Richardson's remaining stock to pay off his notes and the $15,000 house mortgage. She contested the broker's bill, finally compromising for $365 when the court decided that Richardson had not been cheated. When the Traveler's Insurance Co. refused to honor Richardson's $10,000 accidental death policy, Florence threatened them with a court suit. They compromised at $6500. When the final count was made, Florence was left with about $30,000 and a mortgage free house. One of those last bills was from the Wagoner Undertaking Co. – $125 for a black, broadcloth-covered burial casket. James Richardson Jr. did not go out in style. [12]

Although the family was reduced in means, it was not bankrupt. Florence had some money of her own inherited from the Wyman family. Her father had made a sizable fortune shipping goods up and down the Mississippi in partnership with Jay Gould. When he was not engaged in commerce, he was busy founding private schools – four of them by the time he died in 1888. [13] With a financial acumen seldom exhibited by her husband, Florence Wyman Richardson, through astute investments, slowly rebuilt the fallen fortune. When she died in 1920, Hadley found herself executor of a $75,000 estate, which was divided into trust funds for herself, Fonnie, brother James and her two Bragdon nephews. Hadley's share was $15,636. Another $5357 was put in trust for any children she might bear in the future. Yet another $5000 was added to Hadley's inheritance by a curious codicil to the will:

> Should my daughter, Elizabeth Hadley Richardson, be single one year after the date of my death, I give and bequeath . . . the sum of Five Thousand Dollars, to be added to and become a part of the trust therein created for my said daughter.

If Hadley married within that year, the money would revert to the general fund to be shared with Fonnie. When Florence Richardson wrote that codicil in 1918, she was certain that Hadley would never marry and would require more support than Fonnie, who was already married to a university professor. [14]

Various complictions kept Florence's estate from final settlement until 1922, but in October of 1920, Hadley knew that she was heiress to a respectable income. Her trust from her grandfather's will had been accruing interest for twenty-seven years.

What began as $12,000 in 1893 was now worth at least $30,000. When combined with the trusts set up by her mother, Hadley's fortune would be about $50,000, which, safely invested, would provide an income of $3000 a year. In 1920 the average working man was earning only $1342. Three thousand dollars a year was a comfortable income.

While Hadley was struggling with accountants' figures in St. Louis, Ernest was not pining away in his room, nor had he found a job. There was too much happening in Chicago; his summer friends moved at a jazzy pace. Tubby Williams, a friend from the Italian war, tried to get him a job with an advertising firm, but it did not work out. In the evenings Chicago glittered almost as brightly as Broadway. Frequently with Katy Smith on his arm, he took in the shows: Ethel Barrymore in Zoe Akins' *Déclassé*; Belle Bennett in the musical *Happy Go Lucky*; Ann Pennington in *George White's Scandals of 1920*. Pennington, he said, was getting a bit heavy. When he wasn't going to theatre, he was at the Chicago Opera seeing *Andrea Chenier* twice.[15] From his mother's passion for music, he had grown up knowing opera, both melody and story line. *Andrea Chenier*, he said, was like *A Tale of Two Cities*. In Milan he had gone to the La Scala opera house and gotten to know a few of the American singers who were trying to break into the big time. The Chicago Opera put on lavish productions befitting the metropolis that H. L. Mencken called the cultural center of America. The 1920–21 season included *La Traviata, Rigoletto, Lucia di Lammermoor, Jacquerie, La Sonnambula, Il Trovatore* and *Aida*.

Never again would Hemingway have such easy access to movies, theater or opera as he had that year in Chicago, for he would never again reside in an American cultural center. He lived in Chicago for only fifteen months, but as with so much of his life, he lived intensely. The after-effects were curious. Chicago does not appear in his published fiction, but his short course in popular theater left its mark. Like so many American novelists—James, Fitzgerald, Dos Passos, Faulkner—Hemingway wanted to write for the stage. He particularly wanted to write comedy. With his flair for tall tales and his ability to make friends laugh, he thought it might be easy money. Somehow it did not work. What was funny in Kenley's living room failed on paper. With his high-school friend, Morris Musselman, he collaborated on a farce called *Hokum,* which never got beyond typescript. Throughout the Twenties, whenever he hit a dry period, he would start another comedy that usually did not get past the second page. When he finally did write his only play, *The Fifth Column* (1937), the production came off heavy-handed.

When he was not writing, he was reading, always. That fall in Chicago, among literate college men, he began to read heavily in current fiction. His correspondence with Hadley was pleasant, chatty and quite literary. Ernest recommended James Stephens' *Crock of Gold* and Sinclair Lewis' *Main Street,* which was sweeping the country's best seller lists. Hadley promised to read them both. Not to be outdone, she suggested Dorothy Richardson's *Pointed Roofs* and *Black Water.* Although their letters were friendly, Hadley remained cautious. She did not want to appear devastated by him, so she continually phrased her interest in guarded terms. If Ernest and Katy came to St. Louis she would be pleased to show them a good time. She missed everyone: Kenley, Katy and Ernest.[16]

Early in December, Hadley had the chance to return to Chicago for a week. With St. Louis stifling her newly awakened passion for life, she was not going to let the opportunity pass her by. Ernest's letters were filled with energy and the promise of exciting things about to happen. No man had ever written her such letters. No man had ever treated her to such confidences. Fonnie warned her not to go, for unchaperoned she was too naive to cope with the world of men. Hadley knew better. On December 3 she sent Ernest a telegram: "Arriving Saturday."

In November, Ernest and Bill Horne, another ambulance driver from the war, had moved into an apartment on North State Street where Horne paid the rent until Ernest could find work. It was not a bad life, and Hemingway did not exhaust himself with job applications, for the free room gave him time to write. He also spent time at Kenley's apartment, listening to gossip – literary, personal and political – the sort of gossip he always enjoyed. Perhaps it was part of his heritage from Oak Park where gossip was a staple of Village life. As he later said of himself, he was a safe man to tell secrets: they went in one ear and out his mouth. And the *Follies* comedian sang: *"Everybody tells it to Sweeney and Sweeney tells it to me. If there's anything that you'd like to know, I'm the one to see."* Knowing the secrets of others and keeping his own secrets dark were basic character traits that he acquired early and practiced late. At Kenley's there was a lot of gossip, particularly about Kenley's artistic wife, Doodles. Hemingway loved it.

But with Hadley arriving, he must have worried a little about Katy Smith. He had been regularly stepping her out to dances and plays. With Hadley in town, he had a problem to face: how should he treat his two girls when he was a little in love with both? There was also the problem of Marge Bump. Katy, who knew that Hemingway dated Marge at the lake, probably knew that he was still writing her. Would Kate tell Hadley? For a young man, who, four years before, seldom dated any girl, Hemingway was faced with an embarrassment of riches. The problem would plague him all life. He fell in love quickly, and he was usually committed to another woman when he did. His fictional characters do not have such problems, but they fall in love no less quickly. Frederic Henry holds out until he finds Catherine Barkley as his nurse in the Milan hospital. Robert Jordan is deeply committed the moment he sees Maria in the Spanish cave. Colonel Cantwell is like a school boy with Renata in Venice. In the other country of fiction, his tragic lovers led lives nothing like his own. Fortunately for Hemingway, Katy Smith had a sense of humor and Hadley Richardson was more sophisticated than he. She could understand that a man might be involved with two women simultaneously. On moral grounds, Hemingway was usually uncomfortable with two loves; the mores of Oak Park stretched far beyond the Village limits.

Hadley's visit was another non-stop week of parties, music, theater and people. She and Ernest were together constantly though seldom alone, but that did not matter. Anyone who saw them knew they were in love. Together they went to the Art

Institute, where the Hemingway family held a season membership and where Ernest had spent many a Sunday afternoon all his young life. It was there that Hemingway first tasted the Modern. In March 1913, the infamous Armory Show had been on display for almost a month. By 1920 one could see in the permanent collection Cassatt's "The Toilet," Matisse's "By the Window" and Monet's "Cliffs at Trouville." Hemingway's taste in art was and remained rooted in traditional representative painters. Two years later he would discover Cézanne, Picasso, Braque, Klee, Masson and Miró, but when he finally wrote about a painter, Thomas Hudson in *Islands in the Stream*, he made him a realist whose canvases are based on those of Winslow Homer. It was, in fact the Ryerson Collection of Homer that drew Ernest and Hadley to the Art Institute that week. There, for the first time, he saw Homer's brilliant watercolors from his Gulf Stream period: "Tornado, Bahamas," "Breaking Storm," "Gulf Stream" and "Stowing Sail," among others.[17] He loved Homer's ability to catch light on water and fix special moments in his wash of color.

No matter how much he later praised Picasso and Miro, his roots were in the story-telling paintings of the past which were the Art Institute's strong point – paintings like Delacroix's romantic "Cleopatra," "Tiger" and "Wounded Lioness" and El Greco's "Assumption of the Virgin." At his most experimental, Hemingway did not lose sight of the story line. The style he created for his time did not interfere with the plot, nor did it lead him into the excesses of Stein or Joyce. Many of his stories, when stripped of their style on the movie screen, reveal just how romantic he was at heart. In the fall of 1920, Hemingway did not yet understand what Modernism was about. All of his models were spawned in the nineteenth century, but that was about to change radically. Between Hadley's visits he had met Sherwood Anderson, who would begin Hemingway's education in the twentieth century.

Anderson's Modernism, like Hemingway's, began with his exposure to the post-impressionists and cubists. His brother, Karl Anderson, was a graduate of the Art Institute's school. In 1910, his painting "Idlers" was bought for the permanent collection, and in 1919 his "Sisters" won the Alumni Association medal.[18] It was Karl who took Sherwood to the Institute's display of the Armory Show, opening Anderson's mind to the Modern. In turn, it was Sherwood who advocated the Modern to the young Hemingway. In July of 1921, Hemingway saw an exhibition of young Swiss artists, who "under the spell of Cézanne and Van Gogh" had "built up an art as full of the strange investigations of modernism as any art in Europe."[19] The Swiss landscapes were derived from Cézanne and looked no stranger than those Grace Hall Hemingway would be painting by the end of the Twenties after she gave up her music for art.

In September of 1920, an editorial in the Art Institute's *Bulletin* explained to the public what the Modernists were attempting.

> They tended to revolt against the ideal of clever technique characteristic of the nineteenth century and against the more limited standards of design. They have added to the old objective motives a new subjective type of theme. They try to paint their mental reactions to things. . . . they have widened the scope of art. They need not dwell exclusively on "beautiful" things because our mental reactions may be interesting to contemplate even when the things which evoke them are not pleasant. . . . the comprehension of a new art calls for new adjustments, new habits of appreciation.[20]

That fall Hemingway's prose, still grounded in nineteenth century technique, was about to change. Before he was through, he indeed focused on "mental reactions to things." He would abandon the "beautiful" for subject matter quite unpleasant: mules drowning on the quai at Smyrna; a punch-drunk boxer; the horrors of war; prostitutes in a railway station; divorce; bombs dropping on trapped soldiers; hired killers; bulls goring helpless horses; fear and nightmare and all the lovely images from our time. In less than two years, the Art Institute's description of Modernism would fit Hemingway's fiction quite well, and yet he never became completely Modern: a paradox which can be traced back to Oak Park.

The Village, a bastion of Republic values, dependably supported conservative politics throughout Hemingway's life there. Long before the Volstead Act, Oak Park voted itself dry. Moral righteousness flavored every aspect of Village life. Yet the voters and their representatives continually supported progressive measures that elsewhere would have been considered radical. Early in the century Oak Parkers advocated public ownership of utility companies; time and again they harassed privately owned public transportation companies for lower fares, safer crossings and better service. Whatever improved the general welfare, Oak Park supported: improved sanitation, street lighting, safe water, public schools, libraries and parks. Educated and affluent, the townspeople supported welfare programs for single mothers; the plight of the working girl and the Negro stirred them to action. At various public lectures before the war, Oak Parkers digested explanations of socialism and its benefits; at the same time they saw labor unions and strikes as a threat to the nation itself. For these genteel, middle-class burghers, there was no paradox involved. The Village was Progressive Republican and open to certain types of change.

This attitude carried over into the arts, which flourished in Oak Park, The Village was home to a number of artists, architects, writers, musicians and singers, many of whom had modest national reputations. In the drama, for example, Ibsen and Maeterlinck were as accepted as Shakespeare. When the Armory Show opened at the Art Institute, Louis Sharp, a local artist who painted western landscapes for the Santa Fé Railway Company, wrote the first review for *Oak Leaves*.

the authorities of the Art Institute . . . have opened to the public the most curious collection of absurdities within its history. . . . Many there are which seem to be jokes, foisted upon the lovers of good art; gross impertinence reflects from every brush stroke, to say nothing of the childish crudeness of color, line and composition. Many are marked "sold" and one wonders if the card does not refer to the owner.

But let us not be too hasty in judging the works of the cubists and such pictures as "Nude Descending Staircase," or the "King and Queen Surrounded by Nudes." While they are puzzles of intricate forms and lines, yet they show careful thought, each part is definitely drawn and modeled, marked out in detail with seriousness of purpose. Marcel Duchamps deserves our respect if not our approval of his mysteries.

The opposite seems true of Henri Matisse, who apparently has discarded his knowledge of anatomy, and to have forgotten that most people have ten toes instead of eight, and that eyelashes are not black tassels, nor are gold fish cut out of pink paper. . . . One wonders why Paul [sic] Picasso added the mustard pot in his painting of a woman. She appears somewhat worried, even looks a bit broken up about it, or else she has left her powder puff at home. . . .

Taken as a whole the exhibition is exhilarating, stirs one's humor as well as his sympathy, makes him search for new adjectives of praise as well as condemnation, for here are signs of movements and life in the art world and where there is life, there is growth, and influence toward better things. Seriousness of purpose there must be, rank impertinence should be discouraged, and utter crudeness left in the storeroom.[21]

Sharp's split view was typical of Oak Park. He resented but did not completely condemn the show even though it mocked the pictures he himself painted. He found value in the Duchamps painting that so infuriated New Yorkers that it had to be protected from slashers. Whatever Sharp's limitations, he recognized that change was healthy and necessary. No sooner was his review printed than Oliver Marble Gale, a local author of national standing, wrote what he thought to be a rebuttal. Attacking Sharp's smugness, Gale said:

These men are trying or pretending to try . . . to express elemental humanities that their contemporaries ignore for the decadent refinements of conventional art. Admit they are silly, admit they are impudent, admit they are insincere; strip away all their cant and possible hypocrisy, you have left the fact that they are not satisfied with things as they are. And dissatisfaction is the salutary essence of progress; the hope of ultimate truth.

The circumstance that their protest has sent a shivering shock thru the artistic world gives a certain validity to it; it demonstrates that they are attacking something real which dreads the attack. If there had been nothing in existing conditions against which their assault could find legitimate lodgment it would have expended itself innocuously on insubstantial air.

We cannot laugh these men out of the forum. We must credit those who have devoted months of physical and mental labor to the production of creative work with a compelling motive. We do not have to approve dynamitards or condone their deeds to sympathise with the worthy motive that finds expression, however perverted in form. We can merely say we do not know, and wait. Perhaps it would not be amiss to pray a little.[22]

The pictures might be atrocities – silly, impudent, insincere – but their dissatisfaction with the status quo was the essence of progress. In the name of progress any affront to sensibilities could at least be entertained. Sharp and Gale continued to argue in print, not realizing how closely they agreed or how little they understood. Both were open to change if it led to progress, golden words in the Age of Innocence, words which did not weather the war well.

This argument is quintessential Oak Park paradox: the New so necessary for Progress, which all admired, was equally a threat to the Status Quo, which all admired. This type of paradox resides at the heart of Hemingway's fiction. His style and subject matter are Modern; his structure and plot line are traditional. Fiction, he insists, must tell an interesting story. It was on this point that Modernist painters broke with the nineteenth century. Delacroix and Winslow Homer paintings tell stories. Picasso and Miró paintings do not. Even post-impressionist landscapes by Cézanne describe recognizable terrain; cubist and surrealist landscapes do not. Thomas Hudson, Hemingway's fictional artist who lived in Paris with Picasso and Miró, remains a realist.

From Oak Park Hemingway took with him traditional values and a respect for traditional fiction, but his baggage also included a tolerance for the New. Once his model of the writer changed, he was willing to experiment, forging a style and technique for his time. In Chicago he was about to take his first serious lessons from Sherwood Anderson, who would send him to Gertrude Stein's Paris school. The pupil learned quickly, but Oak Parker that he was at heart, he accommodated the New with the Old, holding on dearly to the best of the past. Nowhere is this more obvious than in his values, which, in spite of his subject material, remain traditional: courage, love, honor, self-reliance, work and duty. They are the same values that Teddy Roosevelt lived by and advocated; they are the basis for the morally strenuous life. They are the values which sustain Hemingway's characters in physical and moral crises: the very essence of Oak Park of which Ernest was a native son.

Chicago in 1920 opened to Hemingway new vistas, and Hadley assisted, for she was not only older but less inhibited in many ways than Ernest. Sometimes her language shocked him; he asked her not to use certain words – words which he used commonly enough but which women in Oak Park did not say. Hadley was amused. When she referred to Negroes as "nigs," Hemingway was upset. In Oak Park, where racism was paternalistic, "nigger" was not politely used. She assured him that the finest ladies in St. Louis used no other term, but if it bothered him she would refrain. In St. Louis Hadley grew up in closer contact with Blacks than Hemingway had in Oak Park, where there were only 100 in a population of 20,000. Like most Oak Parkers, Hemingway was an unconscious racist who went out of his way to appear unprejudiced.

As with most social issues in Oak Park, two contradictory racial attitudes existed side by side without bothering the Villagers. Ministers could preach on the necessity of giving the

Black man his equal opportunity at the same time that civic organizations put on annual minstrel shows, singing "real coon songs," and the Nakama Club ladies could masquerade at their cotillion as colored "Aunt Jemimas." In this respect, Oak Park was no different and no more racist than the rest of the country; it was racism so benign that Hemingway, like most Oak Parkers, denied any taint of it. When the Unity Church sponsored a public discussion of the "Negro problem," the spectrum of response said more about the townspeople than it did about the problem.

Rev. Luccock believed that "the races could exist side by side, not in social equity, but to their mutual advantage." Rev. Johonnot admitted that

> the negro was poor, shiftless, ignorant, sensual, and even criminal, but because of these defects, the white man owed him a great duty. . . . [The negro] must either go up or go down, and he could not go down without dragging the white man with him. This consideration ought, he thought, to appeal to the most confirmed "nigger hater."

Mr. Tomlinson predicted that within fifty years the Negro and white population would be equal, with the Negroes educated and financially prosperous, but he wondered if "it would be possible to maintain a republican form of government with the citizenship divided into two such diverse classes, equal before the law, but unequal in social life." Mr. Griffen allowed that he did not care what progress the Negro made; the white man would dominate the country "fifty years from now, 100 years from now, or 500 years from now."[23]

When Oak Parkers visited Tuskegee Institute they were pleased with the spirit of the Black students.

> every person was on his feet joining lustily in the college song, ending with the everlasting, ear-splitting college yell, the visitor could not help but feel that he was in the midst of real, genuine America boys and girls despite their color.[24]

Here was Oak Park benign racism: despite their color the Black students seemed like genuine American boys and girls. The visiting Oak Parkers, so certain that real Americans were white, would have denied any racist charge. Had they not gone to Tuskegee filled with brotherly love? Yes, but the Knights of Columbus still put on a comedy night filled with characters named Honey Boy, Rastus Porkchops, Mushmouth Johnson, Melon Patch, Noah Razor, Uncle Tom, Nose Nuthin, Sambo Jackson, Koka Nutt and Cole Black. Did not Oak Parkers, with a few southern-born exceptions, recognize the rights of the Negro? And did not the Oak Park summer baseball team play Negro teams regularly when most white teams would not? Yes, the college boys did play the black teams and the paper wrote it up.

> The black boys composing the Leland Giants ran thirteen tallies, three of them home runs, and the academically educated white men negotiated but three. The race question did not appear, and if Yale and Harvard ever played a game marked by greater politeness or less friction, it has not been heard of in these parts.
>
> The black experts, and most of them really were black, refused to laugh when the great Skillin was caught napping at third with all bases full and only one out. . . . a good-sized crowd enjoyed the game for there always is comedy when colored men play ball. They improvise dialogs and monologs much to their own entertainment and also for the amusement of the spectators.[25]

In April of 1914 Orren Donaldson, a good Oak Parker, said he was not a hater of Negroes; he simply saw no future for them in America. They should be deported to Mexico where there would be no racial barrier for inter-marriage since all Mexicans were of mixed blood. In America, "the negro must ever be an element of discord in our civilization, a barrier to our oneness and an insurmountable obstacle against an ideal democracy. . . . the few that remained would constitute an ever fading problem, plainly on its way to a final solution."[26]

Few people in Oak Park agreed with Donaldson's "final solution" to the Negro problem, but after the disastrous summer of 1919, they all knew the problem existed. That July a race riot tore Chicago apart. Mobs of blacks and whites roamed like animals, maiming and killing. Six thousand state militia men with rifles and bayonets restored order in the bleeding streets. Joe Lovings was riding his bicycle home through an Italian neighborhood where false rumors of a Negro murdering an Italian girl had excited the residents. Joe Lovings' timing was bad, his skin the wrong color.

> A mob filled the streets when Lovings was sighted. He tried to escape by running down an alley . . . and then jumped back fences and hid in a basement. The mob dragged him out, riddled his body with bullets, stabbed him, and beat him. It was afterward rumored that his body had been burned. . . . This was proved not to be true.[27]

Before martial law took hold, thirty-eight were dead, many of them beaten to death with rocks and clubs; 537 were wounded. Fifteen whites died; twenty-three Blacks, seven of them shot down by Chicago policemen.[28] Oak Park's hundred Negroes kept out of sight; the Village was not touched by the horror, only discomfited by the interruption of commuter trains. And the jazz man sang *"What did I do to be so black and blue?"*

By the fall of 1920, the rents in Chicago's social fabric had not disappeared; the tension was real. No wonder Hemingway objected to Hadley's use of the word "nigger." Hadley's amusement was enhanced by her own family's involvement in the Negro cause. Both her mother and her sister Fonnie had been activists in promoting better race relations and improving the Black living conditions in St. Louis. Between Hemingway and Fonnie no love was lost; she made no pretense of liking her future brother-in-law. Eight years Hadley's junior, he could not possibly be in love with her, Fonnie thought, except for her money. Hemingway's vicious streak responded in his own coin: "Hurray for Fonnie Richardson," a poetic diatribe about his sister-in-law, who, according to the verse, loved "niggers" who raped white women. The proper response suggested by the narrator was lynching and shooting.[29]

Hadley did not bring up the "Negro problem" during her visit. She and Ernest were too busy with each other to worry about the world. Walking, talking, holding hands, they did not mind the cold or the stares of strangers, for this was the new country. And they danced to the music whose tempo increased to match the times. *"This little jazzy Cleopatra has the people gazing at her. She sticks to her partner like a penny postage stamp She's a syncopated vamp."* They went to the opera and the movies, visited Sherwood Anderson, joked and laughed with Katy and Kenley while drinking bootleg liquor that might have been gin. At night, alone on the balcony, they hugged and kissed as lovers do. Around them the national election swirled: Harding versus Cox. They could not have cared less. In Italy, Gabriele d'Annunzio and his army were beseiged at Fiume, but these two lovers were more interested in his romantic poetry. Ernest told Hadley about the Italian's wonderful novel translated as *The Flame.* She promised to read it.

The day after Harding swept into the White House on the promise of no more foreign entanglements, Ernest took Hadley to the train station for the second time. As they stood on the platform, she waited expectantly for his kiss. It did not come, only a quick hug and a flustered goodbye. From the window she watched him disappear. In his next letter he lamely explained that he had not wanted it to be "goodbye," merely "good night." That was why he had not kissed her. His excuse did not ring true. She suspected that Oak Park boys did not kiss in public. Well, there was time to change that; time to change, or at least understand, the secrets he kept to himself or made her promise never to tell. At twenty-nine she was not going to let this chance for love pass by, and he did love her. He said he loved her. In St. Louis she would have to talk to Bill Smith about Ernest's quirks. As the train whistled through the Indiana fields of corn stubble, Hadley was pleased with her trip. She still had not told Ernest about her inheritance. Fonnie had warned her not to say a word.

She smiled, thinking they both had secrets. In her head the singer's words echoed: *"You're on my mind the whole night long. I'm for you, right or wrong."* Wrong or right, she was certain that this was the new country. There was no turning back.

Chapter Seven

THE LAST ROBIN
1921

J IM Gamble wrote two letters.

The first one, inviting Hemingway to visit him in up-state New York, he forgot to mail. That was the letter about Agnes. He told Ernest, "Poor Hemmy, I bet you had a hard time but am glad to see that you had more sense than to pity yourself. It after all is much better. You are pretty young you know and a splendid future before you. . . . Don't get caught on the rebound." Gamble found the unmailed letter when Hemingway sent him a Christmas card in December 1920; he included it with his second letter, in which he invited Ernest to go to Rome with him, all expenses paid. "Come on do it Hemmie," he urged. He wanted to know if Ernest was married yet, which, of course, would make the offer futile. [1]

Hemingway read the letter carefully. *Don't get caught on the rebound.* He thought about the week in 1919 he spent with Jim at Taormina, Sicily. They had such a fine time together in that quaint fishing village. Going back with Jim would solve a lot of problems. Maybe this thing with Hadley was foolish; maybe he was rebounding badly. When she invited him to St. Louis for New Year's Eve, he wrote that he could not possibly come.

Hadley read the letter twice.

He was not coming to St. Louis. After buying presents for all those sisters and family, he did not have the money. She understood that part, but he said he had not been home for Christmas since 1915. Had he been at the war that long? She tried to get the story straight in her head, but somehow he was always vague about dates and places. The story seemed to change. She was not even certain how old he was.

She read the letter once more. He could have lied, he said, could have told her that he had accepted other dates for New Years. But he always told her the truth. She was his secret vulnerability, the chink in his armor against the world. At any time she could drive her sword through his defenses. Hadley smiled. It was just like Ernest to raise the possibility of making her jealous and then protest how vulnerable he was to jealousy for love of her. Her "gentil, parfit knight," complete with chinky armor. Oh, he loved her. Yes, he loved her. He had better love her, for she had let him touch her on the rooftop in Chicago, had felt his hardness against her as their tongues twisted. No one had ever touched her like that before. Then, in the next breath, he could talk about loving Jim Gamble. Not the way he loved her, of course. She tried to understand that part. Jim Gamble, she knew, was another one of the war people, a rich war-person. Now here he was popping up again with some scheme for returning to Italy. She also knew there were other girls. Katy Smith had told her that much. In fact, there was Katy herself to worry about, for there was more between those two than Katy had admitted. In fact, Katy had not come home to St. Louis for Christmas either. In fact . . . in fact, this was not the present that Hadley Richardson had expected to receive the day before Christmas.[2]

The last mail delivery of the old year brought her sketchy details of Jim Gamble's plan. He would pay Ernest's expenses for five months in Rome, giving Ernest time to write fiction. It would mean walking away from his month-old editorial job on the *Co-Operative Commonwealth*, but he said the magazine would buy his free-lance material from Italy. He could always come back to the job. One could always come back. He would come back to her. They could go back to Italy. Hadley was not so certain; going back was not ever the same. People changed.

Places changed. What one did was go on, not go back. She was trying to go back to her music, and it was not the same as when she had dreamed of the concert stage. Five months in Italy with a rich young man paying the bills was a risk. But he said his father thought it a good bet. Certainly a minister would wonder what Jim Gamble got out of the deal besides the bill. Ernest said his father was a minister, or perhaps he sounded like a minister when Ernest spoke of him. There was so much Ernest did not tell her, or told her only in bits, leaving gaps to imagine.[3] No matter what, Hadley knew she could not come between Ernest and his writing. She could not tell him not to go to Rome.

On the first day of the new year, another letter came filled with Rome but couched to catch her sympathy. He was jealous. He could not leave her alone for five months with Dick Rowland hanging about in St. Louis. That was just his way: force her to make the decision for him. She answered him within the hour.

from the way your paragraphs follow each other it sounds as tho being afraid of Rowland had something to do possibly with not going to Rome. It couldn't could it? And I'm not a *fool* Ernest, I don't crave your jealousy. . . . He's lonely and nice. There aren't *very* many girls that are intriguing to him mentally so when he sees me he's mildly and agreeably pleased to be able to talk books. . . . Rome sounds so wonderful – I would be envious of you! . . . I like the sound of Jim Gamble. I wish you could tell me what his proposition was. Maybe can't – don't wanta! I would miss you pretty frightfully unless I tho't it was going to be a great gain to your work.[4]

He was free, of course, to go wherever he wished. Hadley was not going to beg him to stay. To underline her point, she included a list of places in Rome that Ernest just had to see, places she still remembered visiting with her mother in 1910.

His letters were now a daily ritual. He was writing copy and editing the magazine, doing free-lance stories for the Toronto paper, and writing his fiction late and early in the day. Still he wrote her long letters. He was wavering on Rome. Something bothered him. On January 2, she responded: "at first I tho't from the way you talked twas a business idea he had in mind – J[im] G[amble] I mean but if – oh well, I won't say it Ernest – things about the right thing to do are such a bore – what's right is generally what your bottom layer of your heart wants most. . . . You keep the plan so dark, man. . . . I want you here my dear. I know ezzactly what I would do for you – but I can't do it so I won't tell you – did it once."[5] She did not want him to forget the touch of her.

Ten days later Hadley still did not know when Kate Smith was coming to St. Louis, or where Ernest spent the much-discussed New Year's Eve, or the essence of Jim Gamble's proposition.[6] The more Ernest said about Gamble, the less she knew and the more doubts arose in her mind. In the St. Louis winter, she had too much time to think. Then on January 13 his letter came: maybe they should get married and go to Italy. She cried a little as she read it. They would be married. Yes. And they would go to Italy. Yes. Whatever the Jim Gamble thing had been was over. Or was the emphasis on the *maybe?* She could never tell with Ernest, but at least she had not been forced to make the proposal. On Bill Smith's Victrola in St. Louis, she listened to "Avalon," "Cuban Moon" and "Margie."

Ernest wrote the letter twice.

He knew now he must make the break clean, trying not to hurt Marge. It was just his luck that Marjorie Bump would choose Washington University in St. Louis for college. He had written her only a few letters, but he saw that he was leading her on, keeping her in reserve. Three days after he suggested to Hadley that maybe they should get married, he got a letter from Marge. "You asked," she wrote, "if I had seen Bill or the Madame. Yes, I have seen the Madame once. Their home is very nice and comfortable. I have seen Bill once or twice when I was with Edgar."[7] Nothing could have been worse: Marjorie in the house of the Madame – Mrs. Charles – Bill and Katy Smith's guardian aunt who thrived on gossip. Ernest could see the scenario playing out. Mrs. Charles would be the second or third person Hadley would tell of his proposal. If not the Madame, certainly Bill Smith, who would tell his aunt immediately. And Bill knew about Ernest and Marge, knew where she was. He could see how delighted the Madame would be to tell both Marge and Hadley about each other. It had been stupid of him to keep Marjorie on the string right there in St. Louis.

So he did not tell Marjorie about Hadley. Remembering the letter that Agnes Von Kurowsky had written him in 1919, he told her what a fine relationship they had enjoyed, but he felt guilty about leading her on. They would still be friends, and he would never forget what they had shared. She would see some day that he had been good for her, a part of her education. He was going to miss her freckles and red hair.

Then he wrote Hadley that she should not say anything yet about their maybe marriage, nor should she believe everything that Mrs. Charles might say about him. Reading it over, it sounded a bit lame, but he had to keep the Madame dark on the subject. That only left him the problems of Grace Quinlan up in Michigan, Bonnie Bonnell in Toronto and Katy Smith there in Chicago. Grace was just a kid who had been eager to hear him read his stories that winter in Petoskey. She would be easy to handle. But Bonnie and Katy, particularly Katy, would be difficult. And of course he would have to tell his mother, but not yet.

Don't be a fool about the women in his life, she told herself in St. Louis. She was going to marry Ernest Hemingway and those other women would have to disappear. Hadn't he told her about Irene, how she had thrown herself at him and how well he had acted? She told him, "It was difficult for you that way. . . . you see you feel the same way I do about those things – frightfully regretful not to meet such a person's love with your own very best feeling? Tried to didn't you dear. Best sort of person you are."[8] Katherine Smith she tried to treat lightly. Her good friend Kate was right there in Chicago with him; Hadley knew he loved

Katy, but, pray God, not the way he loved her. So Hadley joked about Katy and the sign that her friend once said would hang above the door when she and Ernest married. Hadley read over the letter; the joke sounded weak. She added, "Ernest, you don't have lots and lots of 'infatuations' do you? What could I do if you did? Course if you do I guess you can't help it."[9]

He worried when Hadley found his insistence on secrecy so amusing. He could imagine how amused she would be if Mrs. Charles began talking about Marjorie Bump and those Petoskey rumors from last winter. Hadley's return letter did not reassure him.

> Your terror of what the Madame might tell – is it of your past loves and wickedness in general Ernest? – tickles this child. I *adore* the Madame but course if she started or even finished to tell things about you (she never has – except once – always has nice things to say) course I'd still reserve my own judgment as being the one I have to trust and – we'd not see things – lots of em – in the same proportion.[10]

Two months after what he had thought to be his last letter to Marjorie Bump, he got her reply, which stung him to the quick.

> The long delay in writing was caused by the fact that I have been trying to decide just how your remark that you were good for me could be justified. Two months consideration has failed to show any point where you have been greatly beneficial. In fact I would have been saved from the rather unpleasant sensation of being disillusioned had I never known you.[11]

Conceited, she called him. Abominably conceited. He ripped off a biting letter saying that it was the shape of her mouth which had parted them. But he did not mail it.[12] Instead he wrote a nostalgic letter about the summer of 1919, the best summer of his life. He reminded Marjorie of what they had shared – moonlight swims, fishing off the point, dances, library books – it had all been good. They had shared a perfect summer and fall, but, like the seasons, what they had shared was impermanent. [13]

It was a good lesson to remember: never let anger write the letters. Sometimes he would remember it. Frequently he would forget, and then have to write next-day apologies, until finally, late in life, it no longer mattered to him. But that day it felt good not to have hurt Marjorie by telling her how ugly her mouth was. However, he could not hide his little charity; he had to tell Hadley with what restraint he had acted. Not the whole truth. No need to tell her that Marjorie was in St. Louis. He told her instead how, one summer in Michigan, he had been an older brother to this girl, who had known so little about the world. He had helped her a lot, helped her grow up. But she had misunderstood his brotherly affection. Not exactly the truth. Words were not that reality. Words made a different reality, another truth. With words, the past could be changed. You could always go back and change it. Make it the way it should have been true.

Hadley was not sure what to make of the letter. There must have been any number of girls in his life. Now that was coming to an end for him. That part she understood. But why tell her about them? It was flattering, she supposed, to know how much he cared for her, but the letter also reflected well on Ernest. Whatever girls there had been did not matter to her so long as now there was only herself. She wrote him

> That all does sound magnificent and on top of all your excellent behavior to get a letter from a girl like that! Good thing she has an ugly mouth or you mightn't 'a swollowed it so gaily. Don't you go and write any of these here smarty answers. [14]

She had to see him soon. See him in St. Louis soon. No matter how her sister lectured her on propriety, she knew she must follow her heart quickly. Fonnie told her she was making a fool of herself: she was too old, too frail to marry. She should never have children. What would Mother have said? Hadley knew exactly what Mother would have said – the same things Fonnie told her. Fonnie sounded a lot like Mother. The two of them always thought they knew what was best for Hadley. Didn't they just. But she had danced all night in Chicago without feeling frail.

In Chicago the little Italian restaurants continued to serve red wine in spite of Prohibition. In Chicago the little German restaurants continued to serve beer. A young man could learn a lot in Chicago about the human condition. On Christmas day in Chicago, ten men of good cheer took their presents home at gun point, establishing a new record for armed robberies on a single day. Fourteen other men relieved neighbors of their new automobiles. During that year of 1920 over 500 townsmen had died from collisions with Stutz Bearcats, Essexes, Premiers and Pierce Arrows. In those little Italian restaurants the Cardinella gang had plotted out their murders, while elsewhere the vets were dancing to "Home Again Blues," a little bewildered by the post-war depression. In the Chicago streets and under the elevated tram lines, the unemployed huddled against biting cold that brought tears to their eyes, tears that froze in the wind coming off the lake. Hemingway did well to find a job that winter in Chicago.

Until the end of November he had been living free in Bill Horne's apartment with no particular pressure to find work. But then Bill's job had fallen apart on him. He had left enough money to pay the November rent and buy a few groceries, but Hemingway now had to find a real job. Kenley offered him a free room at his place now that his wife had gone to New York for piano lessons. Good old Kenley. All he needed was food money and Christmas money. From the want ads he applied for an editing position on a trade journal, using his Kansas City and Toronto experience as entrée.

He got the job without understanding how time consuming it would be. The Co-Operative Society of America paid him $40 a week to write copy and assist with the editing of their weekly *Co-Operative Commonwealth*. Hemingway saw it as hack work, but it was better than writing advertising copy in the same office with Kenley Smith, and on $40 a week a man could get by. At the

Atlantic Hotel he could still get a "Dinner Deluxe" for $1.50. When 900,000 war vets were unemployed, $40 a week looked just fine. A man did not have to believe in the co-operative movement to write its copy, and if Harrison Parker, the president of the society, seemed like a con-artist, his money paid the bills.

The midwestern farmers, who were the heart of the co-operative movement, still remembered the Populist uprising of the 1890s and their dream of William Jennings Bryan as President, hopes gone bust in the election of 1896. The railroads and the princes of the grain markets continued to control the farm market place. For a while there during the war years, the farmers almost forgot, but in 1921 mortgages were coming due against depressed prices. Once again in Wisconsin and Iowa and Illinois, they banded together in buying co-operatives to lower costs and selling co-operatives to raise the market. Some said it smelled of socialism. Some said it was not the American way. But when mortgages fall due, even farmers will grasp at straws. Harrison Parker sold them $13,000,000 worth of "beneficial interest certificates" – a bit of money down and a few dollars a month to own a share in the Society. Hemingway did not understand the whole scheme, but he did not need to. For his salary all he had to do was write up the stories that confirmed fears and offered hope.

He told the small rancher why he was losing money every time he independently shipped his cow hides to market: the shoe manufacturers had combined forces to keep the price of leather low and their profits high.[15] The lesson was clear: band together, brothers in the Society. He also pushed the products sold in the Society's co-operative stores. The Pronto fire extinguisher was endorsed, he told them, by the chief of Chicago's fire department, and members could buy theirs at a bargain price through the Society. It was the extinguisher which would best reduce the chances of another movie-theater catastrophe, where the highly flammable movie film was a constant danger.[16] Hemingway, remembering the Iroquois Theater catastrophe of his youth, assumed that farmers shared his concern. With as much authority as he could muster, he began a serial account of the co-operative movement, and interviewed two Polish wrestlers, who gave him a testament of faith.

> Both brothers are great believers in the Co-Operative Society of America and staunch supporters of the Co-Operative movement. Being college graduates and observant men they have watched its course in Europe and seen the great benefits it offers its members and each has taken the maximum number of beneficial debenture certificates allowed a member of the society in order to show their belief in the Co-Operative Society of America. [17]

That last sentence would not have gotten past the blue pencil at the Kansas City *Star*. In Toronto, where Hemingway was still selling free lance features to the *Star Weekly*, Greg Clark would have gotten a laugh out of it. He wrote his copy, pasted up the dummies, read the proof and cashed his check. This was not the writing that mattered.

At night and in the early mornings when he could not sleep, he wrote fiction that *Red Book* and *Saturday Evening Post* would not buy. Each time a story came back, he reworked it, changing bits and pieces to send it out again. Most of the new stories were from the Italian war, using the Dolomite mountain setting that he had known briefly when Section Four had been at Schio. None of them sold, not the one about the fight on Asalone or the one about the Town Mayor who got himself bumped off. [18] His war continued to be a grand adventure filled with funny characters. Archibald MacLeish would later call it "a war of parades, speeches, brass bands, *bistros,* boredom, terror, anguish, heroism, endurance, humor, death. . . . It was a human war." [19] In the winter of 1920, cynicism had not yet destroyed American illusions of having fought to make the world safe for democracy. Hemingway, assuming for his own the heroism of others, was not yet capable of writing about the war either honestly or objectively, and the country was not ready to read about it.

In Kenley's apartment that winter it seemed that everyone was writing something: advertising copy, poetry, fiction. Many of the visitors talked a better game than they played, but they all thought they knew a great deal about writing. With them was Ernest. He read his new stories aloud, eager for praise. Kenley Smith, who thought he saw talent glimmering through the clichés, took Hemingway's "The Visiting Team," first drafted the previous January, to a published friend of his who replied with candor:

> "The Visiting Team" . . . has laughs all through it and a tear at the end. It is so horribly typed no editor would glance at it. Take it to Edna Herron . . . for a 50¢ per thousand words she will type it decently. . . . Then I would send it with a letter setting forth why Hemingway knows whereof he writes to all the good magazines, including [the] Atlantic group and [the] Sat Eve Post group. . . . Hemingway without question has the necessary talent. . . . if he will get books on technique, continue to write about the things he knows, avoid unhappy endings, and write lots of stories with his eye on their availability and worth . . . eventually he will be to sell what he writes. He should do as much humor as possible as that sells easiest.[20]

This advice, neither original nor particularly brilliant but well geared to the market place, was exactly what a hundred other young men, fresh from the war, were following. Those who stuck to it eventually got a few sales, and their names are now forgotten.

Hemingway kept the letter and tried to follow the advice. His stories did not improve or sell, but the typing was much better. He went back over "The Visiting Team," pointing up the collegiate humor of his fictional ambulance drivers. When two rookies arrive at Schio, the old hands haze them as if the war were a fraternity party. One driver curls up on the floor, begging them, "Kick me. I'm a football." The rookies are told he is a victim of shell shock. In the middle of the night they are jolted from sleep as Red, the oldest and most decorated of the group, casually fires pistol shots into the ceiling. The war is described in sports metaphors or as a staged play. College boys all, they smoke, drink and joke their way through the story until the real shelling starts. Red, who has led a charmed life on both fronts, speeds off in the first ambulance only to be blown apart by an Austrian shell. His bleeding body is returned to the field hospital where the doctor says he has but a few minutes to live. Stout-hearted trooper that he is, Red jokes his way right into the grave, his dying words being, "Only the good die young."[21]

It was a war that never happened, and the front-line humor, so funny at the time, fell flat on paper. Invisible editors who rejected "The Visiting Team" were doing Hemingway a favor he could not appreciate. Down deep he knew that he had not understood the war, no matter how bravely he spoke of it, no matter what tall tales he invented. But he remained positive that the war was important to his fiction; it had been the turning point in his life. The more knowledge of it that he acquired, the more certain he became. His new-found Italian friend, Nicolas Nerone, told him some wonderful and real war stories which supplemented his reading. The really detailed war histories were coming out, and he was learning about the Italian disaster at Caporetto, an embarrassment about which few could speak honestly in 1918. He talked to Nerone of that crushing defeat when Italy lost most of her Second Army and much of her pride. Nick had been there. Listening and learning, Ernest took his acquired knowledge to the maps which began to make sense.

Always experimenting, trying on the styles of popular authors, he had not yet given up on the *Saturday Evening Post,* but in Chicago, for the first time in his young career, he was in touch with a literary community, the remnants of a literary revolution. Within three months of his arrival in town, the final flowering of the Chicago Renaissance bloomed in the bookstores along State Street. Floyd Dell's *Moon Calf,* Sherwood Anderson's *Poor White,* Vachel Lindsay's *Golden Book of Springfield,* Edgar Lee Masters' *Mitch Miller,* and Carl Sandburg's *Smoke and Steel* were all published. It was the year when H. L. Mencken dubbed Chicago the literary capital of America.

Mencken was a little late in his discovery, for Chicago's

literary capital had been gradually lured east after the Great War. The exciting years before the war when Burton Rascoe was writing the reviews and Ring Lardner the humor were past history. In those days *Poetry* magazine and *The Little Review* vied with each other to discover fresh talent, much of it right out of the midwest. But it was, in Sherwood Anderson's phrase, a robin's egg renaissance which fell from the nest too early. By 1920 Lardner, Burton Rascoe, Floyd Dell, Robert Herrick, Hamlin Garland and Masters had all gone east. Margaret Anderson moved *The Little Review* to New York. Only Harriet Monroe's *Poetry* remained in Chicago, but she had lost the editing genius of Alice Corbin Henderson, who was responsible for so many of the magazine's discoveries, and she had lost the service of her chief European talent scout, Ezra Pound. In 1920 in New York, Scofield Thayer rejuvenated *The Dial* magazine, to which most of the new talent was immediately attracted. The only great names left in Chicago were Ben Hecht and Sherwood Anderson, both of whom were about to leave.[22]

In October 1920, Hemingway arrived in the afterglow of the renaissance. With the exception of Ring Lardner, whom Hemingway imitated in high school, he was largely unaware of any literary renaissance during those heady pre-war years. Oak Park had been too insulated; he had been too young. There was, however, just enough literary life remaining to change his career forever. Sherwood Anderson was still in town, and he was enough to make the difference. Had Hemingway remained up in Michigan or Toronto another six months, he would have missed Anderson's sad face and sage advice completely. That was the Hemingway luck: timing. He almost missed the war, almost missed Paris, almost missed Pound. He almost missed connecting with that literary network which created the Modern Age. Almost but not quite missing, connecting long enough to make all the difference — that was his luck. Even luckier, the connections were brief. A few weeks at the Italian front gave him all he would ever need of war. A few meetings with Sherwood Anderson were enough to get the point without catching the disease of sentimentalism.

While sharing Kenley Smith's apartment, Hemingway first

met Anderson. Kenley, Bill Smith's older and more sophisticated brother, worked for the Critchfield advertising firm, where Anderson wrote copy to sell tractors. In mid-January of 1921, Anderson, who alternated between his cottage in Palos Park and his apartment on East Division street, was pleased to meet Kenley's friend, this tall, handsome young man who they said was going to be a writer. Anderson was forty-four and at the peak of his career. In 1919, his *Winesburg, Ohio* had sent his literary stock soaring. Now his stories were selling nationally; *The Dial* featured him as an important writer, awarding him in September of 1921 the first *Dial* award of $1000, which, in following years, would go to such writers as Marianne Moore, William Carlos Williams, E. E. Cummings, Ezra Pound and T. S. Eliot.[23] Hemingway also caught Anderson at his most paternal, still wallowing in his Whitmanian phase. Perhaps he spent too many afternoons in the corn fields with his farm-tractor account. In 1917, heralded by his *Mid American Chants,* he advocated "trusting absolutely the knowledge that flows into us."[24] "I have the notion," he said, "that nothing from my pen should be published that could not be read aloud in the presence of a corn field."[25] The "mystery of the grass" had been much upon Anderson during the four years before Hemingway met him, leaving a residual tendency toward mysticism which Hemingway instinctively distrusted. In Oak Park a man did not embarrass himself by letting his deepest emotions out in public. Despite Anderson's romantic bent, he was exactly the man Hemingway needed at that moment.

Far too much has been said about Anderson's influence on Hemingway's style, a real but minor influence. The young novice did not need to meet Anderson in order to read *Winesburg.* Nor did he need Anderson's guidance to learn the value of the Michigan setting or the theme of a young man's growing pains. There were plenty of other writers who contributed to those recognitions. What Hemingway did need in 1921 was someone to influence his reading and someone to tell him how the literary life was conducted, someone who knew about publication pitfalls, contracts, translation rights, someone connected with the leading edge of the literary scene. The tyro could not have found a more helpful tutor than Sherwood Anderson; Anderson could not have found a more apt pupil.

"Of course he likes you," Hadley said, immensely proud that Anderson had taken to Ernest.[26] She had met the older writer some months earlier when Kenley Smith took her for a visit to Palos Park. After meeting Anderson, Ernest's correspondence took a much more literary turn. Almost every other letter had some reference to what he was reading. For the first time Hemingway began to distinguish between popular fiction and literature, and his concept of the true writer's role began to develop during those occasional meetings at Palos Park or East Division Street. Of course, one of the first books he read was *Winesburg, Ohio*, but Anderson also pointed him to American contemporary fiction like Floyd Dell's *Moon Calf* and nonfiction like Waldo Frank's *Our America* and Van Wyck Brooks' *The Flowering of New England* and *America's Coming of Age*.[27] For the first time, Hemingway was exposed to literary nationalism. Anderson personally knew H. L. Mencken and Theodore Dreiser whom Hemingway had not read. Anderson told him that Twain and Whitman were the two great American writers whose roots flourished in native soil. This idea of being an *American* writer was new to Hemingway, for his Oak Park education emphasized only the British tradition. Suddenly Hemingway began to read *The Dial, American Mercury* and *Poetry* magazines. *Saturday Evening Post* was no longer his single standard of literary excellence.

Anderson's reading recommendations, however, were not merely parochial. About the time Hemingway met him, Anderson was in correspondence with a young, unpublished poet in Cincinnati, who was asking for advice and encouragement. Read the Russians, he told Hart Crane, particularly read Dostoievsky. "Had I known you had not read him I should have been shouting at you long ago. . . . The two books I care for most – Karamazov and Possessed. There is nothing like Karamazov anywhere else in literature, a bible. . . . I have always felt him as the one writer I could go down on my knees to."[28] He also sent Crane and

Hemingway to Turgenev and Chekhov, to D. H. Lawrence and George Borrow. All writers needed the past – lifting, borrowing, stealing from the best that had been written and making it their own. At that very moment the arch-thief of the Modern Age, T. S. Eliot, was shoring up his borrowed fragments in *The Waste Land*. Hemingway had half consciously been borrowing from Kipling; now his horizons broadened.

He absorbed Anderson's advice quickly, but its effects were not instantaneous. It took time to read digest and process the new writers. Lawrence, Dostoievsky and Tolstoy he probably did not read until he reached Paris in 1922. Turgenev he may have begun reading in Chicago, but he read and re-read *A Sportsman's Sketches* during the Paris years while he was developing the short-story form that would make him famous. Between the first draft and the revision of *The Sun Also Rises*, he read six Turgenev books. One of them was *Torrents of Spring*, which, ironically, gave him the title for his satire on Sherwood Anderson, who first sent him to Turgenev. Even more obscure was the curious British author, George Borrow, whose picaresque adventures were hidden under the unlikely title *The Bible in Spain*. In the readily available Modern Library edition, Hemingway got his first taste of Spanish life, a taste that he later developed to the full. Anderson praised all of Borrow's work; *Lavarengo* and *Romany Rye* he claimed to have read twenty times.[29] Both of these slightly bizarre collections of gypsy lore and folkways became part of Hemingway's own library, eventually to make their contribution in *For Whom the Bell Tolls*.

Just when Hemingway's sexual life was blossoming, he discovered from Anderson that one could write about it in ways long forbidden. Deviant behavior, Freudian complexes and basic sexual congress – only hinted at darkly by the preceding generation – were becoming the focus of Hemingway's age. This discovery was crucial to Hemingway's development as a writer, but it insured that he could never return to Oak Park, where the sexual bastions remained unbreached well past mid-century.[30] In Chicago, Hemingway continued to read Havelock Ellis, whose *Psychology of Sex* he urged unsuccessfully on all of his friends. In

January he sent a copy to Hadley, whose first attempt at the catalogue of sexual behavior got no further than the chapter titles.[31] But two weeks later she and Ernest were exchanging "essays" on male and female roles. "Is it the Sads or Mads," Hadley asked, "that Ellis says are fond of being in mortal pain? Think all women get sumpen out of it. If a male does it to um – don't you?"[32] By April, Ernest had sent her three volumes of Ellis, which she said was too much; all those fetishes and inhibitions could intimidate a person.[33] This was indeed a new country where a man could discuss sexuality with the woman he loved. This new-found freedom was his passport into the Twenties, and Anderson, if he did not issue the passport, at least stamped the visa.

By April 1921, Anderson had verbally critiqued a number of Hemingway's stories, finding in them a correspondence with Kipling, who, along with O. Henry, the young writer had completely digested.[34] But Anderson's criticism was less import-ant than the fact that he was reading Hemingway and encour-aging him. In the face of the continuing rejection slips, Anderson was the boost Ernest sorely needed. The older writer was also providing important information on the literary life – the importance of finding an honest publisher and the money to be made in foreign translations. It was Anderson who first told Hemingway about cultivating magazine editors and book reviewers, first told him not to give anything away for free. A professional writer must live by his words. If they were good enough to print, then they had a fair price as well. *The Dial*, he told Hemingway, had only one great advantage: Thayer money's.[35] It was a lesson the Oak Park boy took deeply to heart. Professionals got paid; amateurs worked for free. Five years later, when Hemingway first published with Scribner's in New York, some of the professional expatriates felt he had sold out his experimental status for a commercial payday. They simply did not understand the Doctor's son, who had been forced to keep meticulous account of his income and expenditures and who learned from Anderson to value himself highly or no one else would.

At Anderson's apartment and at Palos Park, Hemingway was privy to inside talk, the literary gossip he came to love so much. There he first heard stories about Max Eastman, Anita Loos, Alfred Stieglitz and Georgia O'Keefe. There he met Carl Sandburg, impressing the poet with his knowledge of *The Rubaiyat*.[36] Soon Hemingway began writing his own Chicago poems in free verse. Whatever was said, he listened to; whatever he heard, he permanently recorded. Anderson gave him the same advice he gave all young writers. He told Hemingway that he had to get a room "utterly your own and your ordinary every day life should not be brought into it."[37] In Chicago, two blocks away from the Division Street apartment, Anderson set up separate writing quarters where his wife, Tennessee, did not bother him.[38] No one, absolutely no one – not wife, not family, not God himself – should interfere with the writer's work. The world of business, he told Ernest, was a trap designed to thwart the writer. Hack writing, whether advertising or journalism, could ruin the artist, who must stay simple, his life uncompli-cated.[39] Hemingway listened intently and remembered. A year later in Paris, he rented a separate room where he went each morning to write. Three years later, he quit his journalist's job, telling everyone that such work could destroy a writer. Later during the Spanish Civil War and again during World War Two, he renewed his journalist's credentials when he needed a way into those wars. Despite what first Anderson and then Gertrude Stein told him of journalism's ill effects on his writing, he came to see it as a way of refilling the creative well during dry periods. It was also wonderful publicity. During the Thirties, nothing kept his name so prominent in literary circles as his *Esquire* essays. His news features and essays, in fact, became the raw material and background for much of his fiction. But in 1921, facing the mindless job on the *Co-Operative Commonwealth,* Anderson's advice seemed exactly right.

As with so many of the formative influences, Anderson's impact on Hemingway was sudden, intense and brief. Ernest met the established writer in early January 1921; by mid-April, Anderson left Chicago on his way to Paris, not to return until

November 15. At the end of December 1921, Hemingway himself left Chicago, never to see Anderson again except in passing. During the four months he had access to Anderson's table talk, Hemingway was busy pouring words on to paper: letters, journalism, fiction. His almost daily letters to Hadley could have filled a small book. The *Co-Operative Commonwealth* not only took time to write and edit, but it also sent him scurrying about for stories and interviews. There was little time for talky afternoons with Anderson, afternoons at the Victor House that Bill Horne remembered, "sitting around that back table . . . and Sherwood a bit befuddled and doing a lot of talking and you capping his yarns."[40] Hemingway probably met with Anderson less than once a week during those four months, enough time for Hemingway to absorb what he needed without becoming a disciple.

About the time of their last meeting, Anderson advised a friend about another young writer, advice probably similar to that he gave Hemingway.

There isn't anyone to tell these young men — who might possibly be artists — that they are on the wrong roads — that they should learn some humbleness and most of all learn to face themselves. It will be interesting now to watch this man. Will he go to work to educate himself, to find out what the few real artists in America are talking about and let writing go until he has found out a little about life.[41]

Ernest had already found out more than a little about life on the Kansas City police beat and in the trenches at Fossalta, and humility would never become one of his cardinal virtues. But he was learning to face himself, to deal with his conflicts and fears, to use his own painful experiences as a source for his fiction. Of Anderson's several young protégés, none was more adept than Hemingway in educating himself. Before he was through he would read all the books. But it was more than books. At a crucial moment in Hemingway's development, Anderson was there to show him through precept and by example how an

American writer lived, behaved, spoke, dressed and wrote. Throughout the Twenties, perhaps even later, Anderson's influence was residual. It was not his literary style, which Hemingway could emulate when he wished and also brutally satirize, but Anderson's life style that left its lasting mark. His book, *Many Marriages* (1923), could have been used as an ironic title for Hemingway's life story.

The most immediate result of the newly found literary life was the poetry Hemingway began to write. Not since high school, where he wrote a few satiric poems, had he tried verse. On January 30, in her almost daily letter, Hadley received a "dreamy poem." It may have been the one that said

> Night comes with soft and drowsy plumes
> To darken out the day
> To stroke away the flinty glint
> Softening out the clay
> Before the final hardness comes
> Demanding that we stay.[42]

Over the following seven months more poems flowed, many of them, like the one above, showing a developing skill in rhythm and use of metaphor. Night, depression and love's pain – a young man's subjects – recur frequently.

> Cover my eyes with your pinions
> Dark bird of night
> Spread your black wings like a turkey strutting
> Drag your strong wings like a cock grouse drumming
> Scratch the smooth flesh of my belly
> With scaly claws
> Dip with your beak to my lips
> But cover my eyes with your pinions.[43]

The dark bird of Hemingway's night was not merely affected melancholia. Although he was apt to exaggerate to Hadley his chronic insomnia and fits of depression, they were real problems.

This is not Mother Night gently rocking the cradle; these male night birds, strutting and drumming their mating calls, are homoerotic forms of Death's nightmare. At all cost, Anderson had told him, avoid "the profound shallow smartness and weariness of intellectual and artistic life all over America now."[44] Open yourself up. Find out who you are at the very core. Hemingway was trying to do just that. Under Anderson's influence he began to write about what he knew best: his own experiences and the mind that they haunted. By July of 1921, he was sending some of his verse not to the local market, *Poetry*, but to Scofield Thayer's *Dial* where Anderson frequently published.[45] All the poems were rejected.

More than a few of his letters and poems worried Hadley. Whenever she was sick, he was sicker, usually in the next letter. His throat infections seemed co-ordinated with her own minor problems. What she really could not understand were his secrets: the things she should not tell anyone; the things she felt he was not telling her. She was not supposed to show his writing to anyone else. She was not supposed to say anything about their engagement. She was not supposed to talk to the Madame about him. It was probably Katy. There was something between those two, which did not surprise her. Since they had been twelve together, she had admired Katy Smith and could well understand how Ernest would be attracted to those green eyes. All the boys loved "Ka–Ka–Ka–Katy" as the song said. Well, red hair could compete with green eyes if only she could get him to St. Louis. What else was he not telling her? The Jim Gamble crisis had passed. This too would pass. They were going to be married. She knew that.

He did not tell his parents he was engaged, and he did not tell Katy. He did not tell anyone yet. It was not until the middle of February, when he broke with Marjorie that he finally told Jim Gamble that their trip to Rome was off. When he finally did write Gamble, his letter waffled so badly that Gamble immediately replied, renewing the offer if Ernest decided not to marry. Or maybe he was already married; Gamble could not tell. Ernest quickly drafted a telegram: "Rather go to Rome with you than heaven STOP Not married STOP But am broke STOP." He pulled the sheet out of the typewriter, and scratched out "Not married." He tried again with a second sheet.

> Rather go to Rome with you than heaven STOP Not married STOP Too sad for words STOP Writing and selling it STOP Unmarried STOP But don't get rich STOP All authors poor first and then rich STOP Me no exception STOP Wouldn't we have a great time STOP Lord how I envy you.[46]

In pencil he crossed out *Not married* and *Unmarried.* Once words were on paper with his name signed beneath them, they became a promise. He was going to be married, maybe. He read the telegram once more: another bridge to the past was burning. This maybe marriage was becoming more expensive than he had imagined. Before it was consummated, other good friends would be lost, other bridges destroyed. On paper he had written words which could not be taken back; already those words were having real effects. One could always go back, he insisted now and would insist all his life, and all his life he would discover there was no way back to the past except through more words on paper. For the rest of his life he would be losing friends; for the rest of his life there would be those who felt betrayed by him; for the rest of his life he would find himself betrayed. The world, he was learning, was vaster than Oak Park and more complicated.

During those first two months of 1921, almost daily letters rushed back and forth between St. Louis and Chicago. If Ernest went dancing with Kate, Hadley went walking with Kate's brother, Bill. If Ernest carried on about Kate's problems, then Hadley told him that Bill had said she was the sort of woman he might have married. All the while, mornings and nights, Hemingway struggled with his fiction, wrote his hack work, argued things literary with the various men who passed through Kenley Smith's rooms, read voraciously and somehow found the time and money for the theater. Twice he saw Lenore Ulric in *The Son-Daughter* at the Powers. He caught Charlie Chaplin's feature film, *The Kid,* and saw Willie Collier, live, in *The Hottentot.*[47]

There were bridge games and dances, and always there was Katy Smith. If a man slept only a little he could crowd his days full. Whatever his mind touched interested him – Jack Dempsey, the Russian situation, criminal warfare in the streets, the latest Floyd Dell book – and in all of his interests he was compelled to play the expert, the man with inside information.

Suddenly he was a boxing expert, giving detailed lessons to the men who lived at Kenley's now that his wife Doodles had gone to New York to study piano. Later, in one of his invented lives, he would tell of his youthful trips from Oak Park to Chicago gyms where the pros had given him rough lessons. Sometimes he blamed a brutal thumbing for his weak left eye, which, in fact, he inherited from his mother. No matter how exciting his own life was, his invented lives were better. He probably saw his first professional fight during the previous winter in Toronto when he took the Connable boy to the local bouts. The two fight articles he wrote free-lance that winter for the Toronto *Star* betrayed no real knowledge of ring lore; he hid his inexperience beneath precise observations more concerned with the spectators than the pugilists.

> The society box party smiled and applauded all through the fight. But the hardened fans at the ringside, while they applauded the game fight the Buffalo kid was making, did not smile. For they could see the terrible punishment he was taking. They watched the way Gould kept smashing his left fist on to the kid's broken nose. They knew the way Gould's punches were weakening the kid. They admired his game fight but they didn't smile. But the ladies in the box smiled every minute.[48]

It was not a paragraph to make Damon Runyan nervous, but two years before he met Gertrude Stein, Hemingway was experimenting with repeated phrases to make his point.

Six months later, in a feature on the upcoming Dempsey–Carpentier fight for the heavyweight championship, Hemingway sounded like a man who had lived much among fighters, a man canny in ring history.

> Experts are all victims of "Championshipitis." Whoever happens to be the title holder is the greatest fighter of all time. Thus they write reams about the wonderful superman that is Dempsey.
>
> It is bunk and twaddle of the worst kind.
>
> Jack Dempsey has an imposing list of knockouts over bums and tramps, who were nothing but big slow-moving, slow-thinking set ups for him. He has never fought a real fighter.[49]

Hemingway went on to describe the Dempsey–Willard fight of July 1919 as if he had witnessed it. He wrote of Stanley Ketchel, Gunboat Smith and Battling Levinsky with the familiarity of an old hand. From reading and brief observation, his imagination parlayed his limited experience into expertise. Throughout the Twenties he followed boxing religiously in Paris and kept abreast with American boxers through New York papers. Finally he became the expert he pretended to be.

But boxing and baseball were not enough to give Hemingway an intellectual edge in Chicago, where he found himself among college men who had read not more books than he, but different books, and their interests had a wider scope than his. Most of that group gathering at Kenley's apartment were versed in political theory. They argued the merits of the Russian revolution and the socialist tendencies of organized labor. The safe Republicanism of Oak Park had not prepared Hemingway for such talk.

In Oak Park's Republican bastion, Hemingway's political education was limited. Democrats were a minority and socialists an endangered species. In the 1904 election when Eugene Debs polled a handful of Oak Park votes, a local Republican wrote to the paper:

> Property Owners of Oak Park: The election returns just published show that your property, your homes, your

hearthstones, and even your lives are in imminent danger. You have sixty-eight socialists in your midst. Do not be deceived. All socialists are anarchists, some in thin disguise, others (but few) open and above board, but all anarchists. To such neither your property nor your lives nor the lives of your loved ones are sacred. These Oak Park socialists must be disposed of. . . . Unless you want to see our village covered with flames and deluged in blood you must lend a hand to convert these misled men. This is no childish or alarmist's cry. It is called out by the well known and acknowledged fact that all anarchists are always ready to kill and burn if that will help the propaganda; and that all so-called socialists are full-fledged anarchists.[50]

The usual political discussion in Oak Park was less incendiary. During the 1908 presidential election, the reader of *Oak Leaves* might not have known who the national candidates were, for their names seldom appeared in print. The issues were local: the anti-saloon people versus the Cicero bartenders. But even demon alcohol could not move Oak Parkers to split their ticket for the Prohibition candidate. During Hemingway's youth, drink and annexation were the only raging issues until the fall of 1912 when Teddy Roosevelt splintered the Republican party. Denied his party's candidacy, Roosevelt belligerently formed his own Bull Moose Party, which divided the Republican vote, handing the presidency to the Democrat, Woodrow Wilson. It was the only election in which Oak Parkers did not vote the straight Republican ticket.

As a result, Hemingway understood as little of radical politics as the inhabitants of Sinclair Lewis's *Main Street*, which was sweeping the best-seller lists in 1921 and which both Ernest and Hadley read.[51] That winter in Chicago his political education began in serious. At Kenley's he met Isaac Don Levine, the *Daily News* correspondent who covered the Russian revolution and wrote three books about it.[52] Immediately Ernest began reading Levine's *The Russian Revolution*, which Hadley allowed did not interest her.[53] Hemingway's interest was academic; after the conservative years of Oak Park, it would take something closer to home to create much sympathy in him for the proletariat. But he was coming of age politically. He was beginning to see that the Great War had been fought for economic and political reasons, not for ideals. Like the rest of American youth he had been suckered into it. Now wherever he looked he saw corruption. The Chicago police were in league with the bootleggers; at the state level Lorimer and Thompson seemed above the law; the White Sox had thrown the World Series. In Washington, D.C., Warren G. Harding was about to begin the most corrupt administration since Grant's. It was a lovely eduction for a young man. He would never again be suckered in by what he called Y.M.C.A. idealism. Less than two years later he would be covering the post-war European conferences for the Toronto *Star,* sounding like an experienced and often cynical political reporter. Never a radical, Hemingway became apolitical and remained so for most of his life. When John Dos Passos was radical in the Twenties, Hemingway remained detached. In the Thirties, when Edmund Wilson, Granville Hicks and all the other intellectuals caught the socialist/communist fever, Hemingway went to Africa. Not even the Spanish Civil War in 1936 could make him into a communist. His acquired distrust left him, finally, one of the least overtly political writers of his generation.

What did matter, he learned from Anderson, was to have read the best literature. Before 1921, Hemingway knew nothing of the Russians or the French, except a few stories by de Maupassant and Balzac's *Droll Tales.* He had not read the classic American writers. Of the 1890s Naturalists, he had read only Jack London's adventure stories. He had read a little of Twain but nothing of Henry James. He was ignorant of the new writers: Lawrence, Joyce, Ford and company. It was a little embarrassing, there in Chicago among the college men, to be so innocent of literary knowledge. He covered his ignorance as best he could, bluffed when necessary and read constantly. When he died, forty years later, his personal library would number over six-thousand volumes.

But like so many self-educated men, Hemingway felt insecure among college graduates. With his inborn competitive drive, he could not defer to them; he had to outstrip them. So he read more books than they read and he wore that reading on his sleeve. It would be reflected in his fiction throughout his life: the Doctor finds his son Nick reading beneath a tree; *Torrents of Spring* is filled with literary gossip and satire; Jake Barnes reads Turgenev in Spain and makes cracks about Henry James; Frederic Henry discusses H. G. Wells with the Count at Stresa; while watching the bull fights, the narrator of *Death in the Afternoon* pokes fun at T. S. Eliot; and Colonel Cantwell says that sometimes he is Mr. Dante. More than once during his career, Hemingway felt compelled to hand out lists of great books that any writer should have read. It would be difficult to find so many literary references or the names of writers and books in Stein, Dos Passos or Sinclair Lewis. What started as a defense mechanism became, finally, a habit. That winter of 1920 in Chicago, he told Hadley that he was scheduled for Princeton, but his mother squandered the money on her private cottage at Lake Walloon. Hadley, with only one year at Bryn Mawr, told him he did not need the university, but he continued to retail his alibi until he finally believed it.

Like the Horatio Alger boys whose stories he had loved as a youth, Hemingway continued to create himself anew. In March 1920, he wrote an ironic piece telling the would-be war-hero how to create the façade of a trench veteran. He advised the slacker who had worked in the munitions factory to change towns and buy himself a trench coat. He should also learn a few war songs to whistle on the bus and be modestly taciturn about his service as if it were too painful to talk about. But most importantly he should

> Buy or borrow a good history of the war. Study it carefully and you will be able to talk intelligently on any part of the front. In fact, you will be more than able to prove the average returned veteran a pinnacle of inaccuracy if not unveracity. . . . With a little conscientious study you should be able to prove to the man who was at first and second Ypres that he was not there at all.[54]

It was an art Hemingway himself perfected. Supplementing his brief experience at the front with war histories, he gave the impression of having spent years at the war. When he wrote of revisiting his station at Schio, he did not say he was there for less than a month as a Red Cross driver.

> It was the same road that the battalions marched along through the white dust in 1916. They were the Brigata Ancona, the Brigata Como, the Brigata Tuscana and ten others brought down from the Carso to check the Austrian offensive that was breaking through the mountain wall of the Trentino and beginning to spill down the valleys that led to the Venetian and Lombardy plains. They were good troops in those days and they marched through the dust of the early summer, broke the offensive along the Galio–Asiago–Canoev line, and died in the mountain gullies, in the pine woods on the Trentino slopes hunting cover on the desolate rocks and pitched out in the soft-melting early summer snow.[55]

His facts were correct, but he had gotten them out of books. When those troops marched down that dusty road, the same dusty road that would reappear in *A Farewell to Arms*, Ernest Hemingway was safely enrolled in Oak Park High School.

Little wonder Hadley was confused about his war service: she thought he had been in Italy for at least two years and had taken part in the disaster at Caporetto, but he would never tell her the details. One reason he could not elaborate was the presence of Bill Horne, who had been with him in Italy and whom Hadley knew. But on March 6, he gave her a few invented details about the war which seriously misled her about both his age and his service. By June, when she was trying to draft an announcement for her engagement party, she asked him to make up "a magnificent lie about your age in case anyone is curious enough to inquire – also tell me what events I *can* brag of without being a perfect fool about you and what not."[56] In reply he told that he had served briefly with Ambulance Section Four but had soon transferred to the Italian army, which Hadley agreed must have been much better.[57]

She had only seen him twice, a week each time, and they were secretly engaged, too secretly for her. The more questions she asked, the less sure she was about him, how old he was, who his parents were, the things that had happened to him. He had not come for New Year's Eve, nor in January as he promised. But his letters came every day, up letters and down letters. He loved her madly. Oh yes, he loved her, but he was not there, and words on paper were not enough. And how this strange letter "about the man breaking down a woman's small defenses and leaving her pretty grieving and all." Was he talking about her or someone else? Katy maybe? No, Katy's defenses could never be called small. Someone else then. The girl in Toronto? The Jewess, Irene? It sounded a lot like a guilty conscience. He seemed so sure of himself, so experienced, and yet he wrote these long letters about male and female psychology out of Havelock Ellis. He told her "how men must work and women must weep with sympathetic male insistence on the woman weeping." Well, the world was unfair to women. Yes, and women could become hard as well. She had seen her mother turn suffragist, hardening all the while. . . . Or was he only talking about sex? It was difficult to tell. In some ways he was so old-fashioned about women, almost chivalric, her "gentil knight." Whatever was bothering him could be cured, if only she could get him to St. Louis. What was all of this nonsense about the man being so responsible for what he did to a woman? *"No one,"* she told him, "can really harm a soul – break a heart up pretty much and ruin a body I suppose – but if you are awake you can't be permanently scarred in your soul."[58]

Throughout February, Hemingway kept promising to come to St. Louis and was always putting the trip off. The problem was Katy Smith, who would not or could not get away from her job to come along. Mrs. Charles was certain that Ernest was in love with Katy. She had watched them now for two summers at the lake. It would be an impossible match; she was anxious that Kate get to St. Louis for a little sound advice. When Hadley told Mrs. Charles that she would give Ernest "a terrible rush" when he came, Mrs. Charles said he would not give her a second look, for he was too smitten with Katy.[59] Hadley bit her tongue, but renewed her promise not to tell of their engagement. She was "dying" to be with him, she said "and never say a word – what's the difference."[60]

That was in February. By March, when Hemingway had still not appeared, Hadley knew very well what the difference was. The trip to St. Louis depended on Kate, and Kate kept changing her mind. As lightly as she could manage, Hadley warned him not to fall for Kate. "Think what the Madame would say or do," she joked.[61] She, however, was not laughing, for she also heard that Hemingway's friend, Howie Jenkins, advised him not to marry her. On top of which, there were all of Ernest's questions about her family background, which sounded like questions her sister Fonnie would ask. Or maybe his mother. Enough was enough. On March 8, she told him that as soon as he arrived, if he ever arrived, she was going to "tell them Charleses about yoon me, and how we feel bout each other."[62] She had kept their secret long enough. Once it was made public, there would be no turning back. The next day she told him, "I'm afraid I'm getting pretty disgusted but I'm dead sure of the game in the end luckily."[63]

Down on the St. Louis levee, the jazz singer said, "*Aggravatin' papa, treat me kind or let me be, I mean just let me be. Listen while I get you told, stop messin' round, sweet jelly roll. Aggravatin' papa, don't you try to two-time me.*" Two days later on March 11, Ernest and Kate arrived by train in St. Louis for the weekend. It was not much time, but enough for Hadley to make their marriage plans clear to Kate and Bill and Mrs. Charles.

Chapter Eight

SON AND LOVER
SPRING, 1921

AFTER his trip to St. Louis, whatever it had been between Ernest and Katy Smith was over. That simplified his life: Grace Quinlan, Bonnie Bonnell, Marjorie, Irene, Kate – that was all finished. Hadley was everything now. All his early life he had been a male surrounded by women: a doting mother and all those sisters, about each of whom he felt as possessive as a male lion with his pride of females. For two years now he had gathered up a second pride – substitute sisters who flattered him simply by their presence. Now that was over. He was ready to be married, to play the papa role. Everyone told him – Grace Quinlan, Bill Horne, even his sister Sunny told him – he was too young to marry. Sometimes he even told himself. But those doubts, too, were over. He had promised and the promise was public. It would be different now and much simpler. If Hadley's sister, Fonnie, did not care for him, it did not matter, for he did not much care for her propriety which was too much like Oak Park. Besides, he and Hadley would not live in St. Louis anyway. Toronto, maybe. He could always work for the *Star*. Or another magazine. That was a possibility until his fiction began to sell, which he never doubted. If a man worked at it hard enough, the sales would come. All his life he believed quite seriously in the virtue and rewards of hard work.

And all his life he would have troubles with women, troubles of his own making. He needed their attention, and always it got him in trouble, even with his sisters, all of whom but Marcelline wanted to be his favorite. Ahead of him waited three divorces, each of which was triggered by his falling in love with another woman. Each time he floundered pathetically in his dilemma, until the women made the decision for him. Unable to bed a woman without marrying her, the Doctor's son did not play the adultery game with panache; fornication within his social class was never without responsibilities.

In May, Kate wrote her brother Bill in St. Louis, trying to explain her feelings for Ernest. Another serious mistake. Hemingway could not imagine that Bill would just leave the letter lying in his room where Hadley would find it while searching for a cigarette. Bill was angry. Hadley was angry. Ernest tried to explain to her about loving people. To his relief, she seemed to understand.

> And how sorry I felt for you when you told me about Kate. Very, very sorry and frightfully admiring of Butstein [Kate] for the way she's been. Can't say enough so won't go on about it at all. Course you love her – love her like mad. At the same time I'm "always to remember you don't love anyone but me"? Course I love Kenley – greatest fun and nice and mysterious, he is. Terrible devil in them grey eyes, oftimes blue. Still – you know who I love – s'you. *Think* I know, honey, how you feel about Katie – hope I understand it right, hope it's all right. [1]

In fact Hadley came to understand his needs better than he did. He needed to be married but he needed the support of many women. What she did not yet understand was how much he blamed his own mother for what he took to be his father's suffocating married life. Nor did Hadley know how much his mother's son Ernest actually was. How, like her, he needed to create, and, like her, resented whatever constrained his freedom.

In his fiction, married couples are more practiced in martial than in marital arts. With the exception of Harry and Marie

Morgan in *To Have and Have Not*, Hemingway's characters do not fare well in their marriages. Mr. and Mrs. Elliot, who cannot make a baby, resolve themselves into separate lives – he with his poetry, she with her good female friend. Another wife leaves her husband for a lesbian lover. In "Canary for One", husband and wife return to Paris to separate, the world gone dead around them. In "Cross Country Snow", the skiing husband must give up his sport to take his pregnant wife back to the States. "It's hell, isn't it," his friend says. "No, not exactly," Nick tells him. Not exactly, but almost. Margot Macomber, after cuckolding her husband with their white hunter guide, puts a bullet through her husband's head, perhaps by accident but effective nevertheless. Harry, dying of gangrene in Africa, sees his slow death as a metaphor for his rotting career while married to a rich woman. When the shell-shocked Nick Adams cannot sleep, his orderly tells him he ought to be married: he'll never regret it. Nick imagines how the women he knows would be in bed, but when they begin to blur, Nick fishes in the dark down imaginary trout streams that remain distinct. He knows that married men "missed a lot" of life. In "Three Day Blow," Bill tells Nick:

> "Once a man's married he's absolutely bitched . . . He hasn't got anything more. Nothing. Not a damn thing. He's done for. You've seen the guys that get married. . . . You can tell them. . . . They get this sort of fat married look. They're done for."[2]

In Hemingway's fiction, marriage usually bitches a man one way or another; it either kills him or cripples his work. As Hadley wrote to Hemingway in May 1921, the worst thing "would be to discover the man she loved would have gone further without her."[3]

In fact, the only sexual relationships that work well in Hemingway's novels take place outside of marriage. Frederic Henry and Catherine Barkley create their separate peace, fornicating the world away in Italy and Switzerland. Only her pregnancy ruins their life together. High in the snowy Spanish mountains, Robert Jordan and Maria joyfully couple, and the good earth moves out from under them. Colonel Cantwell and the teenaged Renata strain his failing heart and our credulity in their Venetian gondola, stirring the waters. These happy, unmarried lovers, however, are all parted by death. This dilemma haunts Hemingway's writing to the end: only fornicators enjoy sex, but fornication is stalked by death. On the other hand his married couples rarely enjoy sex. Beneath the surface, supporting what some called shocking fiction, was an implacable social ethic that would not allow unending fornication nor long abide adultery.

During his March 11 visit to St. Louis, he slept in Hadley's bedroom, where, as she had warned him, she made frequent trips for things she had forgotten. If he harbored any doubts about their relationship, that weekend erased most of them. No sooner had he returned to Chicago than Hadley made plans to return the visit, which infuriated Fonnie. Hadley, she said, simply could not go without a chaperone. Hadley could hear her mother speaking from the grave. So she took Ruth Bradfield with her and stayed at the Plaza Hotel for propriety's sake, but most of her days and all of her evenings she was with Ernest. They cuddled and petted on the roof. They kissed in the streets. No one, she wrote later, was better at petting than he. The imagist poem he sent her captured their happiness as they made a world for themselves.

> At night I lay with you
> And watched
> The city whirl and spin about.[4]

With Katy, Ruth Bradfield and Bill Horne they dined and partied and talked. He took her for the first time to meet his parents in Oak Park, where Mrs. Hemingway invited them back for a Sunday meal. Yes, they would return on Sunday. But when the meal was cooked and the table set, the two lovers did not appear. Lost in their own world, they somehow managed to forget the invitation. It was that kind of week, every moment intense, every touch prolonged.

Years later Ruth Bradfield still remembered Hemingway as:

> a beautiful youth. He was slender and moved well. His face
> had the symmetry of fine bony structure and he had a small
> elastic mouth that stretched from ear to ear when he
> laughed. He laughed aloud a lot from quick humor. . . .
> His focused attention to the person he was talking with was
> immensely flattering. . . . He generated excitement because
> he was so intense about everything, about writing and
> boxing, about good food and drink. Everything we did took
> on new importance when he was with us.[5]

Most of that attention, of course, was focused on Hadley.

Before she returned for St. Louis, Hadley was certain they
would marry. Fonnie had warned her not to tell Hemingway
about her money, but now she felt it safe to tell him that she was
an heiress with a combined trust fund totaling about $50,000.
Invested in low-risk stocks, it would provide $3000 a year; they
could live wherever they wanted to live. They could go to Italy
for a year. Back in St. Louis, she wrote him about it:

> Think of how in Italy there won't be anything but love and
> peace to form a background for writing and what with all
> this seething writhing mass of turbulous creation going on
> inside of you now and bursting loose now and again in spite
> of lack of ideal opportunity – why you'll write like a great
> wonderful sea breeze bringing strong wiffs from all sort of
> strange interior places you know.[6]

They had not set the date, but whatever *maybes* had remained in
Hemingway's mind disappeared.

It was working out better than he had hoped or imagined.
Even the meeting with his parents went better than he had
expected. His mother had been almost too gracious, his father
too animated. They had not seemed nearly as terrible as he had
warned Hadley. To balance their impression in Hadley's mind,
he wrote her a long letter explaining how his mother had

destroyed the love that once flourished in their home, wearing away his father's enthusiasm for life. It was sad now to watch his father dying from angina, lonely in that house that had been once so happy. But the Doctor would leave them, he said, an inheritance in his will. Part of what he said was true. His father was gloomily predicting his death from heart disease, but the inheritance was a fiction. Perhaps Hemingway wanted to believe it, but more likely he invented it to balance out the real inheritance that Hadley was bringing to their marriage. He did not tell her about his father's "nervous condition," which was more responsible than Grace for the changes in his personality. He did not say that the previous summer's conflicts were largely forgotten inside the family or that he wrote his mother affectionate letters during her two-month Christmas trip. There was a lot he did not tell her.

Hadley sympathized with him, apparently believing his every word.

> I do love you so dearly and I feel all sort of wrenched in my heart for you to have been jerked about – had a lot of wonderful young affection just simply worn away by un-necessary – something. I don't believe there's any use in people marrying unless they make up their minds to pull together.[7]

In spite of Hemingway's diatribe on his mother, Hadley instinctively liked and was wary of the Doctor's wife, who reminded her a little of her own mother. In Grace Hemingway's need for her own identity outside of marriage, Hadley saw her mother's furious attack on a male-dominated society. But she could not have known how much their independent mothers shared in common. Both women had been suffragists; both had a streak of mysticism deep within. Grace was apt to donate money to almost any strange religious cause. The older she got, the more she dabbled in mystic religious books, remembering her English forebear who was once visited by a bright, speaking light. Hadley's mother had become a Theosophist who led St. Louis meetings for twelve years. Both women had a strong drive to improve their surrounding cultural climates. Florence Richardson began the Piano Club in St. Louis, and the first meeting of the Symphony Society took place in her living room. Grace Hall Hemingway supported the Chicago opera and symphony, and instilled a love of the fine arts in her children so deeply that all but one of them became public performers of one kind or another.

Both of these women, with their strong personalities, chafed at the restrictions of marriage. Both tended to dominate their husbands, and both husbands committed suicide. Grace Hemingway, providing as she did a substantial part of the family income, simply insisted on her separate vacations, her separate cottage and her usual housemaid and cook. Florence Richardson, married to the weak, alcoholic heir of the Richardson drug fotune, was the strongest will in the household. Before James Richardson's suicide in 1905 she had been outspoken, but after his death, while she was repairing the depleted fortune, she furiously attacked male society. It was not only her suffragist campaign, but her public writing as well which had a marked effect on her daughters. In *Reedy's Mirror* she published a poem attacking the issue of birth control, to which she was opposed but not for the reasons one might suspect. In the *New Republic* she made her rationale perfectly clear. Contraception simply allowed the man to satisfy his lust upon his wife's body without restraint. Birth control, she said, was:

> based upon the . . . fallacy of extreme sexual necessity and marriage as its natural expression. . . . Only eradication of the cause will avail – the destruction of the root-evil which is no other than abnormal, inordinate, unsane sensuality, primarily of men. The one possible cure for the whole evil is continence.[8]

Sex, she said, should be reserved for creating children and rarely exercised. Any other use was an impure attack on the wife. Hadley and her sister Fonnie had listened to this diatribe all their adult lives. Mrs. Richardson preached "continence," but "destruction of the root-source" sounded something like castration. Hadley, somehow, reacted quite differently. In Paris, Ernest boasted of her skills in the amatory arts, while in his notebook keeping careful track of her menstrual periods.

To Hadley, Grace Hemingway seemed a much freer spirit than her mother Florence had been. Grace was less concerned with social guidelines and public decorum. Back in St. Louis, Hadley felt guilty that she and Ernest missed the Sunday meal in Oak Park. She wrote Ernest for the address, which he seems not to have sent, perhaps not wanting Hadley exchanging confidences with his mother. Instead Hadley wrote Grace a bread-and-butter note which she sent to Ernest to forward. In it she apologized: "Being a housekeeper and cook myself I know how disturbing and annoying it must have been to have cordially invited guests fail to turn up for Sunday." The blame, Hadley said, should all fall on her. She thanked Grace for singing for them, enclosing a piano program of her own to let her future mother-in-law know that her son's fiancée was no amateur. It was a friendly, open note, but Hemingway apparently never delivered it.[9] He probably had already invented some covering story for their missed meal which Hadley's letter would have jeopardized. No sense in overtaxing the Village grapevine, which he knew would have plenty to say about Hadley.

Oak Parkers, like all small-town people, loved to gossip; behind decorous curtains, tongues wagged and heads nodded. Everyone's life was public domain. When Dr. Hemingway evicted Ruth Arnold from his house, knowing looks were exchanged up and down Kenilworth. Mrs. Loomis, neighbor in the village and at the lake, never forgot the rumor that Ruth had disrupted the marriage. Hemingway learned the art of gossip early and practiced it late. In 1921, it was gossip that cost him one friendship and damaged another.

It all began with Kenley's wife, Genevieve, whom everyone called Doodles. When she left for New York to study piano, Hemingway was taken aback: a wife's place was at her husband's side. That was the rule in Oak Park for everyone except Mrs. Hemingway, who took her vacations separate from the Doctor.

When Doodles departed for New York, Ernest spoke his concern about Kenley's marriage, perhaps because he saw what he thought to be a destructive pattern. When Doodles returned, her piano technique unimproved, Hemingway became even more concerned, for she was flirting outrageously with Don Wright, who, like Ernest, was living at Kenley's. Hemingway wrote Hadley about the affair and apparently told more people than he should have. His concern, he emphasized, was for Kenley, who did not understand what was going on while he was at work.

It was Hemingway who did not understand. At thirty-five Kenley Smith was not only much older than Ernest, he was also more sophisticated or jaded, depending upon one's perspective. His father, William Benjamin Smith, was a mathematician and biblical scholar whose revisionist essays and books on the Bible shocked many traditionalists. When Katherine Merrill, his wife, died in 1899, Professor Smith gave up his children to be raised by his sister-in-law Mrs. Charles who blamed him for her sister's death. For a long time now Kenley had been on his own, and his marriage with Doodles was certainly less traditional than the models Hemingway had in Oak Park. If Doodles wanted to flirt with Don Wright, that was her business. If Kenley wanted to have an affair that was his. Three years later their marriage dissolved in a front-page scandal when Kenley's mistress, after failing to shoot Doodles, committed suicide in Detroit.

In the summer of 1921, Hemingway was telling mutual friends how shabbily Doodles was treating his good friend Y. K. When the gossip returned to Kenley, he was furious with Hemingway, who had, as he frequently would, poked his nose into the business of others. Later, in Paris, Hemingway was exposed to even more unconventional relationships, but he did not condone them. In *The Sun Also Rises,* he catalogued the costs of such liberated sexuality. Jake Barnes' hopeless love for the liberated Brett Ashley costs him all his dignity, ruining forever the festival at Pamplona. "Such a hell of a sad story," Hemingway called it, and certainly no guide to moral behavior. Hemingway invariably felt guilty for his own adulteries, and did not forgive others their transgressions.

By late August, Ernest and Hadley no longer planned to live at

Kenley's after their marriage. With the viciousness that marked the end of so many of his later friendships, Hemingway told Kenley that he was not welcome at the 'Oak Park wedding reception. The two men never again spoke to each other, and his response almost cost Hemingway his close friendship with Bill and Kate as well. Hemingway's love of gossip had gotten his foot too far into his mouth to amend the situation easily, nor would it be the last time he made such a mistake.

With Hadley back in St. Louis toward the end of March, Hemingway's life returned to something like normal. Between April and June he sold three more stories to the Toronto *Star*, ground out his copy for the *Co-Operative Commonwealth* (which was beginning to give off the faint aroma of a con-game), went to movies and plays, worked on his own fiction, wrote Hadley almost daily letters and read incessantly. Back and forth they recommended books to each other and frequently Hemingway sent her copies she could not find in St. Louis. In February he suggested the play *Married* by August Strindberg, who Hadley said made her mourn. "Only the happily married can afford to read Strindberg," she told him. Like Ernest, Hadley was usually reading at least two books at the same time.[10] Together they read Sinclair Lewis's *Main Street*, which was on all the best-seller lists, and Chesterton's life of Browning, a poet Hemingway admired early. Much of this reading they bought in the cheap Modern Library editions published then by Boni and Liveright.

In April Hadley read Anatole France's novel, *The Red Lily*, which Hemingway told her about in Chicago, having made his discovery through Anderson. It was a strangely prophetic book for the two of them to be reading. Filled with romantic passion and poetic figures, *The Red Lily* also described the hate, pain and anger that are the underside of love. France's theories of Beauty's significance appealed briefly to Hemingway. But Hadley saw direct parallels between their life and the book.

I think we're awfully like Jacques and Therese – their feeling has length and breadth and thickness and an un- known fourth dimension just like ours. T'was terrible the

thing that happened – how Jacques ruined the happiness of
Therese, but we're primarily interested in the quality of the
emotions and what happens differently to different people.

The idea of a fourth dimension was much discussed in those days,
for Einstein's theories of relativity turned him into an international figure whose face appeared in newspapers, magazines
and news reels. Years later, when Hemingway needed a phrase to
describe his art, he said that he was trying to achieve in fiction a
fourth dimension, which he left vaguely undefined but which
probably meant the timeless quality of great writing.

Caught in her own comparison, Hadley amended it by saying,
"Know you couldn't be like him and I wouldn't have been as
quiet and kind up to the end as she was."[11] In the novel Jacques,
the sculptor, ruined the perfect love of Thérèse through his own
blind jealousy. Having loved him more passionately than she
thought possible and having suffered more pain than she deserved,
Thérèse finally walks away, ashamed, indignant and empty. No,
Ernest would never treat her like that, Hadley thought, but if he
did, she would not suffer the indignity so long. Five years later,
the fictional roles would be played out in their lives, and Hadley,
the injured party, would walk away from their marriage equally
hurt and indignant.

Perhaps she had been drawn into her comparison by Ernest's
suggestion that marriage was something of a trap, not exactly
what a fiancé was expected to say. "Biologically speaking,"
Hadley told him, "'tis a trap – or socially rather – biologically of
course just there being two sexes is the trap." When Hemingway's
fictional heroine, Catherine Barkley, tells her lover, Frederic,
that she is pregnant, she asks him if he feels trapped. "You
always feel trapped biologically," he replies.[12] Catherine does not
appreciate his comment. How like Hemingway to give Hadley's
observation to the male protagonist, and how like him to
remember a good line. The blighted love of Jacques and Thérèse
was a running theme in Hadley's letters through April and May.
"Jacques," she said, "had a terrible quality like a nail, a steel nail
that forced him to ruin the most marvelous happiness."[13] On

May 17, Hemingway sent her a copy of the novel so they might own rather than borrow it. Hadley joked that he was marrying her for her library.

Another book of which Hadley and Ernest were inordinately but explicably fond was the hopelessly sentimental Kipling tale, *The Brushwood Boy*. Therein, a young British war veteran returns to England vaguely discontent with life and haunted by a dream in which he finds a beautiful woman beside a brush pile on the beach. When he one day discovers just such a woman beside just such a brush pile, not even the reader is surprised to find that she has had the recurring female version of the same dream. They are deliriously happy to have the dream come true. Whatever residual effects the war might have had disappear as they fall deeply in love. Hadley and Ernest naturally identified with the two characters, for he was the disturbed veteran and she was the cure. He did not tell her that three years earlier, Agnes Von Kurowsky had addressed him fondly as her "Brushwood Boy." Eight years later, when Hemingway finally published his novel of the Great War, he rankled at Lewis Galantière's review which called *A Farewell to Arms*, "The Brushwood Boy at the Front." [14]

During high school, Kipling was one of Hemingway's favorite authors, whom he read and reread in his parents' library. Much of his early writing was heavily influenced by the British author whose fingerprints were detected by both Sherwood Anderson and Bill Horne in Hemingway's work that spring of 1921. [15] In 1916, Hemingway knew *The Jungle Book* well enough to quote from it by heart, remembering the sad poem the animals say when Mowgli leaves the jungle to marry:

> Through the night when thou shalt lie
> Prisoner from our mother sky,
> Hearing us, thy loves, go by;
> In dawn when thou shalt wake
> To the toil thou cans't not break
> Heartsick for the jungle's sake. [16]

If Ernest remembered this warning in 1921, he did not bring it to Hadley's attention.

Instead he sent her Gabriele d'Annunzio's *The Flame* – a book filled with turbulent, passionate love, a book for breathless lovers, but a questionable model for a young writer. During his six months in Italy, Hemingway first heard of d'Annunzio, one of the few romantic heroes of the war and a throwback to an earlier age. In the Great War, the balding poet:

> delighted in a kind of individual enterprise in which, together with some chosen Ulyssean companions in a motor-boat, he would glide into an Austrian harbour by night, and fire off torpedoes, at shipping or at shore. . . . Officially a commissioned officer in the army, he adopted on his own authority a naval title, *Commandante*. . . . He fought in the air, on the sea, on the land. . . . His theory was that fear is natural to the body, and that courage to control it belongs to the mind.[17]

His daring adventures, fiery public speeches and epic love affairs made d'Annunzio an Italian hero and an international figure. At a time when Hemingway was looking for models of how an author behaved in public, how he conducted his life, there was d'Annunzio, a romantic to the core and a difficult act to follow.

Hemingway's own military adventures in World War Two were to bear a striking resemblance to those of the Italian writer. D'Annunzio led single-boat raids on the Austrians; Hemingway outfitted his fishing boat to attack German submarines single-handedly. D'Annunzio flew bombing missions; Hemingway flew intercept missions with the R.A.F. as a reporter. D'Annunzio gathered his own army to liberate Fiume after the war; Hemingway gathered his band of irregulars after the Normandy invasion and was the first military group into Paris.[18] From d'Annunzio, T. E. Lawrence of Arabia and Lord Byron, Hemingway gradually developed a public role for the writer in his time: a physical, passionate, active life balanced against the contemplative life while actually writing. The public role that developed was nothing short of disastrous for American literature: the writer not only had to write well and honestly, he also had to test himself in the crucible of fear and danger. He eventually defined for his time how an American writer should live, and more than a few post-Hemingway writers would destroy their talent trying to follow in his large footsteps.

It was a self-destructive model, but the American models available to him in his youth were simply no longer viable. Twain, James and Howells were then the giants of American writing. No boy raised on the deeds of Teddy Roosevelt could be expected to follow the sedate and sedentary lives of either Henry James, taking his ease among the British gentry, or William Dean Howells, comfortably lodged in his editor's easy chair. Of the three, only Twin was a remote possibility, but the West of Twain's youth was no longer available to Hemingway. Sherwood Anderson, who might have become a literary father to the young Hemingway, appeared, for all his wisdom, a little too soft, a little too sentimental and vulnerable. Hemingway was not looking to be wounded by life, nor did he want to take all of America to bed. He needed a strong, masculine public model and America had none to provide. Roosevelt was dead and his idealism for the war even deader. Hemingway needed a mask behind which to write, a mask to cover his own fears and inexperience, a mask sufficiently opaque to hide what he did not know. Because he could not find one in the American market place, he invented his own, piecing it together from the rag-tag residue of European romanticism. It would take him ten years to perfect the part and another five to make it public domain. By the time he was thirty-five, the mask was no longer removable, and he had become the writer he invented.

The earliest model for his invented persona was this aging romantic, Gabriele d'Annunzio, vestiges of whom would appear late in Hemingway's fiction. When he wrote *Across the River and into the Trees* (1950), he called his young Italian beauty Renata, taking her name from d'Annunzio's character in *Notturno*. But the book that most impressed him after the war was *The Flame,* an autobiographical account of d'Annunzio's love affair with the famous actress Eleonora Duse. Ernest had given Dorothy Connable a copy of the book the previous winter, and in May 1921 he sent

Hadley her copy which she found to be slow reading. Set in what would become Hemingway's beloved Venice, the novel is a Nietzschean fantasy inside a Wagnerian opera. Here the aging, famous actress gives herself completely to the poet–hero, understanding, as only a fantasy could, his passionate love and his equally passionate need to remain independent. The flame of their sexual union is barely dimmed by his eye for a younger dancer. The actress knows the poet can never marry, no matter with what Venetian brightness their flame burns. In the courtly love tradition, only amourists outside of marriage can achieve love's heights. If Hadley found anything disturbing in *The Flame*, she did not mention it to Hemingway. She should have read more closely, for there was a disturbing pattern in *The Red Lily* and *The Flame*. Bright burning love was a self-consuming artifact. Jacques' "terrible quality like a nail" destroyed Thérèse's happiness. The poet and the actress burn incandescently but they also burn out. Love in those books did not last. One way or another, the male lover destroyed what he professed to desire most. Hadley was reading prophetic passages but chose to ignore them.

However much Hemingway admired d'Annunzio, he did not read the Italian's fiction for either style or subject matter. He was working toward his own pithy style, and for timely subject matter, there was plenty of that right there on the Chicago streets. Prohibition had spawned a network of gangsters who fed Chicago's thirst for alcohol. By 1921 territorial disputes were already producing gang wars. Bloody bodies piled up, their killers, for the most part, uncaught. The Irish might control Chicago politics, but the Italians were running its liquor and hold-up trade. The previous December, Hemingway had done a feature for the *Star* on "Plain and Fancy Killings, $400 Up," in which he supposedly interviewed a "hired gun," who told him:

He's heard that most of the *guns* were *Wops* – Dagoes, that is. Most *gunmen* were *Wops*, anyway. In the U.S.A. they nearly always *worked* out of a motor *car*, because that made the *getaway* much *easier*. That was the big thing about doing a *job*. The *getaways*. Anybody can do a *job*. It's the *getaway* that counts. A *car* made it much *easier*. [19] (my italics)

Gun, Wop, worked, job, car, getaway, easier – repeat and repeat the key words for effect. Already he was learning how to do it, but could not yet get it into his fiction. When he got to Paris, Miss Stein would give him some pointers, but he already had the hang of it. That winter in Chicago he was keeping his journalism and his fiction in separate categories; within the year he would begin to see that they overlapped.

On April 15, in a newsy letter to his father who was vacationing without family on Sanibel Island, Florida, Hemingway noted casually:

They hanged Cardinella and Cosmano and some other Wop killer today. Lopez, who was to hang, was reprieved. Cardinella is a good man to swing I guess. Passed the County Jail this morning and there was a big crowd standing outside waiting for the event. [20]

It did not seem important to get the names right for a letter, but Hemingway followed the Cardinella story closely in the *Tribune*, which regularly featured the city's violence. Sam Cardinella, Joseph Costanzo and Sam Ferrara, who died on the rope that spring morning, had been the brain and the brawn of the Cardinella gang which specialized in armed robbery, extortion and murder for hire.

Another gang member had been hanged the previous October just as Ernest arrived in town. He used some of the details in a poem written in early January. The *Tribune* had reported:

Campione and Reese, a Negro wife slayer, plunged through the trap together the first double hanging in nearly three years.

As the two men stepped up to the scaffold, Campione nearly collapsed.

"Please let me go," he sobbed. . . .

Reese, standing tall and smiling beside the craven white man, seemed almost jubilant.

"I am going to rest." . . .

Campione's knees swayed beneath him while Father Shields tried to make him repeat a prayer.[21]

Out of his imagination, which was fascinated with executions and the demeanor of the executed, Hemingway fashioned a sardonic little poem in which the narrator is actually present beside the scaffold.

There were two men to be hanged
To be hanged by the neck until dead
A judge had said so
A judge with a black cap.
One of them had to be held up
Standing on the drop in the high corridor of the county jail.
He drooled from his mouth and slobber ran down his chin
And he fell all over the priest who was talking fast into his ear
In a language he didn't understand.
I was glad when they pulled the black bag over his face.
The other was a nigger
Standing straight and dignified like the doorman at the
    Blackstone
"No Sah – Ah aint got nuthin to say."
It gave me a bad moment,
I felt sick at my stomach
I was afraid they were hanging Bert Williams.[22]

Bert Williams, the black star of Ziegfield's *Follies* and master of the "Cake Walk," was a national performer whom Hemingway had seen on the Chicago stage. Eddie Cantor would say that he learned everything he knew about vaudeville from Williams, who taught him that less being more, the minimal could achieve large effects. With that minimal and unexpected last line, Hemingway jammed death, fear, courage and comedy together as if the execution were a vaudeville routine. In the summer of

1921, he reworked the poem, reducing it to its essential element, fear, and called it "Ultimately."

> He tried to spit out the truth;
> Dry mouthed at first,
> He drooled and slobbered at the end;
> Truth dribbling his chin. [23]

In the first version he had used the word "nigger," a word he strongly objected to when Hadley used it. [24] After the 1919 race riots in Chicago, East St. Louis and points south, "nigger" was a word much in the mouths of violent, reactionary men. In Mississippi, Alabama and Texas the Ku Klux Klan was resurgent; in 1925, 50,000 Klansmen would march in white costume down Pennsylvania Avenue in the nation's capital. Across the south, black men were being lynched at an alarming rate. In February, 5000 Georgia whites watched a black man burn at the stake. Hemingway felt he could use "nigger" in the poem because the speaker was not himself but a narrative voice overheard, an authentic voice of the times. Through his newspaper interviews he had become adept at catching individual rhythms and speech patterns, at characterizing individuals by what they said. It was one of several journalistic techniques which he carried over into his best fiction.

The Cardinella execution, which he mentioned so lightly to his father, etched itself in his mind. Two years later in Paris, when he needed more incidents to complete the vignettes for *in our time,* he remembered the *Tribune*'s specific details of the 10:00 a.m. hanging.

> For hours before the death march, Cardinella paced his cell, wringing his hands, moaning and sobbing. . . . When the death march time arrived, he fought his guards like a maniac until he was exhausted. Finally he was carried to the scaffold in a chair, unable to stand erect, and, gibbering insanely in Italian, half insensible from fear, still cringing in the chair, he was executed. . . . Cardinella died in eleven minutes, his neck broken.

The article also told of the two other whites and three black men who were to follow "Devil" Cardinella to the scaffold.

For his vignette, Hemingway changed the time to "six o'clock in the morning," and, perhaps not remembering correctly, changed the number of victims to two whites and three blacks. But he remembered absolutely the way Cardinella had gone out. "They were carrying Sam Cardinella. He had been like that since about four o'clock in the morning." As the guards placed the hood over his head, he "lost control of his sphincter muscle." Disgusted, they strapped him into a chair, for he could no longer stand on his own. "Sam Cardinella was left sitting there strapped tight, the younger of the two priests kneeling beside the chair. The priest skipped back onto the scaffolding just before the drop fell."[25] That skipping priest, doing a little buck-and-wing, serves the same purpose as Bert Williams did earlier. This is the black comedy of death, the dance awaiting all of us. The point was how to face it. In Italy, his leg mangled by the trench mortar, young Hemingway had stared at his own death, felt his soul slip out of him as if on a wire, and he had known real fear. Now, in Chicago, he was trying to deal with the fear on paper.

Campione and Cardinella went out sobbing hysterically with priests at their side. That was one possibility. In May he sent Hadley the carbon copy of his latest Toronto *Star* piece which focused on another way of dying. On May 11 Tony D'Andrea, an Italian politician, was shot down in front of his own house by his opponent's hired guns. Picking up the details from the Chicago papers, Hemingway imagined the bloody narrative in wide open journalese.

Reaching back with his left hand to press the door bell, he was blinded by two red jets of flame from the window of the next apartment, heard a terrific roar and felt himself clouted sickeningly in the body with the shock of the slugs from the sawed-off shot gun.

This subjective account he did not find in the *Tribune*; it came straight out of his own wounding at Fossalta. As he would later insist, the best writing was imagined but it had to be based on experience. Here the sequence of light first, then sound then sensation was exactly what he knew from being blown up. The treatment was pulp fiction but the sequence was right.

The story continued.

> But it was not quite the end. For the pale-faced D'Andrea, his body torn and huddled, his horn-rimmed spectacles broken, but hooked on, pulled himself to his knees and looking with his near-sighted eyes into the darkness jerked five shots out of his automatic pistol in the direction of the shot gun that had roared his death warrant.[26]

Melodramatic, yes, but the movies had not yet made such scenes into clichés, and Hemingway clearly admired the dying man's last effort: fight it all the way. With his own myopic eyesight, he could vividly imagine the scene, live it, in fact, in his mind. Better to die like D'Andrea than Cardinella. His own characters – Harry Morgan, Robert Jordan and Thomas Hudson – all go down to gun fire bravely, choosing their time and place. His bull fighter, Manuel Garcia, takes his fatal goring while the crowd pelts him with cushions and bottles. But he is there in the sandy ring, fighting on his chosen terrain, losing with a special kind of bravery. What Hemingway learned at the war without realizing it became clearer that year in Chicago: man loses and winners take nothing. All one could hope for was to lose with a touch of grace, a little dignity.

Frequently, when sending stories to Hadley, he cautioned her to let no one else read them. The D'Andrea story was different. "You bet you needn't care who sees the D'Andrea story," she told him. "T'was a most powerful thing and I'm madly proud of it. Just showed it to Ruth and she's all for your journalistic style – eliminates everything she says except what's necessary. . . . I'm wild over the way you pounce on a strong word and use it in the right places without any of this darned 'clever' effect most present day writers have."[27] Yes, he was learning quickly now: eliminate the dross; get the effect; repeat the key words. Looking back at "The Ash Heels Tendon," his gunman story of the year before, he saw how phony it sounded. He had invented all of it but there had been no foundation, nothing in his own experience to build on. Now he was getting the hang of it all right.

The repetition of a phrase, turning it over and over on the page, he developed that year in Chicago. He used it in his journalism and occasionally in his letters. When Marcelline had her appendix out, he wrote her an apparently affectionate letter, which began:

Hope the [ab]'domen is feeling in good shape. Gee I was sorry when I heard that you were *to go under the knife.* There's nothing that bothers me like having a dear old friend or relative *go under the knife.*

Conversation with the male parent however elicited the information that you had *come out from under the knife* in nice shape.

The men are going to screed [write] you and I will be out shortly to see in what shape you have *come out from under the knife.*[28] (my italics)

Variations on "Going under the knife" are repeated ten more times throughout the letter as Hemingway experimented with its comic effects.

His first impulse was frequently toward satire and comedy that always misfired. Several of the stories he worked on that year were comic parodies or had comedic twists at the end. More than once he tried to write humorous plays which seldom got beyond the third page. As Hadley, who liked everything he wrote, told him, "your way of saying it is ingrained in the style of your serious stuff – and I think from your not having written as much funny stuff yet – that [it] hasn't got your vitality in it as steadily."[29]

The only outlet he found for his humor was the Toronto *Star*. In "Condensing the Classics," which satirized the efforts of Andrew Carnegie to put classic literature into nutshells, Hemingway suggested that "The Rhyme of the Ancient Mariner" might appear as:

ALBATROSS SLAYER FLAYS PROHIBITION

"Water, water everywhere and not a drop to drink" is the way John J. (Ancient) Mariner characterized the present prohibition regime in an address before the United Preparatory Schools here yesterday. Mariner was mobbed at the end of his address by a committee from the Ornithological Aid Society.[30]

It was the sort of humor that amused friends at parties but did not hold up in print. Almost everyone who knew him in those early years remembered Hemingway's broad and sometimes vicious humor, but the closest it would come to working was in his *Esquire* essays, where it was frequently misunderstood as braggadocio. He was much more adept at satire, parody and imitation – sometimes doing it so cleverly that few even noticed.

Whether Marcelline was amused or not by her brother's "going under the knife" routine is not recorded. She did not speak of it in her own memoir – *At the Hemingways: The Years of Innocence* (1961) – but there was much that she did not tell in that effort to sanitize the Oak Park years. She did not tell us of her "nervous" collapse during the 1921 summer, or of her beau whom her brother undermined with their parents, or of her absence from her brother's wedding. She did not say how distant she and Ernest had become by 1921, or how intense their mutual dislike grew over the years. Perhaps the split began in the summer of 1919 when Ernest had told his parents that Marcelline's constant male companion was a liar and not to be trusted. Perhaps the antagonism was fed by association, for of all of Grace's daughters the one most like her was Marcelline. It was Marcelline who moved into the Oak Parkish suburb of Grosse Pointe, Michigan, and bought a summer house at Lake Walloon, carrying on the family tradition there with her children.

After 1921 there were only a few letters between the two oldest children in the Hemingway family. Within the silences, the division widened. In 1939 in a letter to her mother, Marcelline bitterly recalled her brother's attitude at their father's funeral, where – in his Catholic phase – Ernest told her that suicide was a mortal sin that condemned the Doctor forever to hell. Ernest, she said, had never forgiven her for having had a year at college. About 1937 she wrote him trying to borrow and repair the old rowboat which had rotted at Windemere, where he never returned. He replied that she could paint, caulk and use the boat if a reliable witness were present both when she took the craft and when she returned it, but those were the only conditions under which she could ever set foot on the property. He was, she said, a changed person whom she no longer knew. She did not hate him; she simply could not respect him.[31] During that spring and summer of 1921, the division between brother and sister was merely a crack in the wall that would widen over the years into a gaping fissure. In *At the Hemingways* – a book she would not have published while Ernest was alive – Marcelline skillfully papered over the split, trying to put the family's best face to the world. The funeral meats from her brother's burial were barely cold when she launched her defense of the family and especially Grace, who appears more saintly therein than most remembered her.

First Marcelline, then Leicester and Sunny all published their versions of life at the Hemingways as if to offset what Ernest might have left to be published posthumously – the book on Oak Park he never wrote. He never wrote about delivering *Oak Leaves* up and down Kenilworth, slogging through rainy football practice on the lightweight squad, or learning to dance. He never wrote a word about Uncle Tyley, a drinking man, who late in life proposed marriage to the Hemingway maid. He never revealed his mother's peculiar dabbling in vaguely Christian mysticism. Nowhere in his books do we find family reunions or Christmases crowded with siblings. He did not tell us about Ruth Arnold and the Doctor's wife. He did not mention being cared for by a succession of maids and cooks. Not one of his characters bathes naked in the lake at evening with his sisters. This man, surrounded all his early years by sisters, who grew as possessive of them as a father, never approving of their marriages, gives his fictional Nick Adams only one sister, Littless, who suggests an incestuous version of *Swiss Family Robinson* that young Nick briefly entertains but knows to be impossible. Only when both Clarence and Grace were dead could Hemingway write the story, which he left unpublished at his death.

He never wrote about his mother giving birth in what would be his marriage bed at Windemere cottage. For a writer whose mother was pregnant four times before he was fifteen and whose father was an obstetrician, Hemingway's fictional birthings are strangely abhorrent: women whelping like animals in the dark or huddled in the back of a wagon; women clutching dead babies or hemorrhaging to death or being delivered with a jack knife and no anesthetic. These were his metaphors for our time, the time after the Great War. The secure, leisurely and firmly rooted world that he knew in Oak Park ended for him that night when the mortar shell roared out of the sky at Fossalta. That was the beginning of Modern Times. There would be no more cows of his youth munching harmoniously in the yards of Oak Park. Hemingway's generation, which some would misname "Lost," knew precisely where it was and where it had been. The only thing it ever lost was the secure world of its youth before the Great War. For all of its apparent excesses, it secretly harbored the memory of that first world. It would live in other countries and sample the wares. It would anatomize the new age of automobiles, alcohol, promiscuity, divorce and violence. As William Carlos Williams would say, "Divorce, divorce is the sign of our times." But that generation of writers, Hemingway included, did not approve of what it saw, nor would it ever feel completely at home again. Like Fitzgerald's Nick Carraway, many of those writers preferred their first world, a world more stable, a world standing forever at moral attention.

The mortar shell that ended Hemingway's first world was merely the punctuation, the period at the end of the chapter. By the time Hemingway was in high school, the Board of Education banned "close dancing" like the Tango and the Turkey Trot or any dance which was "questionable or even suggestive." In 1914, a detective was employed by the high-school principal to track down the rumor that the banned "secret societies" had been resurrected within the school. In 1915, over thirty sons and daughters of the Village's most respected families were expelled for belonging to such societies.[32] When Hemingway was a junior, the students complained that the "classics" were waning in importance; Greek and Latin could not compete with "practical education."[33] Try as they might, Oak Park parents and their representatives could not stop the children from dancing, smoking, going to movies, riding in automobiles, or sneaking across the village limits to the saloons in Cicero; they could not stop their children any more than they could stop the developers with their banner of progress. It was the new century and the cost was high.

Inside the stuccoed house on North Kenilworth, the casualty rate was even higher. Just when Ernest was becoming aware of how other fathers behaved, the father he loved was gradually disappearing into the darkness of hypertension, depression and paranoia. The arguments, the snapping tongues, the tears and apologies diminished the Doctor in his young eyes. As his father's enthusiasm for life gradually drained out of him, Ernest saw only that there was a war going on inside the house, a war his father was losing.[34] Wherever he looked in his time – at home, in the village or at the front line itself – he found conflict: sexual, social, cultural and physical conflict. It was neither a conflict of his choosing nor one for which his youth in Oak Park had prepared him.

A part of him always wanted a simpler, more stable system of values, a rigid code of conduct where right and wrong were clearly marked. In those early years back from the war, he could still read the medieval romances of Maurice Hewlett with admiration.[35] Hadley was right when she dubbed him her "gentil, parfit knight." Like Chaucer's soldier with his rust-stained armor, Hemingway appreciated the code of honor and service, and, like that faithful warrior, Hemingway found the values of his youth outdated in modern times. Small wonder then that war became his metaphor and conflict his stock in trade. Time and again he would create characters mismatched with an age they had not wanted, forced to forge their own code of conduct in a world without universal values, and like Roland at Roncesvalles, fighting a holding action against impossible odds.

On April 20, 1921, Hadley first heard about the war novel that Ernest said was "busting loose" in his brain. After a dull month in which he had written no fiction worth saving, he had, in a rush of energy, written three chapters about a wounded American soldier on the Italian front. Several times now he had tried to begin such a novel using his own experience in the war as Anderson advised. Drawing on his knowledge of the classical epic, Hemingway began in the middle of things with a burst of dialogue. It was probably juvenilia, he told Hadley, but he had to begin somewhere. Hadley, of course, was enthusiastic. "Some young one's gonna write something young and beautiful," she said. "You go ahead. I'm wild over the idea, Ernest – and the *start*! That's the way for a novel to start with real people talking and saying what they really think."[36]

Kenley Smith, before his break with Ernest, read part of the novel but did not think it would find a market. A literary agent told him that it was "impossible to sell war stories *except* where the war appears as a background more or less dimly suggested." Eventually there would be a change in reader reaction. When that happened, he was sure Hemingway would be able to sell his war fiction.[37] Well, the war was in the background there in the Milan hospital. That was the part Hemingway knew best, for he had been at the front line for less than one month but in the hospital for five. He was using some of the real people, like Catherine De Long, the career Red Cross nurse who was un-amused by his sense of humor or his drinking. Some of the people he was inventing or at least fictionalizing slightly, but the wounds were his wounds, and the novel would be closer to his own experience than anything he had yet attempted.

With the exception of his poetry, the novel consumed his late spring and all of his summer. When he could steal time from the hack journalism which was paying the rent, he worked on his Italian war. For the next year and a half, in Chicago and Paris, Hemingway worked on the novel, trying to blend his reading of war histories with what he knew from his own experience. But in

1921 he simply did not have enough sexual experience to create the heroine of *A Farewell to Arms,* Catherine Barkley. He had been in love with a number of women, fondled more than one and proposed marriage to several, but he had not yet experienced the intimacy of living with a woman. In 1921 he was still fascinated with Havelock Ellis' sexual theories, which Hadley found interesting in small doses but indigestible in quantity. Her sister, Fonnie, worried about Hadley's presumed sexual ignorance had given her "a posthumous book on Sex Relations," which she had been unable to finish. It was too "dictatorial," Hadley said. She told Ernest that Ellis was right: "mature people gauge things for themselves." They "were crazy enough about each other to look out for one another if things aren't good for us." Instruction was fine, but in "the beautiful country" of sexuality, two lovers could figure much out for themselves.[38]

What is more, as Hemingway was learning from Anderson's *Winesburg, Ohio,* a man could write about those discoveries no matter how fumbling, raw or inexperienced they were. No more could he write about war-heroes who went into the boxing ring to win the love of an idealized woman. That was past. Anderson pointed him to Lawrence's *Sons and Lovers* and Joyce's *Dubliners,* both of which were excellent models for handling the sexual awakening honestly. It would take Hemingway only a while longer to digest the lesson. That April he was still enamoured with the misty, romantic and idealized sexual adventures of d'Annunzio. Using Hadley's money for the most part, he was buying lira for their escape to Italy. Toward the end of April, Anderson, out of hospital from a tonsilectomy, urged Hemingway to consider Paris instead. That was where the action was. That was where Gertrude Stein held forth. He told Hemingway to read *Tender Buttons,* but had recommended so many books that Ernest had not gotten to all of them, and Paris did not yet excite him. He did not speak a word of French and he did not know the terrain. Italian he knew, at least a little to get by on, and there were places he wanted to show Hadley, places he had known and places he remembered from his Roman history in high school. In Italy his war medals would still have some meaning and there was all that classical art to see. Anderson tried to tell him about Cézanne and Gauguin, but Hemingway had not yet developed a taste for post-impressionism. The Italian settings he remembered and the ones he had visited in *The Red Lily* and *The Flame,* living them in his mind, were like a magnet pulling him back.

"He could always go back," Nick Aams tells himself in "The Three Day Blow." Even when Hemingway knew that "going back" was a mistake, even when he had proved it to himself more than once, he always made the trip. In 1922 he went back to Italy to be disappointed by Fossalta, its war-torn dignity completely lost. He went back to Africa in 1954, trying to find the people, the places and the beauty he had first known in 1934. It was a bust: two plane crashes, concussions and burns. In 1959 he went back to Pamplona and the San Fermin bull fights to find thousands of tourists searching for the life he had created in *The Sun Also Rises.* Where once his lovely, bitchy Brett Ashley turned men's heads, he found a bust of himself, a mockery of "going back." And at the very end, in *A Moveable Feast,* he went back to Paris in his mind, which as he knew, was the only way to recover the past, to redeem, revise or exorcise memorious time.

Chapter Nine

CITY LIGHTS
SUMMER, 1921

IT was hot in the summer in Chicago and the dark came very late. Then the electric lights came on and paired lovers walked along the boulevard looking in the shop windows. He imagined himself doing the things that they had done but walking home alone at night in the streets with the lovers stopping in front of the closed shops; he knew that he could not do such things now. The town was empty for him in August and he was very much alone. Hadley was in Wisconsin. Bill Smith would not answer his letters, and he could no longer talk to Kenley. Sherwood Anderson was in Paris. Irene and Kate were out of town. Along the boulevard, lookers had raised their skirts another inch, letting their black silk bloomers peek out below the hem line. And Hadley was in Wisconsin.

He wrote her pitiful letters complaining of sore throats, insomnia and loneliness. She sent him pictures, and said he was mistaken "in thinking the side of the bed on the roof is empty – I must be with you – always go to sleep with my arms around you and all warmed by your loving self."[1] That gave him something to think about, but it was not the same as the black silk he saw on the streets and he was never good at being alone. So he thought about Hadley and how their life would be together, and he thought about the streams, the Sturgeon and the Black, and how the trout rose at evening to the bait. "Guy loves a couple or three streams all his life," he said, "and loves 'em better than anything in the world – falls in love with a girl and the goddam streams can dry up for all he cares. Only the hell of it is that all that country has as bad a hold on me as ever. . . . you know how it's always been – just don't think about it at all daytimes, but at night it comes and ruins me – and I can't go."[2] That had been in April. Now in August he felt the loss of the north country day and night. Except for the war, he had been at the lake every summer of his life, and were it not for his impending marriage, he might have quit the *Commonwealth* for the trout. He told himself there would be other summers, but there never were. Lake Walloon, its streams and woods, the heart's source of his first good fiction, was passing into memory's precarious keep.

Now and again there was time to ride the tram line down the lake shore to the new Field Museum of Natural History. It was newly opened but not new, just moved further south along the lake. Nothing had changed from the old and temporary Columbian Exposition building they put up in 1893. The Greek temple had been duplicated, this time in marble to last. Inside the heavy brass doors, it was exactly as he remembered it; you could go back to museums that way; things stayed where you left them. As soon as he entered, the two enormous bull elephants in fighting stance still loomed up under the rotunda, dominating the vast room. As a boy he had pushed through those doors more than once. On school trips and with his father, mostly with his father, Hemingway had been coming to those elephants since his earliest years.

Once more he walked under the rotunda, past the elephants and into the Hall of African Mammals. In semi-darkness, where father and son had often stopped, he now stood alone in front of the sealed glass cubes in which family groups of African animals, softly lighted, stood forever stilled against their natural settings: cheetah, gazelle, zebra, wart hog, wildebeest and black leopard. There, first, as they should be, were the lions – maned male, female and cubs. To the right, two large-horned rhinos. And there, just past the rhinos, stood five greater kudu, their beautiful, spiraling horns, the color as he would later say, of walnut meat. The explanatory label called them the finest of the antelope tribe. And there were the five African buffalo, their boss and horns shiny black, their noses up, scenting the stilled air. Beyond, poised on their reddish sandstone lair, tails almost twitching, were the two infamous man-eating lions of Tsavo. One crouched, ready to spring; the other stood with his right foot slightly raised. Their eyes were fixed on him, and on the boy he had been, as he read once more that these beasts had killed and eaten over one hundred human beings, including several white men. In 1913, Colonel J. H. Patterson's book *The Man-Eaters of Tsavo* was one of several featured by the Oak Park library. It was the sort of book that the young Hemingway would have read more than once.[3]

Deep in the African hall, where the only light came from inside the glass cubes, he stopped in front of the spotted hyenas, frozen in the act of digging up a native grave to feed on the dead. The Field's description had made a lasting impression; he could almost quote it by heart:

This Hyaena is exceedingly cowardly, and does its best to save its malodorous body from getting into any danger, but it is a great sneak and woe betide any unfortunate native it comes upon sleeping in the night, for with one snap of its powerful jaws it will carry away the whole face of the victim. . . . The power of a Hyaena's jaw is tremendous, and with a single snap they [sic] are able to inflict dreadful wounds.[4]

Years later, Hemingway's fictional writer, dying of gangrene on the African plain, knows that death can come with the stinking breath and wide snout of a hyena. The fearful images a boy collects can last him a lifetime.

More than any other man in Hemingway's youth, it was Roosevelt who opened East Africa to the American imagination. In the popular magazines Hemingway followed the Colonel's safari, etching the photographs into memory. When the movie of Teddy, performing "strenuous stunts peculiarly his own," played

Oak Park in 1910, the young boy was there in the dark, collecting more images for his imagination. That same year Roosevelt came to Oak Park on a whistle-stop tour.

> Amid the lusty cheers of five hundred admirers, [he] was carried majestically thru the center of the village about 5 o'clock Thursday. . . . [The train], scheduled to stop, merely slackened speed and rolled smoothly past the station platform on which were gathered scores of school children and business men.[5]

Standing beside Grandfather Hemingway, a staunch Roosevelt man, Ernest had cheered and waved his safari hat, the newest addition to the costumes he wore as a boy – army uniforms, Indian garb, and now a khaki outfit exactly like the Colonel's. Africa and its dangerous game caught and held his imagination forever. At the Scoville Institute library he read Stewart Edward White's five African books – travelogues, novels and short stories. In *Rediscovered Country*, he devoured the maps and the details of the safari: how to hire porters; where to hunt; what to take and where to buy it; how to survive. His eyes lingered over the photographs of bare-breasted native girls.

When Hemingway turned thirteen, Oak Park literally teemed with African interest. Almost every church sponsored lectures on the African wilds. As the local paper reported it,

> these lectures have awakened great interest and especially in view of the fact that Africa is the subject that Oak Park people will study in preparation for their part to be performed in the World in Chicago exposition.[6]

Oak Park practiced seriously for its part in the exposition, which was to celebrate missionary work worldwide. Specifically, several hundred Oak Parkers were:

> to serve as stewards, or explainers, in the Africa section of the exposition. They will wear the native costumes and be

prepared to give information to visitors, telling of Africa, the land, the people. . . . To do this requires a course of preliminary training to make each explainer familiar . . . with the country. . . . Each lecture will have seventy or more colored slides.[7]

At the Third Congregational Church, Grace Hemingway was the Pageant Secretary and directress of the vested choir, in which young Hemingway sang. In March 1913, she conducted the choir's celebration of the David Livingstone centenniel.[8] By that time there were:

nearly 400 in classes in the churches studying Africa and reading about it. . . . In the Africa section, besides the models of the African huts and other scenery showing native life, there will be a large collection of curios . . . in charge of a native Zulu, who is at present studying at one of the colored schools of the south.[9]

On June 7, 1913, this same Zulu, Madecana Cele, whom the paper reported to be "a fine specimen of his race," appeared before the Third Congregational, dressed in his native costume, to "sing native songs and tell the story of his conversion."[10] Young Hemingway, in his pew, was more interested in Cele's costume and songs than his conversion. Unlike his father, who regretted not becoming a medical missionary, Ernest showed not the slightest interest in heathen health or souls. Along with his sisters Marcelline and Sunny, he participated in both the Chicago exhibition and the pageant, which enjoyed a run of several weekends in a row, playing so well that Oak Parkers were loathe to give it up. At the end of May, Grace trotted out her troops before the Third Congregational for a farewell performance, including the vested choir's "chorus scenes in Africa" and the Young Ladies quartet, which sang "in the Congo dialect."[11]

The African passion continued into 1914. In January, Dan Crawford, an African explorer, addressed the congregation on his:

twenty-three years among the savages of the most primitive sort. He was the first white man to visit the grave of Livingstone, and he penetrated 1,000 miles farther into the interior than Livingstone himself. He has shot more lions than Theodore Roosevelt ever saw, and has witnessed scenes of incredible cruel and savage brutality. [12]

Hemingway was pleased that Crawford did not dwell on converting the natives.

A year later Hemingway was promising himself such a life. He would become a natural historian, exploring the last frontiers, those empty white spaces on the world's maps. There might be no more American West, but the strenuous life was out there waiting for him still. As Roosevelt urged, Ernest had promised himself to become physically fit, resourceful and self-reliant. Standing once again among the African animals, he remembered that promise, which he would never renounce.

In 1933–34, with millions of Americans out of work and another Roosevelt in the White House, Hemingway, in a burst of conspicuous consumption, fulfilled his boyhood dream of hunting East Africa. The roots of his safari were buried in the crannied wall of Oak Park, where he had absorbed the words, images and voices that lured him to the Rift Valley. His African journey was an act of faith: life could imitate the imagination. The point was not merely to kill animals. The point was the "new country," where, across the frontier, a man might once again test himself, where self-reliance was still a virtue and society imposed few restraints. Growing up as he did during that transitional period before the Great War, Hemingway admired inordinately the survival skills and individual courage that powered the mythical heroes of the American West, a West over and done with before he was born. Raised on the old soldiers' stories of the Civil War and the Indian wars, he would all his life be looking backward, for, other than criminal warfare, he could not find an urban equivalent for the frontier experience.

Teddy Roosevelt had left his lasting imprint on the boy who had first stood there in the half darkness studying the kudu, the hyena and the lion. Let one be beauty; one, fear; one, courage. It was easier in those days before the war; anything, in theory, was easy. Standing once again in that darkness, he now knew that nothing was ever easy or simple or even over. He had told lies about his life, trying to make it match his dreams. That, after all, was the promise of America: with wit and grit any boy could rise in the world. Later, remembering to forget right, he would say that all his life in Oak Park he had worked hard: delivering papers, slopping trays in the lunch room, digging potato fields, selling vegetables, working all summer.[13] He was always working hard. Those long afternoons on the football practice field had been work to no purpose, but he was correcting that now that he had his growth on him. He was the boxing expert, the fighting writer who gave lessons. He worked hard at the war, which had not turned out well, but he was imaginatively remaking that accidental wounding into more heroic stuff. It was not San Juan Hill, but it would serve his purpose.

When Hemingway finally understood the war, understood the failure of the old ideals, he would write sarcastically of Roosevelt:

> Workingmen believed
> He busted trusts,
> And put his picture in their windows.
> "What he'd have done in France!"
> They said.
> Perhaps he would –
> He could have died
> Perhaps,
> Though generals rarely die except in bed,
> As he did finally.
> And all the legends that he started in his life
> Live on and prosper,
> Unhampered now by his existence.[14]

The hand that wrote those words would start a few legends of its own, legends more fecund than even a young man could dream that summer of 1921.

With everyone he knew on vacation, Hemingway sweated out the Chicago summer. He had not been out of the city since Memorial Day weekend when he and Bill Horne had gone to St. Louis, a trip not without its problems. No matter who said what to whom, it got back to just the person who should not hear it. Bill had not been sanguine about Ernest's getting married. The gossip chain sent that news back to Hadley who was furious. If people wanted to carp about their wedding, then they should say it to her. Then she had read Kate's letter to Bill, and Ernest had to smooth that over, trying to make light of his love for Kate. It was one damn thing after another. He had asked Hadley not to talk to Kate about him. Lies and evasions had a habit of catching up with him. On his birthday, Hadley thought he was twenty-three, a year older than he actually was. And she, as Fonnie continually reminded her, was thirty.

Fonnie Richardson, still playing the role of the disapproving sister, was certain that "iniquities" had taken place between the two lovers. She lectured Hadley on keeping their intimacies dark from the world. "Some awfully funny expression was used – not keep a naked sword on guard but something like that."[15] He recognized that naked sword from Maurice Hewlett's *Forest Lovers,* which he and Marge read two summers past. He would remember it again when he wrote about Nick Adams. Nick would say:

> "It's a swell book. What I couldn't understand was what good the sword would do. It would have to stay edge up all the time because if it went over flat you could roll right over it and it wouldn't make any trouble."
> "It's a symbol," Bill said.
> "Sure," said Nick, "but it isn't practical."[16]

Well, they had not needed a naked sword when their only sanctuary was the roof at Kenley's. There they had petted under the constant possibility of intrusion. Soon they would be married, and it would be the beautiful country. Alone together in Italy, maybe on Lake Garda or Maggiore, maybe at Capracotta, maybe even Taormina where he had gone with Jim Gamble, but in Italy together, alone, where no one knew them, it would be the new life.

Meanwhile, in Chicago, he was truly alone. Katy Smith had been there in June, but now the town was empty for him. Every day he wrote Hadley. When he missed her daily letter, he was despondent and morose. His chronic throat ailment returned as did the insomnia. He was becoming more like his father, wearing his loneliness like a hair shirt. When Hadley was there with Ernest, life was lovely. When she left, he wrote poems like "Flat Roofs."

> It is cool at night on the roofs of the city
> The city sweats
> Dripping and stark.
> Maggots of life
> Crawl in the hot loneliness of the city.
> Love curdles in the city
> Love sours in the hot whispering from the pavements.
> Love grows old
> Old with the oldness of sidewalks.
> It is cool at night on the roofs of the city. [17]

It was one of the poems he had sent to *The Dial*. A few days back from her July visit to Chicago, Hadley got her copy in the mail. *Love curdles, love sours, love grows old.* Was he trying to tell her something? She ignored several obvious replies, saying only that she found "dripping and stark" a chilly line. [18] There was much about his moodiness she did not understand; much about his "secrets" that worried her. She had little experience with men to judge by, and Ernest was like no man she had ever known. Certainly not like her father. Not anything like her sister's safe husband, Roland Usher the university professor. When they were together, Ernest was buoyant, funny, intense and talking, always talking, making up stories and spinning dreams of their life in Italy. He made her feel beautiful and young. When she was with him, the dust of St. Louis fell magically away and she was free.

Let Fonnie think them iniquitous; the safe world of St. Louis and Oak Park was a jail, and they were breaking out. For Ernest's twenty-second birthday in July, she bought him his first type-writer, a Corona; the Doctor sent his customary five-dollar birthday check.

July was a ritual month for Hemingway: born in July, wounded in July, he would one day blow off the top of his head in July. Always his birthday had come at the lake, where parents and sisters set up the birthday tree, and his father would ceremoniously hand him the five-dollar gold piece. Then the Doctor stopped coming to the lake in summer, and the money arrived by post. On his nineteenth birthday he awakened in the Italian hospital, his legs full of shrapnel. On his twenty-first birthday, his mother ordered him away from Windemere cottage, calling him a threat to youth. July was birth and death for him, but he could not explain that to Hadley, not in a letter. He could not even explain it to himself, but it was there. Two Julys later at Pamplona, Spain, he would discover the ritual bull fights on the feast of San Fermin; there for several summers he would celebrate the day of his wounding, July 8, watching the gaudy spectacle of courage and death.

For this July there was no celebration, only work. His father's five dollars came at a good time. He had lost forty dollars betting on Carpentier to beat Jack Dempsey. It was Dempsey the slacker, the war-deferred champion, against the French veteran who flew against the Huns. Hemingway admired the Navy pilots he knew in the Milan hospital just as he secretly feared that anyone who knew he had merely been a Red Cross driver might think him a slacker. He knew he was not brave in Italy, merely foolish. His war wounds were a fortunate accident, about which he could invent courageous fictions. He wore his façade of bravery like a borrowed suit a size too large, a suit he was determined to fit.

Earlier that year he met Nicholas Nerone, a certified war-hero working in the Chicago Italian consulate. Nerone had earned four silver crosses as well as the Croce de Guerra on his way to becoming Captain. His wound stripes were authentic. In 1917, he was on the Alpine front when the Austrians broke through at

Caporetto.[19] Drinking red wine with Nerone in small cafes, Hemingway listened to stories about the disastrous retreat to the Piave river. He was so impressed with the young Italian that he revised his early story, "The Woppian Way," to include some of Nerone's experience and gave his hero Nerone's name. Nick was equally impressed with Hemingway's fictionalized war effort; they had been together on the Piave and also at Vittorio Veneto, or so Nerone was led to believe. They knew the same bars and cafes in Milan, had drunk the same wines. When Hemingway told him that he was going to Italy in the fall, Nerone was enthusiastic about arranging details for the trip. At the consulate he was busy just then putting together the visit of General Diaz, the hero of Vittorio Veneto, who was coming to Chicago in November. When Nerone discovered that Hemingway never formally received his war medals, he proposed that the General himself decorate Ernest, who simply must delay his Italian journey.

Hemingway wrote Hadley about Nicholas in glowing terms. They were heartsick for the Italian life, which he and Nick were reminded of in the Italian section of Chicago. Kate told her that Nick was "mad" about Ernest. Hadley, already thinking of babies, wrote Ernest, "Isn't Nicholas or Nick Hemingway too charming?"[20] But the name was made flesh only in Hemingway's fiction, where Ernest was both father and mother to the man he called Nick Adams.[21] During that summer of 1921, Nick Nerone was an unexpected gift, an antidote for Hemingway's fitful moodiness.

As was Hemingway's habit, he was reading continuously that summer from the best-seller lists. He and Hadley read Floyd Dell's *Moon Calf* and his newest novel *Briary Bush*, both Chicago novels; W. L. George's *Bed of Roses*; Knut Hamson's *Hunger*, about which Ernest was enthusiastic; and Somerset Maugham's *The Moon and Sixpence*. Hadley thought that Maugham's "complete acquiescence to the melancholy of life" was a little like the Russian writers she knew. She did not comment on the plot wherein the young artist leaves his wife and children for the South Seas in order to paint as he must. Also on their list was the latest Maugham novel, *Mrs. Craddock,* in which a marriage is unable to sustain the intensity of the wife's passion. Both read Rose Macaulay's satire, *Potterism,* which was then sweeping the country. Neither particularly cared for this English *Babbitt* which attacked the smug, safe and complacent middle class. Parents and complacency were in need of satire, but when Macaulay poked fun at Johnny Potter, the young veteran who wanted to become a writer, Ernest found it difficult to laugh. Johnny Potter, who wanted to write poetry and best-selling novels, supported himself with hack journalism. That was too close to the bone. The problem with the book, he told Hadley, was the characters: all the normal ones were treated as abnormal.[22] He saw nothing wrong with the young journalist's ambitions, nor did he find anything funny about the middle class placing creature comforts about radical ideas.

As the Twenties avant-garde and the Thirties proletarian critics would discover Hemingway was neither a literary theorist nor a radical. Except for his brief Thirties involvement with the Spanish Loyalists, political causes, for the most part, did not interest him. Government and its agencies – F.B.I., Internal Revenue Service, Army bureaucrats – were generally suspect. Like Owen Wister's Virginian, he believed firmly in unrestricted self-reliance, and like Teddy Roosevelt, he believed in a natural elite. He was a benign racist, no more and no less prejudiced against Jews and Negroes than most Oak Parkers, which was less than the average White American at the time. He may have rejected the involvement in local issues that suburban Oak Parkers so enjoyed, but in large part he never rejected their middle-class ideals. The homes he owned in Key West, Cuba and Idaho were Oak Park establishments with servants and cooks. For his sisters, brother and children, he wanted the best education possible. And like most Oak Parkers, he took pleasure in knowing the rich, the famous and the accomplished. He never traveled second class when he could afford to travel first, either literally or metaphorically.

Not all of Hemingway's reading that summer was popular fiction. He continued to read Joseph Conrad, whom he had discovered in Toronto. In 1921, just in time for post-war American writers, Boni and Liveright reissued Conrad's *The Nigger of the Narcissus* with its now famous Preface. In late August, Hemingway sent a copy to Hadley.[23] It was the right book at the right time. Anderson told Hemingway that it was possible to write well without compromising values or style, that there was more to the literary life than the seasonal fluff that no one would remember. As much as he admired Anderson, Hemingway was not ready to accept him as an idol. Anderson was too much his contemporary and too much an American writer. Hemingway had no particular appreciation for the American tradition, particularly the effusive Whitmanian strain. With the exception of Jack London and Twain's *Huck Finn*, he was largely ignorant of nineteenth-century American novelists. At the crucial moment when Hemingway was changing his role model for writing, Conrad was there.

Conrad's work echoes throughout Hemingway's fiction. Hemingway's favorite plot – the American isolated "in another country" for a test of values – comes primarily from Conrad. Hemingway's Jake Barnes (1926) is an American isolated in Europe where his values are tested to the breaking point. Frederic Henry's trials in *A Farewell to Arms* (1929) are a study of isolation's effects. Robert Jordan's American values are pushed to their limits behind enemy lines in Spain (1940). And Santiago, lonely old fisherman, alone on the Gulf stream for three days with his giant marlin, is broken but undefeated, his values intact. As Conrad ended the life of Lord Jim with a pistol shot, so Hemingway would end the lives of Robert Jordan, Harry Morgan and Thomas Hudson.

From Conrad also came the theme of the "secret society." Those characters in Conrad who share a moral code are bound together in a special brotherhood. Sometimes the trust is broken, as in *Outcast of the Islands*, or sorely strained, as in *Lord Jim*, but the moral code itself is reaffirmed, even by negatives, and the credit of paid-up members is always good. As Marlow reiterates, Jim was "one of us." That phrase plays ironically through *The Sun Also Rises*. In Hemingway, the secret society may be the war wounded as it is in *The Sun Also Rises* and *Across the River and Into the Trees*, or it may be a select group that shares a particular expert knowledge of fishing or bull fighting. Whatever the criteria, the members are easily recognized.

All of that, of course, came later. First he had to find his style, and Conrad's Preface to *The Nigger of the Narcissus* gave him a maxim which became the foundation of his tight, intense paragraphs. Conrad said that the writer's task was "to make you hear, to make you feel . . . to make you see. That – and no more, and it is everything."[24] As Hemingway explained it to his father in 1925, "I'm trying in all my stories to get the feeling of the actual life across – not to just depict life – or to criticize it – but to actually make it alive. So that when you have read something by me you actually experience the thing."[25] And again in 1934, he told his readers, "For we have been there in the books and out of the books – and where we go, if we are any good, there you can go as we have been."[26] He learned it first from Conrad.

While rejection slips from *Red Book, Cosmopolitan, Saturday Evening Post* and *The Dial* piled up, he was learning. Whatever he read, he studied the technique and the style. Even from sorry novels one could learn what not to do. Like young Ben Franklin, whose *Autobiography* he read in high school and would carry with him to Key West and Cuba, Hemingway was teaching himself to write by imitation. He saw now that his first models were flawed. With practice he could master the popular short story, but Sherwood Anderson changed his focus. Slick fiction, Anderson said, was a "perversion of life." Oh, it was skillfully done; the characters had an "exterior semblance of life," but they were not human. The trick was giving enough mechanical details to make the reader think he was getting life itself. Then "you simply make these people do and say things no human being has ever really been know to say or do." This dishonest writing was not the fault of the writers, but of the market place. With decent conditions, some of the hacks could be artists.[27] After a generation of intellectual drought, Anderson was certain that Modernism was the future. Hemingway could be part of it, or he could follow the slick fiction writers into history's dustbin. It was his choice.

Being a writer was no longer enough. Now he wanted to become a great writer. As he read through the chapters of his war novel, he saw what Anderson meant. The characters talked well enough. Doing interviews, he had developed a quick ear for people talking. But it was not life, and the plot line, the narrative, the technique did not read as well as *Moon Calf*. It was juvenilia, no matter how much Hadley encouraged him. In August, he tried to replot the action, using some of the techniques he had been studying. In *Potterism*, Macaulay had told her story in chronological sequence but shifted the point of view for each chapter. He probably did not know enough about the characters to pull that off, but he considered fragmenting the story, jumping back and forth between letters and narrative maybe.

The structure was ragged, jumpy, but open, allowing him to work in his war poetry and some of the letters which he had saved. To Hadley, the plot sounded "if anything *too* patchwork." She reminded him how she had wanted "a long stretch of the same form when Fitzgerald got to pitching from letter to narrator." But she did not want to discourage him. *This Side of Paradise*, misspelled words and all, had the "vital throb of youth;" she did not want Hemingway to squash that throb. But the important thing was to have a tight narrative thread holding the novel together. She reminded him of W. L. George's narrative structure in *Bed of Roses*, which they had both read that spring.[28] Maybe she was right, but he saw that the loose structure had an advantage: a lot could be left out that way. Stringing together fragments could work; he and Bill Smith had seen that when they played with the concept for "Cross Roads." Masters did it with *Spoon River* and Howe used it with his *Anthology of Another Town*. It was a good idea that he finally put to use in 1924 when he wrote *In Our Time*.

When the war novel got stuck that July, Hemingway ripped off on his new Corona a satirical fable that he called "A Divine Gesture." God, looking a lot like Tolstoy, and his angel Gabriel, who might have been d'Annunzio, find their Garden deserted by Adam and Eve. She's out, they are told. Won't be back until four. There are only broken flower pots; simpering, "faithful" bootjacks, who mindlessly chant "We mustn't squirm today;" and a cortège of talking bathtubs filled with water. God "like many leaders was very deaf at times," and is not amused by his creation. Obscure, comic and irreverent, the satire read a bit like *Alice in Wonderland,* a bit like one of the fables of Lord Dunsany or George Ade. The angel Gabriel trying to correct the Lord God's grammar – "there is only twenty-four hours in a day" – sounded like Alice trying to correct the White Rabbit.[29]

Hadley loved the piece without indicating that she understood it completely.[30] Ernest was amused. Later that fall when Anderson returned from Paris, he told Hemingway about a new magazine in New Orleans called *The Double Dealer* which might publish the fable. He needed the encouragement. For two and a half years now he had been sending out stories without a single acceptance or even a hint of interest. His Oak Park classmates were college graduates, selling bonds, real estate and automobiles, making their way in the world; some were now getting out of medical or law school, setting up practice, buying homes like the ones Uncle George was building on speculation in Oak Park. His old acquaintances were becoming respectable, getting on with their lives. He was a twenty-two-year-old high-school graduate, still holding on to his war experience when the rest of the country was putting up monuments to the war dead in order to forget. Writing hack pieces for a possibly fraudulent journal, he needed all the encouragement he could get.

Six million Americans were still unemployed, and the *Tribune* ran a special daily column to help the demobilized vets find jobs. *Ain't we got fun.* The *Tribune* also carried full-page ads placed by the Knights of the Ku Klux Klan, who were looking for "100 Per Cent Americans . . . None Others Need Apply."[31] Twelve thousand Chicagoans answered the call: the scars of the 1919 race riot had not healed. *In the meantime, in between time, ain't we got fun.* From Europe, bodies of the American dead continued to arrive home for ceremonious burial while the Peace Conference muddled on, and American soldiers still occupied the Rhineland. The Navy scrapped its warships and the Army cut back to 150,000 troops just when everyone knew that "a conflict of force with Japan is inevitable." *In the meantime,* Greek soldiers were marching off for a war with Turkey. The Marines were back in Panama to protect the Canal, and the Black Shirts were sweeping Mussolini to power in Italy. In Russia millions were starving while U.S. Senators assured American businessmen that the revolution there had failed. The Senators did not say that something had failed much closer to home, but then they did not ask "Big Bill" Haywood, the I.W.W. labor leader who had fled to Moscow to avoid jail. They did not ask Eugene Debs, the socialist presidential candidate who polled a million votes and who was now in prison as an enemy of the people. The world was safe once more for business if not for ideas. *Oh, the rich get rich, and poor get poorer,* when the stock market began to respond to normalcy. U.S. Steel was selling at 73. Brokers thought it would go higher. No one had yet noticed that Harding's "Ohio Gang" was doing with the Navy's oil reserve at Teapot Dome – no one except Harry Sinclair who profited quite nicely.

While Hemingway hacked away for the *Co-Operative Commonwealth,* the Chicago streets were bleeding. Bodies were piling up at a record rate: sixty-nine murders; thirty-seven manslaughters; sixty-one justifiable homicides. *In between time* no need for undue alarm. Worry more about wayward daughters and truculent wives, who had not returned to normalcy. Having tasted independence during the war and now armed with the vote, the ladies were not acting like ladies. Washing machines, refrigerators and vacuum cleaners were not enough to lure them back to normalcy. On a windy day along Michigan Boulevard, a man could see bobbed hair where once long tresses flowed. Much easier and quicker for a working girl, who was now rolling her stockings below the knee. *In the mean time, in between time* women were smoking in public. Polls showed that women approved and men did not. In August women began walking down the boulevards in pants, which were called knickerbockers, but they were pants. *Ain't we got fun.*

In St. Louis, Hadley finally set the date and place for the wedding, and Ernest sent a list of friends to invite, including Agnes Von Kurowsky and Ruth Brooks from the Milan hospital as well as several other women whose names Hadley did not recognize. Fonnie mailed the engraved invitations to the September 3 wedding at Horton Bay. The date was two weeks past the first anniversary of Mrs. Richardson's death, barely long enough for Hadley to collect on the codicil which specified an extra $5000 for her trust fund if she stayed unmarried for one year. September 3 was also one day before Dr. Hemingway's fiftieth birthday. At Windemere, Grace was varnishing floors and fixing the roof for the honeymooners, who would spend their wedding night in Grace's bed. She reminded Ernest to bring a birthday gift and note for his father's surprise party.[32] As August began to run out on him, Hemingway must have felt that too much was coming together there in Horton Bay: wedding day and birthday and the lake; Hadley and the summer people. All his early lives were melding into this wedding, where he would be son, friend and lover all at once, where he would row his bride home to the cottage his father had built and his mother had thrown him out of, where he and Hadley would finally lie down all naked in his mother's birthing bed.

His father was not making it easy for him. From the lake he wrote:

> Please tell me, dear boy, exactly what you want and *who* of our own family you wish to be present at your wedding. I have been told you did not wish me present – say so to me and I will know it is so. Then I will go on home and be there to receive Sunny. Let me hear soon. Lovingly, Dad.[33]

If the Doctor had been told that, Ernest knew that his mother must have said it. He could imagine another of their fights that had ended with her saying, "Well, Ernest doesn't even want you at the wedding." It was the sort of thing she was good at, the sort of wound that would fester in his father's mind. Or maybe it was only the Doctor's increasing paranoia. Ernest wrote back to assure his father of his affection, to which the Doctor immediately replied. "You can expect to receive One Hundred Dollars as the

Wedding Gift as I promised you. We will have Windemere all in good shape for you *two*."[34]

His mother was his mother still — exuberant, willful and gossipy. "It seems a long time since I have heard from you," she wrote in August. "Here's hoping all your plans are going well and that SHE still loves you. . . . Write mother *soon* and tell her EVERYTHING."[35] She circled her final period to indicate the kiss that sealed the letter. Whatever the anger of a year past, it was as if it had not happened. His mother did not dwell on the past the way his father did, or the way he did, for that matter. His mother was having too much fun planning the wedding, tuning the cottage piano for Hadley, and being the center of local attention. Nevertheless, she understood her children better than did her husband. It must have been Grace who arranged that Sunny, the seventeen-year-old sister more than half in love with Ernest would not be at the wedding. The weak excuse was Sunny's summer camp, but it served. Sunny had not taken the engagement at all well, and Grace did not want her to create a scene.

Nor would Marcelline be at the wedding of her oldest brother. She had started the summer as a camp counselor, but was forcd to quite in August because of her health. As Grace explained it to Ernest, "I'm worried about Marcelline. Had to [quit] her Camp job and go to the Voses in New Hampshire and go to bed. Nerves all gone to smash. Won't you write her."[36] No one knew exactly the nature of her illness, but it was the first indication that Dr. Hemingway's "nervous" condition might have passed on to the children. Twenty years later Marcelline would be subject to fainting spells, low blood pressure and "depths of inadequacy." At the same time, her own daughter began to behave strangely — weeping, morose and withdrawn. In her senior year in high school as an honor student, Marcelline's child suddenly began dreading class, saying "I wouldn't know what to do. I couldn't remember what class to go to." Marcelline took her out of school, but she did not improve. Depresion and hysteria increased. Marcelline's own headaches, a family trait, increased and she developed ulcers as her daughter's memory began to disappear.

245

After nine months, the daughter was diagnosed as a low thyroid case.[37] She was neither the first nor the last of the Hemingway line to suffer depression, "nerves," insomnia and erratic behavior. Genetically, Ernest had inherited a time bomb which he carried unknowingly into his marriage.[38]

At the end of August, Hemingway packed his bags for what would be his last trip up Lake Michigan to Horton Bay. He also boxed up the remainder of his belongings at Kenley's apartment, for he and Hadley could not return there. He told Bill Smith that he would rather move Hadley into the second floor of a Seney, Michigan brothel than sleep under the same roof with Doodles. The problem, he said, was Don Wright, who had poisoned his relationship with Bill's brother. He and Wright were no longer speaking, and Doodles, at every chance, was telling Kenley vicious lies about Ernest. He wanted Bill at the wedding to best-man him through the ordeal, so he tried not to offend him. It was not Kenley's fault, but Doodles' and Wright's.[39]

Into one of the boxes Hemingway carefully stacked two years of his life – drafts of Toronto stories, notes, rejected manuscripts, poetry, the war novel and a new story that he had begun in July about Pauline Snow. He had gone back to the "Cross Roads" sketches that he and Bill started over a year before. Using Anderson's *Winesburg* stories as a model, Hemingway tried to write about Pauline Snow's loveless seduction up in Michigan. He changed her name to Liz Coates and played with the point of view, trying to tell the story at least partially through her eyes. It did not come out right the first time or the second, but it was better than anything else he had yet written. Trapped in the July heat of Chicago, he got a lot of it right about the people at Horton Bay. The lake was there and the boat dock and the cold autumn night and the people he knew from the Village. It was not a nice story, not a story for a bridegroom in waiting, but he was proud of it.

"Up in Michigan," as he eventually called the story, did not flesh out until he got to Paris, but there in Chicago he got the bones of it right. When Gertrude Stein read it, she told him it was unprintable. When Boni and Liveright read it, they asked him to take it out of *In Our Time*. When Marcelline read it in *Three Stories and Ten Poems*, she was shocked. "It was Ernest's apparent lack of any decent consideration for the feelings of the people whose names and detailed descriptions he had used in the story," she said, "that horrified me."[40] She would not be the only Oak Parker horrified by her brother's fiction. And more than one of his biographers would assume that Liz Coates' seduction was the story of Hemingway's first sexual experience.[41] But he had invented it, just as he would invent the best of his fiction. It was not until after his marriage in September that he got the story right. Once he had been to bed with Hadley, he could imagine and invent the seduction of any woman: their parts were the same, located in the same places. He did not take the story with him to Horton Bay, for it was not the gift a bride expected on her honeymoon. But he did take his fishing rods; when he got to Windemere, there was just enough time to escape on the river for his last days of bachelor fishing.

By summer's end the Sturgeon river trout were wary, the days hot and the nights laden with mosquitoes. The trout season was about to close, but it did not matter. If a man loved a river deeply enough, nothing else mattered. The Sturgeon, the Black, the Fox, each bend and pool, the curl of water moving across the sunken log, the glitter of water all silver in the afternoon, the murmur at evening with the feeding trout raising circled ripples on the blue–black slick of it: all as he remembered and would remember always. The smell of pine smoke or the odor of fresh coffee could bring it all back to him no matter how far distant. Another summer in another country, with only his map and its blue markings to remind him, he would write of "Big Two-Hearted River," fishing with his mind that water which he had married young. He could not know that he was fishing it now for the last time, would not have believed it anyway. A man, he thought, could always go back.

Chapter Ten

THE BEAUTIFUL COUNTRY
FALL AND WINTER, 1921

"**Y**ES," she said, "I do."
He had been in swimming and was washing his feet in the wash bowl after having walked up the hill. The room was hot and Dutch and Luman were both standing around looking nervous. Nick got a clean suit of underwear, clean silk socks, new garters, a white shirt and collar out from the drawer of the bureau and put them on. He stood in front of the mirror and tied his tie. Dutch and Luman reminded him of dressing rooms before fights and football games. He enjoyed their nervousness. He wondered if it would be this way if he were going to be hanged. Probably. He could never realize anything until it happened. Dutch went out for a corkscrew and came in and opened the bottle. [1]

"Yes," she said, "yes, I do." And they were married in the clapboard church at Horton Bay with odor of bittersweet and balsam boughs in the air, while Kate and Bill, families and old friends, looked on. Ernest Hemingway, the youngest of the summer people, was married to Hadley Richardson, eight years his senior. It was four o'clock in the September afternoon; after the photographing and the eating, shadows were long and the air beginning to chill. From his mother's cottage at Longfield, he rowed his bride across the still lake toward Windemere. Late-feeding trout silently broke the water ahead of them. It was almost too dark to see the point where he and Marge had often fished only two summers before. He pulled on the oars, facing backward in the boat, navigating off the lights of Grace's cottage. Less than a year after they met, they were married, and now, for the first time, they were truly alone together in the virgin country of their love, about which they had written so much and explored so little.

There, on the newly tuned piano, they found a Grace note – her own words and music to "Lovely Walloona." *"Heaven's face is seen smiling in thine own placid summer seas. But grand is thy wrath, when lashing winds ruffle thy breast, then dashing waves swirl shoreward repenting, relenting, till all's sweetly at rest. . . . Oh, Lovely Walloona."*[2] If Hadley played the piece, it was not while Ernest was in the cottage. As the honeymooners were staking out their territory at Windemere, Mother Grace resided at her Longfield cottage, waiting for them to call. A full week passed before they came to lunch. The invitation she left for them at the cottage was, they told her, never found. Later Hadley would say that because of Ernest's bias, she was not able to appreciate her mother-in-law, who had been kind and good to her.[3] But that September she could not see Grace clearly for the trees that Ernest's anger had raised. Eventually Hadley would realize that it was Grace's unconventional attitude toward wifehood that most irritated Ernest. Like most Oak Park men he expected a wife to be wife – mother, cook and homemaker – a role that Grace never enjoyed. Her strong streak of independent feminism, her need for creative accomplishments, her talent for finding the local limelight would not allow Grace to disappear behind the Doctor's career. Hadley discovered, as did all of Hemingway's wives, that being Mrs. Ernest Hemingway meant giving up all other ambitions.

Four days after their marriage, Hadley appeared before the notary in Petoskey to sign her new name for the first time. As executor of her mother's will, which would not be finally settled for several months, she was not so lost in the new country as to ignore her best interests. She changed the name to Elizabeth Hadley Richardson Hemingway. The clerk mistakenly dated the instrument "7 September 1920." In October the estate, honoring her mother's codicil, duly transfered $5000 in bonds and notes to her trust fund. Until then Ernest had no clear idea how much money Hadley's trusts would provide. Now he added it up. At the *Co-operative Commonwealth* he was making $200 a month; Hadley's income would eventually come to just under $300 a month. In a year when lamb was selling at eight cents a pound and a Hart, Schaffner and Marx suit for only thirty-five dollars, Hadley's income was more than adequate. With the exchange rate so favorable in Italy, they saw that they could live comfortably in Rome on her income alone. As soon as the estate was settled, he could quit his job to write full time.

Instead, the job quit him. While he and Hadley were at Windemere, the bubble of the Co-operative Society of America burst. Harrison Parker, president of the company, filed for bankruptcy. By October 7 the Society was in receivership, and a fine aroma of massive fraud was scented by the *Tribune*. Thirteen million dollars of "beneficial interest certificates" had been sold to stockholders – mainly farmers, widows, small business men and small-town residents – little people who paid half down and half on time to belong to the movement. The Co-operative's stores had been milked almost dry; the invested capital gone to paper companies. Parker had set up the Great Western Securities Company to receive eleven million dollars from the certificates, and the money was gone. His wife, whom he had made treasurer, had also disappeared with almost three million dollars. Judge Evans turned the evidence over to a Grand Jury that indicted Parker, his wife and associates.[4]

Hemingway continued his editorial duties to the bitter end. In the October 1 issue of the *Commonwealth,* he did the Co-Op Notes, Personal Mentions and the Insurance Notes. His story on "The Ice-Berg Patrol," written completely from secondary sources, ran on page 4. It was a filler, having little to do with the Co-Operative movement, but it did tell the reader about the dangerous submerged portion of the ice-bergs, the seven-eighths of the ice mountain that lurked beneath the surface supporting the visible peak. Years later, he would come back to that image as a metaphor for his own technique.[5] For the following issue on October 8, he dutifully wrote about the missing Liberty bonds that Judge Parker had not been able to find among the Society's listed assets. The mystery, Hemingway wrote, "was knocked into a cocked hat today when it was announced that Mrs. Edith S. Parker, treasurer of the Great Western Securities Corporation, fiscal agent of the Co-Operative Society of America is on her way back to Chicago with securities estimated at between $2,000,000 and $3,000,000." Harrison Parker was quoted as saying, "This absolutely blows the bankruptcy proceedings up in the air. Our enemies have nothing left to stand on."[6] Nothing could have been further from the truth. Mrs. Parker and the bonds never appeared, and the magazine went under.

When Ernest and Hadley returned to Chicago in mid-September, they moved into bare, rented rooms. After his job sank beneath him and the Society's con-game became a daily feature in the *Tribune,* Ernest laid low. He had not been directly part of the fraud, but he had written much of Parker's propaganda. From the moment he took the job he had suspected something was wrong. In December 1920, he wrote his mother, "I ought not to play the role of the rats deserting the sinking ship yet – the odor from the ship is just beginning to be perceptible. . . . 'Nother words I haven't all the confidence in the world in the [Co-operative] Movement."[7] Whatever his scruples, they did not prevent him from writing copy for the final issue. It was not a part of his life that he cared to remember. Years later he said, "I worked until I was convinced it was crooked, stayed on a little while thinking I could write and expose it, and then decided to just rack it up as experience and the hell with it."[8] As with much of the early life that did not fit his self-image, he chose to remember wrong. A man could always go back and revise.

With the demise of the *Commonwealth,* money became a problem. Hemingway's check on the first of October had been for $150, one week light. Editor Stockbridge had given him three weeks off to get married, but only two with pay. If he got paid at all for his October work, it would have been only $50. Their family finances were not desperate, but there certainly was not enough ready cash to buy tickets for the long-planned Italian journey. He had another $100 from his father as a wedding gift; Hadley had some monthly income from her grandparents' trust funds, but her mother's estate was still in probate, not to be settled until early in 1922. On October 1, the two of them put up a brave front in Oak Park for the twenty-fifth wedding anniversary of the Doctor and Grace Hall Hemingway, who were proud to show off their handsome son and his new wife. Yes, they told everyone they were going to Italy in December. Yes, they were nice to everyone, smiling and small-talking in the North Kenilworth house oppressive with the odor of roses.[9] It was the last time that Ernest and Hadley would be there together, the last time but one that the Doctor's children would gather so smilingly. Riding the trolley back into Chicago, the couple cuddled against the chill, joking about the proper people of Oak Park. Somehow they were going to break loose. Maybe the estate would get settled in time, but if it did not, a man had to find work.

Back in March, on Greg Clark's advice, Hemingway had written John Bone at the Toronto *Star,* offering to return to the paper on April 1 for a salary of $85 a week. Quite casually, he said the *Commonwealth* was paying him $75 a week, which was only a $25 fib. Clark had told him to ask for no less than $70.[10] Bone did not take the bait. Now, at the end of October and with no pay checks in sight, Hemingway once more wrote Bone about returning to the *Star* either in Toronto or in Italy; this time he said less about salary.[11] Before Bone's reply could reach him, the Hemingway luck intervened. Two crucial events, both beyond his control, changed forever the course of Hemingway's career. First, an uncle of Hadley's died, leaving her almost $10,000. They could skim enough from that to buy their tickets to Italy, investing the remainder through Hadley's St. Louis bank.[12] Second, Sherwood Anderson returned to Chicago just in time to change the course of American writing.

Paris, he told them, the place to go was Paris, where pleasant rooms and good wine were cheap, the cathedrals beautifully crafted stone on stone, and the lovers all along the Seine kissed unashamedly. Paris was the city for lovers, he told them. In the public gardens and sidewalk cafes, Anderson said he was able to write in his notebook; the story ideas flowed, American stories that he saw clearly in that city of bridges. There were bookstores in Paris, a myriad of them, as frequent as bars once were in Chicago. He found his *Winesburg* in the window of one run by a Sylvia Beach, who knew everyone in Paris. And my God, there were writers there who had not given up the fight for their art and their craft. James Joyce, a "handsome man with beautiful hands," had come by one day to see him, Sherwood Anderson, because of *Winesburg*. Joyce told him about his new book *Ulysses* which no one outside of Paris would publish. Anderson told Hemingway that it might be "the most important book that will be published in this generation." If Hemingway really wanted to become a writer, he simply had to go to Paris.

Anderson could help. He had met Ezra Pound and Lewis Galantière. He had met Gertrude Stein, "a strong woman with legs like stone pillars sitting in a room hung with Picassos."[13] Hemingway could learn something from Gertrude. He could learn something from the Picassos as well. My God, Picasso! He was the center of the revolution, "the most powerful living man among the painters of France." Dada was all over, done with. Picasso was the future.[14] Hemingway must see Picasso. Anderson would write letters to them all, and they would help. Until Ernest and Hadley found rooms of their own, they should stay at Hotel Jacob, clean and cheap, and filled with Americans without much money.

Hemingway hesitated. For two years now he had dreamed of going back to Italy. Nick Nerone was setting up some contacts there, and Hemingway knew a bit of the language. He did not know a word of French. That was no problem, Anderson assured him. He got along fine without a clue to the language. It was even better that way for a writer. In Paris he would see America clearly. There the dross would wash away; there he would find his style. In Paris a craftsman could take pride in his work; he could experiment. He could find new forms just as Picasso was painting in new forms. The American writer must "be and remain always an experimenter, an adventurer."[15] In Paris, he assured Hemingway, the experiment was affordable, for a man could live a year there on $1200, not giving in to the "success disease" that plagued American writers.

Anderson's enthusiasm, buoyed no doubt by his recently accepted *Dial* prize and publication of his *Triumph of the Egg*, turned Hemingway away from Italy. Paris obviously had done wonders for Anderson's spirit; Hemingway had never seen him so healthy, so full of juice. As he and Hadley walked back through the cold streets of October to their rented rooms, they talked about Paris. She wanted what he wanted. Paris or Rome, either would suit her so long as he had his chance to write, but she *had* studied French for eight years, which might be an advantage. It would all come back to her quickly. Then she could deal with the grocers and landlords; he could write. They would be a team in Paris. Walking down North Dearborn Street, they passed the darkened offices of Charles Kozminski, the Chicago agent for the French Line. Shivering in the cold, they read the window ads for liners crossing the Atlantic.

After all the Italian planning, Nick Nerone was going to be disappointed. After all those nights together refighting the war, Hemingway found it difficult to tell Nick they were going to Paris. John Bone made it easier. He wanted Hemingway on the Toronto paper; if the European trip was on, he offered Hemingway a position as a roving reporter doing feature material, but he had to work out of the *Star*'s headquarters in Paris. He would pay "regular space rates for all the stories they printed" as well as legitimate expenses.[16] It could not have worked out better as far as Hemingway was concerned. No time clocks to punch. No fixed routine. He could write for the *Star* those pieces he did best, human interest features, saving the best material for his own fiction. He told Nick he had to go to Paris; a man had to have a job.

Nicholas Nerone was disappointed but he understood about a man's responsibilities. The red wine helped his understanding. There was a lifetime ahead of them with plenty of time for Italy. Hemingway promised that he would not leave Chicago until after General Diaz's visit at the end of November; after everything

Nick had done to get Hemingway decorated by the General, that was the least he could do. Diaz, who was on a goodwill trip to America, was coming to Chicago from the east coast where he was laying memorial wreaths and speaking of the fraternal bonds between America and Italy. In Boston, two Italian immigrants who had not gone to the war were on trial for their lives. General Diaz did not speak of Sacco and Vanzetti when he laid the wreaths. "The leader who took the Italian army after its disastrous defeat at Caporetto and molded it into the fighting machine that routed the Austrians" could not afford to make any waves, not when the reallocation of war-captured territory was still in the balance. Italy needed America's support at the European conference tables.[17]

Nick Nerone, working at the Italian consulate, helped plan the parade down Michigan Avenue to honor the General, helped plan the banquet at the Congress Hotel. Included in the plans was his good friend Ernest Hemingway. On November 20, the *Tribune* ran a large spread on the activities, featuring pictures of Diaz, Nerone and Hemingway, who would be "decorated by General Diaz for bravery while serving with the Italian army." Ernest had buried the Red Cross forever, erased it. The General was there to decorate real heroes, not Red Cross men. In his conversations with Nerone, Hemingway led Nick to believe that he had transfered to the Italian army's Ancona Brigade, taking for his own the stories he had heard in Milan. Nick believed him. Nick, a war lover who volunteered in 1916, was wounded that year three times in a single battle; he fought on until removed from duty. He recovered in time to fight again at the battles of Gorizia and the Isonzo, where "he received the bronze medal on the field with a citation for taking with his platoon an important entrenchment." When the Italian army moved up toward the Bainsizza plateau, Nerone was there at Plava and Mount Kuk. And he was there in the mountains on the morning of October 23, 1917, when the Austro-Hungarian forces broke the Italian line at Caporetto. As the snow turned to rain and much of the Italian army turned into a defeated mob, retreating badly down the valleys toward the Tagliamento river, Nick Nerone earned his captaincy. When the Second Army was throwing down its rifles and shouting "Andiamo a casa!" Nerone fought as well as he could while retreating and, more importantly, survived to fight again when 265,000 Italian soldiers disappeared, either killed or captured. At war's end, Nerone was there at Vittorio Veneto, earning finally his War Cross.[18]

Nick and Ernest, brothers in arms, had shared each other's stories, and now they were both going to be on display before their Chicago friends. If Ernest was worried what Art Newburn, who was in Italy with him, might think about his fabricated Italian army experience, he did not mention it. After leaving Section Four at Schio, Hemingway operated his mobile kitchen mostly alone. No one from the ambulance gang knew for certain what he had done. Listening to Nick's authentic war stories, Hemingway kept mental notes. The war novel that he was writing had a character called Nick, who was part Nerone and part himself. The problem was that Nerone's experience in Italy pre-dated almost all of his own: how to combine them was the question, which he was too inexperienced to solve.

Eventually Hemingway would realize that he had two stories: Nick Nerone's Italian war and the ambulance driver's at Schio. In 1928 he came back to the material once more, knowing more about the war and with his style perfected. He did not see Nick Nerone again after they parted in Chicago, but he never forgot his stories of Gorizia, the Isonzo and Caporetto. Having read the war histories, Hemingway changed his Nick character into Frederic Henry, an ambulance driver with the Italian army who was at the war from the very beginning. He called the story *A Farewell to Arms*. In it nothing of Nick's heroism remained, for the world was weary of heroes and disillusioned by the war's aftermath. After he finished *A Farewell to Arms,* having used up his own wounding and his romance with Agnes Von Kurowsky, he tried once again to tell the story of Schio.[19] It was a disaster. Frederic Henry's experience he could invent based on everything he knew, but when he tried to write about the ambulance drivers of Section Four, he was too close to the truth, and it came out stilted and juvenile. He never did write about the hair-pin turns with the Fiat brakes smoking and the sheer mountain walls dropping a thousand feet below the back wheels as they skidded at the edge of the road.

Nor did he ever write about General Diaz. After the grand news story the banquet did not turn out well. In fact, it did not turn out at all. At the last moment there was not enough time to squeeze Hemingway on to the agenda. *Oak Leaves* buried the story on page 77:

The ceremony for decorating Ernest Miller Hemingway by General Diaz, commander of the Italian armies when Mr. Hemingway was on duty in Italy, was omitted, as the general's program was so crowded. Mr. Hemingway had the decoration for longer than a year, but it had never been formally presented.[20]

In 1923, when he returned briefly to Toronto, Hemingway showed his medals to Greg Clark at the *Star*, saying that General Diaz had personally decorated him.[21] It was not true, but it should have been. As Sherwood Anderson was fond of saying, "It is only by lying to the limit one can come at truth."[22] In those years back from the war, Hemingway invented himself, not from the whole cloth, but through embroidery and artful rearrangement. Late in life, with fame bringing him under close biographical scrutiny, he would become seemingly irrational about his early years, telling friends and family not to answer any questions. He knew that his fictional early life would not match historical fact, but did little to correct it when he had the opportunity. When Sylvia Beach wrote her memoirs of the Paris years, she sent Hemingway a draft, full of inaccuracies, asking him to make whatever corrections were necessary. He returned it without substantial change. In his interview with George Plimpton, Hemingway changed Uncle Willoughby from a medical missionary into "an explorer along the Chinese border who led very much the life . . . he imagined himself as following."[23] In his correspondence with Malcolm Cowley, Hemingway intimated that he and one of his sisters had committed incest. As late as

1960, he prefaced his own memoir of the Paris years with the caution: "If the reader prefers, this book may be regarded as fiction. But there is always the chance that such a book of fiction may throw some light on what has been written as fact."[24] He was making up his life to the very end.

Whatever Truth he had to tell us was in the fiction; whatever biographical truths he bent, scrapped or recast were in the American vein, where immigrants were renamed on Ellis Island and men moving West frequently abandoned personal baggage at every stop. The promise of America was that any boy could become what he believed himself to be; Hemingway took the promise at face value. Growing up in Oak Park where only the extraordinary gained attention, where a single loss made a football season less than satisfactory, the only public attention he ever got in high school was through his writing. Now, having chosen to make it his profession, he could settle for nothing less than fame. Everyone he knew thought of him now as Hemingway the writer, but in three years he had not sold a single piece of fiction. Still his friends believed in him, for he talked a good game and his enthusiasm for his work was infectious. Hadley believed so strongly that she staked her future on him. Anderson believed strongly enough by November 28 to write Lewis Galantière in Paris, asking him to help the young writer settle in the City of Light. On December 3, Anderson gave Hemingway a letter of introduction to carry to Gertrude Stein's salon.[25] He might be without sales, but Hemingway had, in three years, transformed himself from a Red Cross ambulance driver with a limp into a war-hero with great promise as a writer. After only infrequent high-school dates, he returned from the war an impulsive lover; in three years he went through several romances to marry Hadley. Now that was done. Now he must begin to write the fiction that would meet the expectations he had created, that would match the persona he had invented for himself. Later he would say that it was easy; anyone willing to work hard could do it. There in the Chicago winter of 1921, he truly believed hard work eventually succeeded. It was well that he did, for it would be another four years before he published *In Our Time*.

As he and Hadley prepared to leave Chicago that winter of 1921, they had to travel light. By November 28, they booked passage on the French Line aboard the *Leopoldina*, scheduled to sail from New York for Le Havre on December 8. Six days before they left Chicago, the Doctor drove into the city to pick up several boxes of possessions to be stored: wedding gifts, kitchen gear, Ernest's war-shredded uniform, and a box filled with news stories, clippings from Kansas City, Toronto and the *Commonwealth*. There was one other box that Hemingway left behind, the box holding "The Mercenaries," "The Woppian Way," "The Ash Heels Tendon," "Cross Roads," as well as several early untitled manuscripts and a handful of poems.[26] They were all stories he had written before he met Anderson in the fall of 1920, before he had revised his concept of the short story. With him he took all the new fiction he had written in the previous year, much of it short stories set on the Italian front.[27] He also packed the first version of "Up in Michigan," and the novel he had begun in the spring.

On a cold Wednesday morning at the Chicago station, Ernest and Hadley waved goodbye to friends and family; they would arrive in New York with barely enough time to board the ship for France. Marcelline waved from the crowd, tossing her gloves to Hadley as a farewell present. As the train pulled out of Chicago, it passed the stockyards where two thousand policemen controlled the meatpackers' strike that was edging toward violence. As Captain Russell told the *Daily News*, "The patrolmen have been instructed not to shoot unless necessary. They have been advised to use their fists and clubs freely. However, they have also been told that if the occasion should arise for shooting, they must shoot quickly and accurately. That policy has had excellent results already." One man was dead, several were wounded. It was a good time to be leaving the city, to be leaving the country. The stockyard strike, as everyone knew, or at least thought they knew, was yet another communist plot to undermine the nation's economy. The Red Scare had abated but had not died, nor would it in our time. Easing through the South Side where two years before Blacks and Whites had bloodied the streets, the train began to pick up speed. At the window Ernest and Hadley watched Gary slip past, its steel mills smoking, its ore boats riding low in the water, waiting to unload. Through the smoke and grey December day, Ernest took a goodbye look at Lake Michigan at whose far end lay Horton Bay.

Oak Park took no special notice that another native son had left the Village, for Ernest Hemingway was never a particularly "promising youth." Fannie Biggs, who once tried to get him a job on the *Tribune,* remembered little about the writing class she taught him. "When he was in it, there were more athletes than usual, mostly his crowd. They imitated sports writers in their talk . . . and prefered a fast colloquial style, whatever the subject." She remembered much more about Mrs. Hemingway than about her pupil Ernest. Everyone remembered Mrs. Hemingway. "Thinking of his mother's exuberant vitality, the rich curves of her every move, the warmth of her vital personality," Miss Biggs said, "I have wondered if Ern would find a wife with the lush motherhood he knew."[28]

While Ernest and Hadley rolled eastward toward the Hoboken pier, other Oak Park mothers gathered in the name of common decency to establish The Friends of American Writers, whose premise was that "all education should be based upon good, clean literature." Mrs. John Bohr, behind her steely glasses, took careful notes on the discussions, which centered around the detrimental influence that Jazz was having on the arts. "On all sides organizations had formed to counter-act the evil, but no one was especially interested . . . in literature which seemed . . . to be the most essential." What the ladies wanted was a literature filled with "high ideals and a desire for higher life."[29] Across the Atlantic, T. S. Eliot, a nice boy from a proper St. Louis family, was shoring up the fragments of his poem, *The Waste Land.* In Paris, Sylvia Beach was agonizing over yet another set of Joyce's revisions to *Ulysses.* The ladies in Oak Park were going to be disappointed by the Modern Age. Had they known what Ernie Hemingway, the Doctor's son, was going to write, they might have tried to stop the east-bound train. It would be years after his death before Oak Parkers took pride in their local boy. By that time, the old families had gone under and their "high ideals" with them. The families, who "sought a place far enough removed from the moral filth of the big city to give influences for the good a chance to work in the lives of their boys and girls," woke from their dream to find their sons and their daughters beyond their command.[30]

Chuffing up the gangplank of the *Leopoldina,* neither Hadley nor Ernest cared that the sky was grey or the air cold. The *Olympia,* just docked from London, reported gale winds of 90 miles an hour loose upon the Atlantic. All across Europe, political storm clouds were ominously forming, but these two, ignorant in their innocence, were undeterred by weather reports. Breaking loose as they had planned, they were never happier than now, on the edge of the new life, the new country. At 3:00 p.m., the old ship was guided slowly out past the Statue of Liberty and pointed eastward as the grey day sank into dark. The two lovers at the railing, under the care of no special Providence, hugged tight against the chill. They were in for rough passage.

NOTES

Introduction: TIME WAS

The sources for this chapter are *Oak Leaves* newspaper 1900–20; Oak Park Board of Education minutes (1910–16); the Village Council minutes (1900–20); *Revised Ordinances of the Village of Oak Park* (Oak Leaves Co.: Oak Park, 1911); *Glimpses of Oak Park*, pub. by Frank June and George R. Hemingway (Oak Park, Ill., 1912); *The Oak Park Code of 1916* (Oak Park, Ill., 1917); *Annual Reports of the Village of Oak Park* (1903, 1904, 1908, 1911, 1912); *Blue Book* (Chicago: 1910); *Oak Park Directory* (1906, 1908, 1910, 1915, 1919, 1923); "Historical Survey of Oak Park," compiled by Federal Works Progress Administration, Project No. 9516.

Chapter One: THE END OF SOMETHING

1. *American Ideals* (New York: G.P. Putnam, 1901), p. 42; *A Book-Lover's Holidays in the Open* (New York: Charles Scribner's Sons, 1916), p. 105; *The Strenuous Life* (New York: Century Co., 1904) p. 155.
2. *A Farewell to Arms* (New York: Scribner's, 1929), p. 184.
3. "Several Aviators Return," *New York Times*. January 22, 1919.
4. New York *Sun*, January 22, 1919.
5. *Oak Leaves*, August 10, 1919.

6. *Oak Leaves*, October 5, 1919.
7. See Robert W. Lewis, "Hemingway in Italy: Making It Up," *Journal of Modern Literature*, 9 (1981/82), 209–36.
8. *A Farewell to Arms*, p. 63.
9. *New York Times*, November 19, 1919.
10. Theodore Roosevelt, *The Foes of Our Own Household* (New York: George H. Doran Co., 1917), p. 47.
11. Roosevelt, *The Strenuous Life*, p. 3.
12. Edmund Morris, *The Rise of Theodore Roosevelt* (New York: Coward, McCann & Geoghegan, 1979), p. 323.
13. April 27, 1912.
14. October 13, 1913.
15. Roosevelt, *The Strenuous Life*, p. 160.
16. Morris, *The Rise of Theodore Roosevelt*, p. 63.
17. "Remembering Shooting-Flying," *By-Line: Ernest Hemingway* (New York: Scribner's, 1967, p. 189.
18. Roosevelt, *The Strenuous Life*, p. 282.
19. Ernest Hemingway to Clarence Hemingway, September 6, 1917, Lilly Library, Bloomington, Indiana.
20. High School Note Book, March 21, 1915, Hemingway Collection, J. F. Kennedy Library, Boston, Mass.
21. September 11, 1910, Lilly Library, Bloomington, Indiana.
22. September 13, 1910, Hemingway Collection, Kennedy Library.
23. Major General Eric E. Dorman-O'Gowan (né Dorman-Smith) to Carlos Baker, n.d. (c. 1960) in Baker's files, Princeton, N.J.
24. Grace Hall Hemingway to Ernest Hemingway, July 21, 1918, Humanities Research Center, University of Texas, Austin, Tex.
25. *American Ideals*, p. 42.
26. Item 604, Hemingway Collection, Kennedy Library.
27. Bicholride of Mercury was widely used in the Great War as a germicide and antiseptic. In highly diluted solution, it was also used in injections for the treatment of syphilis. As a poison, it was slow-acting but deadly. See *Useful Drugs*, ed. R. A. Hatcher, eighth ed. (A.M.A.: Chicago, 1930), pp. 86–8; *Poisoning*, W. F. Oettingern (W. B. Saunders: Philadelphia, 1958), pp. 417–18; and *A Reference Handbook of the Medical Sciences*, ed. A. H. Buck (William Wood & Co.: New York, 1890), vol. I, pp. 384, 687.
28. "In Another Country," *The Short Stories of Ernest Hemingway* (New York: Scribner's, 1953), p. 270.

Chapter Two: HOME AS FOUND

1. *Oak Leaves,* January 25, 1919.
2. George Fitch, "The Greek Double," quoted in *Oak Leaves,* March 18, 1911.
3. High School Note Book dated 1915, on loan to Alderman Library, University of Virginia, in 1977 for "in their time/ 1920–1940" exhibit.
4. Marcelline Hemingway Sanford, *At the Hemingways* (Little, Brown & Co.: Boston, 1961).
5. *Oak Leaves,* November 25, 1916.
6. *Oak Leaves,* March 3, 1917.
7. Item 717c, Hemingway Collection, Kennedy Library.
8. *Oak Leaves,* March 24, 1917.
9. Information on Hemingway's enlistment in Missouri National Guard in the Fenton Collection at the Beinecke Library, Yale University.
10. *Oak Leaves,* April 14, 1917.
11. Ernest Hemingway to Jim Gamble, March 3, 1919, Knox College Archives and Manuscript Collection.
12. Item 489, Hemingway Collection, Kennedy Library.
13. Acquisition Records, Oak Park Public Library.
14. Hemingway Collection, Kennedy Library.
15. Item 634, Hemingway Collection, Kennedy Library.
16. Grace Hall Hemingway to Ernest Hemingway, December 4, 1926, Hemingway Collection, Kennedy Library.
17. *Oak Leaves,* October 13, 1917.
18. *Oak Leaves,* January 25, 1919.
19. *Oak Leaves,* February 1, 1919.
20. *Oak Leaves,* February 8, 1919.
21. Memorial Committee records, Oak Park Library.
22. *Oak Leaves,* February 1, 1919.
23. *Oak Parker,* March 22, 1919, reporting on March 12 meeting. See also Carlos Baker, *Ernest Hemingway, A Life Story* (New York: Scribner's, 1969), pp. 58–9, 574.
24. *Oak Parker,* March 14, 1919.
25. *A Farewell to Arms* (New York: Scribner's, 1929), p. 54.
26. Undated clipping from miscellaneous file, Hemingway Collection, Kennedy Library.

27. Item 532, Hemingway Collection, Kennedy Library.
28. See Hemingway short stories, "Three Shots," "Indian Camp," "The Doctor and the Doctor's Wife," "Ten Indians" and "Fathers and Sons" in *The Short Stories of Ernest Hemingway* (New York: Scribner's, 1953).
29. "The Woppian Way," Item 834, Hemingway Collection, Kennedy Library. The story went through several versions, only the last of which has survived. It was essentially finished by the spring of 1920, but the name Nick Neroni was added to the surviving version sometime in 1921 when Hemingway met Nicholas Nerone in Chicago.
30. Baker, *A Life Story*, pp. 30–1.
31. "Return of the Authors," *New York Times*, January 5, 1919.
32. Ernest Hemingway to Jim Gamble, March 3, 1919, Baker File, Princeton University.
33. Interview with author, October 1972.
34. *American Ideals*, p. 53.
35. Item 416, "In the gallerias of Milan . . .," Hemingway Collection, Kennedy Library.
36. *Oak Leaves*, February 8, 1919.
37. Clarence Hemingway to Grace Hall Hemingway, May 26, 1919, Humanities Research Center, University of Texas.

Chapter Three: SUMMER PEOPLE: PART ONE

1. *Oak Leaves*, August 19, 1911.
2. *Oak Leaves*, September 5, 1902.
3. Clarence Hemingway to Ernest Hemingway, March 8, 1925, Hemingway Collection, Kennedy Library.
4. Ursula Hemingway to Ernest Hemingway, May 20, 1919, Hemingway Collection, Kennedy Library.
5. Ernest Hemingway in Grace Hall Hemingway Scrap Book, May 11, 1913, Hemingway Collection, Kennedy Library.
6. Baker, *A Life Story*, p. 61.
7. Constance Montgomery, *Hemingway in Michigan* (Vermont: Crossroads Press, 1977), p. 118.
8. Grace Hall Hemingway to Clarence Hemingway, [spring, 1919], Humanities Research Center, University of Texas.

9. Grace Hall Hemingway to Clarence Hemingway, July 30, 1915, Humanities Research Center, University of Texas.

10. Clarence Hemingway to Ernest Hemingway, July 31, 1915, Hemingway Collection, Kennedy Library.

11. Ernest Hemingway to Carissinus [high-school friend, nickname?], July 17, 1915, Hemingway Collection, Kennedy Library.

12. F.B.I. File obtained under the Freedom of Information Act and shared with Jeffrey Meyers who claimed it for his own.

13. Reprinted in *Ernest Hemingway's Apprenticeship,* ed. M. J. Bruccoli (Washington, D.C.: N.C.R. Microcard Editions, 1971), pp. 96–7; originally published in *Tabula* 22 (Oak Park High School) (February 1916), 9–10.

14. Ibid., pp. 101–3.

15. Grace Hall Hemingway to Clarence Hemingway, August 2, 1919, Humanities Research Center, Texas University.

16. Grace Hall Hemingway to Clarence Hemingway, August 9, 1919, Humanities Research Center, University of Texas.

17. Marcelline Hemingway to Grace Hall Hemingway, August 26, 1919, Humanities Research Center, Texas University.

18. Marcelline Hemingway to Grace Hall Hemingway, August 30, 1919, Humanities Research Center, Texas University.

19. Ursula Hemingway to Grace Hall Hemingway, n.d. (c. September 1919), Humanities Research Center, Texas University.

20. Ursula Hemingway to Grace Hall Hemingway, September 22, 1919, Humanities Research Center, University of Texas.

21. Ruth Arnold to Grace Hall Hemingway, 1909, Humanities Research Center, Texas University.

22. Ruth Arnold to Grace Hall Hemingway, August 4, 1919, Humanities Research Center, Texas University.

23. Grace Hall Hemingway to Clarence Hemingway, n.d. (noted by C.E.H. "ans to Aug. 2 letter fr CEH"), Humanities Research Center, Texas University.

24. Ruth Arnold to Grace Hall Hemingway, August 30, 1919, Humanities Research Center, University of Texas.

25. Marcelline Hemingway to Grace Hall Hemingway, August 31, 1919, Humanities Research Center, University of Texas.

26. Patrick Hemingway at the Hemingway Conference, Northeastern University, May, 1982.

27. "A Way You'll Never Be," *Short Stories,* p. 407.

28. Marcelline Hemingway to Grace Hall Hemingway, September 16, 1919, Humanities Research Center, Texas University.

29. Clarence Hemingway to Grace Hall Hemingway, January 10, 1904, Humanities Research Center, Texas University.
30. Grace Hall Hemingway to Clarence Hemingway, October 18, 1908, Humanities Research Center, Texas University.
31. Grace Hall Hemingway to Clarence Hemingway, October 17, 1908, Humanities Research Center, Texas University.
32. Clarence Hemingway to Family, October 26, 1909, Humanities Research Center, Texas University.
33. Coroner's Inquest, held December 7, 1928, Oak Park, Ill.
34. This abbreviated medical history has been compiled from the several published biographical sources available, but the most significant parts were found in the Hemingway family collection at the University of Texas.

Chapter Four: STILL LIFE WITH PARENTS

1. William Smith to Ernest Hemingway, January 24, 1920, Hemingway Collection, Kennedy Library.
2. Item 581, Hemingway Collection, Kennedy Library.
3. "The Ash Heels Tendon," Item 254, Hemingway Collection, Kennedy Library.
4. William Smith to Ernest Hemingway, November 7, 1919, Hemingway Collection, Kennedy Library.
5. William Smith to Ernest Hemingway, November 13, 1919, Hemingway Collection, Kennedy Library.
6. "Cross Roads," Item 347, Hemingway Collection, Kennedy Library.
7. "Cross Roads," Item 348, Hemingway Collection, Kennedy Library.
8. William Smith to Ernest Hemingway, November 7, 1919, Hemingway Collection, Kennedy Library.
9. *Saturday Evening Post,* March 20, 1920, p. 128. Howe's story was serialized in the *Post* beginning in the November 7, 1919 issue.
10. *Saturday Evening Post,* March 20, 1920, p. 14.
11. Ralph Connable to Ernest Hemingway, January 12, 1920, Hemingway Collection, Kennedy Library.
12. Theodore Brumback to Ernest Hemingway, April 23, 1920, Hemingway Collection, Kennedy Library.
13. Carl Edgar to Ernest Hemingway, February 20, 1920, Hemingway Collection, Kennedy Library.

14. Bonnie Bonnell to Ernest Hemingway, May 20, 1920, Hemingway Collection, Kennedy Library.
15. Baker, *A Life Story*, pp. 68–70.
16. Clarence Hemingway to Ernest Hemingway, March 28, 1920, Hemingway Collection, Kennedy Library.
17. Clarence Hemingway to Ernest Hemingway, January 24, 1920, Baker file, Princeton University.
18. Item 384, Hemingway Collection, Kennedy Library.
19. "Fathers and Sons," *Short Stories*, p. 496.
20. Grace Hall Hemingway to Ernest Hemingway [February 9, 1920], Hemingway Collection, Kennedy Library.
21. *Oak Leaves*, November 4, 1905.
22. Ernest Hemingway, "The Art of the Short Story," *The Paris Review*, 23 (Spring, 1981), 92.
23. Ruth Arnold to Ernest Hemingway, July 16, 1951, Hemingway Collection, Kennedy Library.
24. *Oak Leaves*, November 7, 1920.
25. Ernest Hemingway to Marcelline Hemingway, September 13, 1910, Humanities Research Center, Texas University.
26. *Oak Leaves*, June 4, 1904.
27. *Oak Leaves*, March 22, 1913.
28. "Father and Sons," *Oak Leaves*, November 11, 1905.
29. *Oak Leaves*, May 30, 1910.
30. See Rev. William E. Barton to Ernest Hemingway, May 25, 1920, Hemingway Collection, Kennedy Library.
31. Clarence Hemingway to Ernest Hemingway, June 4, 1920, Hemingway Collection, Kennedy Library.
32. Marjorie Bump to Ernest Hemingway, February 5, 1920, Hemingway Collection, Kennedy Library.

Chapter Five: SUMMER PEOPLE: PART TWO

1. "On Writing," *The Nick Adams Stories* (New York: Scribner's, 1972), p. 235.
2. Clarence Hemingway to Grace Hall Hemingway, July 30, 1920, Humanities Research Center, Texas University.
3. Clarence Hemingway to Grace Hall Hemingway, July 22, 1920, Humanities Research Center, Texas University.
4. "The Summer People," *The Nick Adams Stories*, p. 218.

5. *Oak Leaves.* November 27, 1915.
6. "Fathers and Sons," *The Nick Adams Stories,* p. 259.
7. William Smith to Ernest Hemingway, April 7, 1920, Hemingway Collection, Kennedy Library.
8. "Fathers and Sons," p. 258.
9. Theodore Brumback to Ernest Hemingway, April 23, 1920, Baker file, Princeton University.
10. *The Oak Park Code of 1916* (Oak Park, 1917), p. 822.
11. "The Summer People," p. 227.
12. See Townsend Luddington, *John Dos Passos* (New York: E. P. Dutton, 1980), p. 265. Bill Smith said his sister never had an affair with Hemingway.
13. See "Fathers and Sons," "Up in Michigan," and *For Whom the Bell Tolls* (New York: Scribner's, 1940).
14. Theodore Brumback to Ernest Hemingway, April 23, 1920, Hemingway Collection, Kennedy Library.
15. See Albert J. Guerard, *Conrad the Novelist* (New York: Atheneum, 1967), pp. 255–73.
16. "The Mercenaries," Item 572, Hemingway Collection, Kennedy Library. The earliest version of this story was called "Wolves and Doughnuts."
17. James Gamble to Ernest Hemingway, December 11, 1918, Baker file, Princeton University.
18. Eric Dorman-Smith (Dorman-O'Gowan) memoir, Baker file, Princeton University.
19. James Gamble to Ernest Hemingway [March 16, 1919], Hemingway Collection, Kennedy Library.
20. James Gamble to Ernest Hemingway, May 23, 1919, Hemingway Collection, Kennedy Library.
21. Clarence Hemingway to Ernest Hemingway, June 4, 1920, Hemingway Collection, Kennedy Library.
22. Ruth Arnold to Grace Hall Hemingway, June 19, 1920, Humanities Research Center, Texas University.
23. Clarence Hemingway to Grace Hall Hemingway, June 25, 1920, Humanities Research Center, Texas University.
24. Grace Hall Hemingway to Clarence Hemingway, August 6, 1920, Humanities Research Center, Texas University.
25. Ruth Arnold to Grace Hall Hemingway, June 26, 1920, Humanities Research Center, Texas University.
26. Ruth Arnold to Grace Hall Hemingway, July 7, 1920, Humanities Research Center, Texas University.

27. Katherine Norris A. to Grace Hall Hemingway, August 13, 1933; A.C.S. to Grace Hall Hemingway, April 13, 1934, Humanities Research Center, Texas University.

28. Sophia Ebann to Grace Hall Hemingway, December 25, 1938, Humanities Research Center, Texas University.

29. Marcelline Hemingway Sanford to Grace Hall Hemingway, December 14, 1940, Humanities Research Center, Texas University.

30. Blanche Fletcher to Grace Hall Hemingway, June 2, 1942, Humanities Research Center, Texas University.

31. Grace Hall Hemingway to Marjorie Andree and Clara Harell, July 10, 1934, Humanities Research Center, Texas University.

32. Clarence Hemingway to Grace Hall Hemingway, July 18, 1920, Humanities Research Center, Texas University.

33. Quoted in Baker, *A Life Story*, p. 71.

34. See ibid., pp. 71–2; Grace Hall Hemingway to Clarence Hemingway, July 27, 1920, Humanities Research Center, Texas University.

35. Grace Hall Hemingway to Ernest Hemingway, dated July 24, 1920 but hand delivered on July 27, Humanities Research Center, Texas University.

36. Clarence Hemingway to Grace Hall Hemingway, September 2, 1920, Humanities Research Center, Texas University.

37. Clarence Hemingway to Grace Hall Hemingway, September 15, 1920, Humanities Research Center, Texas University.

38. Clarence Hemingway to Ernest Hemingway, September 18, 1920, Hemingway Collection, Kennedy Library.

39. Clarence Hemingway to Grace Hall Hemingway, September 19, 1920, Humanities Research Center, Texas University.

40. Grace Hall Hemingway to Ernest Hemingway, October 4, 1920, Hemingway Collection, Kennedy Library.

41. Ernest Hemingway to Mrs. Jasper J. Jepson, July 30, 1943, Hemingway Collection, Kennedy Library.

42. Grace Hall Hemingway to Ernest Hemingway, July 21, 1946, Humanities Research Center, Texas University.

Chapter Six: CHICAGO

1. See Jim Hinkle's "Note on Two-Timing at Zelli's," *Hemingway Newsletter* No. 4 (July, 1982), 3–4.

2. Hadley Richardson to Ernest Hemingway, November 5, 1920, Hemingway Collection, Kennedy Library.

3. "The End of Something," *In Our Time* (New York: Scribner's, 1930), p. 34.

4. Grade Record Books, Mary Institute, St. Louis, Mo.

5. Item 409, Hemingway Collection, Kennedy Library.

6. Catalogs 1900–1910, Mary Institute, St. Louis, Mo.

7. Note: misspelled names have been corrected. Carlos Baker, ed. *Ernest Hemingway Selected Letters* (New York: Scribner's, 1981), p. 44.

8. William Hyde and Howard L. Conrad, *Encyclopedia of the History of St. Louis,* vol. III (St. Louis: Southern History Co., 1899), pp. 1909–10; W. B. Stevens, *St. Louis the Fourth City: 1764–1909,* vol. I. (St. Louis: S. J. Clarke Publishing Co., 1909), pp. 833, 937.

9. Holograph will of James Richardson, d. 1893, Probate Office, Civil Court Building, St. Louis, Mo.

10. Probated will of James Richardson Jr., File No. 31077, Probate Office, Civil Court Building, St. Louis, Mo.

11. Medical Examiner's File No. 1360, James Richardson Jr., Medical Examiner's Office, St. Louis, Mo.

12. Probated will of James Richardson Jr.

13. *Encyclopedia of the History of St. Louis,* vol. IV, p. 2558.

14. Probated will of Florence Wyman Richardson, File No. 53491, Probate Office, Civil Court Building, St. Louis, Mo.

15. Ernest Hemingway to Grace Quinlan, November 16, 1920, Hemingway Collection, Kennedy Library.

16. Hadley Richardson to Ernest Hemingway, November 11, 20, 25, 1920, Hemingway Collection, Kennedy Library.

17. *Bulletin of the Art Institute of Chicago,* 14 (7) (October 1920), 90.

18. *Bulletin of the Art Institute of Chicago,* 13 (1) (January 1919), 11–12.

19. *Bulletin of the Art Institute of Chicago,* 15 (5) (September–October 1921), 156.

20. *Bulletin of the Art Institute of Chicago,* 14 (6) (September 1920), 82–3.

21. *Oak Leaves,* March 29, 1913.

22. *Oak Leaves,* April 5, 1913.

23. *Oak Leaves,* January 22, 1904.

24. *Oak Leaves,* March 4, 1904.

25. *Oak Leaves,* April 29, 1914.

26. *Oak Leaves*, April 29, 1914.
27. *The Negro in Chicago* (University of Chicago Press, 1922), p. 659. This is the Chicago Commission's detailed report and analysis of the riot.
28. See William M. Tuttle, *Race Riot* (New York: Atheneum, 1975).
29. This poem was not published in *Ernest Hemingway 88 Poems,* ed. Nicholas Gerogiannis (New York: Harcourt Brace Jovanovich, 1979). Like T. S. Eliot's equally racist "King Bolo Poems," Hemingway's poem will remain dark for some time.

Chapter Seven: THE LAST ROBIN

1. Jim Gamble to Ernest Hemingway, December 27, 1920, Hemingway Collection, Kennedy Library.
2. Ernest Hemingway to Hadley Richardson, [December 23, 1920], Hemingway Collection, Kennedy Library.
3. Ernest Hemingway to Hadley Richardson, [December 29, 1920], Hemingway Collection, Kennedy Library.
4. Hadley Richardson to Ernest Hemingway, January 1, 1921, Hemingway Collection, Kennedy Library.
5. Hadley Richardson to Ernest Hemingway, January 2, 1921, Hemingway Collection, Kennedy Library.
6. Hadley Richardson to Ernest Hemingway, January 12, 1921, Hemingway Collection, Kennedy Library.
7. Marjorie Bump to Ernest Hemingway, January 14, 1921, Hemingway Collection, Kennedy Library.
8. Hadley Richardson to Ernest Hemingway, January 8, 1921, Hemingway Collection, Kennedy Library.
9. Hadley Richardson to Ernest Hemingway, January 8, 1921, Hemingway Collection, Kennedy Library.
10. Hadley Richardson to Ernest Hemingway, February 15, 1921, Hemingway Collection, Kennedy Library.
11. Marjorie Bump to Ernest Hemingway, April 7, 1921, Hemingway Collection, Kennedy Library.
12. Ernest Hemingway to [Marjorie Bump], [April 1921], Hemingway Collection, Kennedy Library.
13. Ernest Hemingway to [Marjorie Bump], [April 1921], Hemingway Collection, Kennedy Library.
14. Hadley Richardson to Ernest Hemingway, [April 15, 1921], Hemingway Collection, Kennedy Library.

15. Item 764, Hemingway Collection, Kennedy Library.
16. Item 331, Hemingway Collection, Kennedy Library.
17. Item 722, Hemingway Collection, Kennedy Library.
18. Bill Horne to Ernest Hemingway, November 29, 1927, Hemingway Collection, Kennedy Library. These two stories were taken to Paris and eventually lost.
19. Review, *New Republic*. September 20, 1933, reprinted in Malcolm Cowley's *Think Back on Us* (Southern Illinois University Press, 1967), ed. Henry Dan Piper, pp. 35–6.
20. R.W.B. to Kenley Smith, n.d. (c. January 1921), Hemingway Collection, Kennedy Library.
21. Item 670B, Hemingway Collection, Kennedy Library.
22. See Bernard Duffey, *The Chicago Renaissance in American Letters* (Michigan State University Press, 1956), and Ellen Williams, *Harriet Monroe and the Poetry Renaissance* (University of Illinois Press, 1977).
23. See William Wasserman, *The Time of The Dial* (Syracuse University Press, 1963), and Nicholas Joost, *Scofield Thayer and The Dial* (Southern Illinois University Press, 1964).
24. Sherwood Anderson to Waldo Frank, January 10, 1917, Newberry Library, Chicago.
25. Sherwood Anderson to Waldo Frank, October 1917, Newberry Library, Chicago.
26. Hadley Richardson to Ernest Hemingway, January 19, 1921, Hemingway Collection, Kennedy Library.
27. Sherwood Anderson to Lucille Cox, December 13, 1921, Newberry Library, Chicago.
28. Sherwood Anderson to Hart Crane, March 3, 1921, Newberry Library, Chicago.
29. Sherwood Anderson to Waldo Frank, May 1919, Newberry Library, Chicago.
30. For sources of Hemingway's reading see my book, *Hemingway's Reading* (Princeton University Press, 1981), and James Brasch and Joseph Sigman, *Hemingway's Library* (New York: Garland Publishing Co., 1981).
31. Hadley Richardson to Ernest Hemingway, January 28, 1921, Hemingway Collection, Kennedy Library.
32. Hadley Richardson to Ernest Hemingway, February 14, 1921, Hemingway Collection, Kennedy Library.
33. Hadley Richardson to Ernest Hemingway, April 24, 1921, Hemingway Collection, Kennedy Library.

34. Hadley Richardson to Ernest Hemingway, April 8, 1921, Hemingway Collection, Kennedy Library.

35. Sherwood Anderson to Waldo Frank, [c. 1920], Newberry Library, Chicago.

36. Hadley Richardson to Ernest Hemingway, January 7, 1921, Hemingway Collection, Kennedy Library.

37. Sherwood Anderson to Karl Anderson, December 28, 1918, Newberry Library, Chicago.

38. Sherwood Anderson to Waldo Frank, March 11, 1918, Newberry Library, Chicago.

39. Sherwood Anderson to Waldo Frank, [summer, 1919], Newberry Library, Chicago.

40. Bill Horne to Ernest Hemingway, n.d. (c. 1926), Hemingway Collection, Kennedy Library.

41. Sherwood Anderson to Lucile Cox, December 13, 1921, Newberry Library, Chicago.

42. *88 Poems.* p. 22.

43. "Bird of Night," ibid., p. 36.

44. Sherwood Anderson to Jerry Blum, January 7, 1921, Newberry Library, Chicago.

45. Hadley Richardson to Ernest Hemingway, July 12, 1921, Hemingway Collection, Kennedy Library.

46. February 24, 1921, in Carlos Baker, *Selected Letters.* p. 45. The first draft is in the letter file, Hemingway Collection, Kennedy Library.

47. Ernest Hemingway to Grace Hall Hemingway, January 10, 1921, Hemingway Collection, Kennedy Library.

48. "Toronto Women Who Went to the Prize Fights Applaud the Rough Stuff," Toronto *Star Weekly.* May 15, 1920, p. 13.

49. "Carpentier Sure to Give Dempsey Fight Worth While," Toronto *Star Weekly.* October 30, 1920, p. 8.

50. *Oak Leaves.* November 29, 1904.

51. Hadley Richardson to Ernest Hemingway, February 24, 1921, Hemingway Collection, Kennedy Library.

52. Ernest Hemingway to Grace Hall Hemingway, January 10, 1921, *Selected Letters.* p. 45.

53. Hadley Richardson to Ernest Hemingway, January 7, 1921, Hemingway Collection, Kennedy Library.

54. "How to be Popular in Peace Though a Slacker at War," Toronto *Star Weekly.* March 13, 1920, p. 11.

55. "A Veteran Visits Old Front, Wishes He Had Stayed Away," *Toronto Daily Star*, July 22, 1922, p. 7.
56. Hadley Richardson to Ernest Hemingway, June 6, 1921, Hemingway Collection, Kennedy Library.
57. Hadley Richardson to Ernest Hemingway, June 8, 1921, Hemingway Collection, Kennedy Library.
58. Hadley Richardson to Ernest Hemingway, February 11, 1921, Hemingway Collection, Kennedy Library.
59. Hadley Richardson to Ernest Hemingway, February 14, 1921, Hemingway Collection, Kennedy Library.
60. Hadley Richardson to Ernest Hemingway, February 19, 1921, Hemingway Collection, Kennedy Library.
61. Hadley Richardson to Ernest Hemingway, March 3, 1921, Hemingway Collection, Kennedy Library.
62. Hadley Richardson to Ernest Hemingway, March 8, 1921, Hemingway Collection, Kennedy Library. See Baker, *A Life Story*, pp. 77–8.
63. Hadley Richardson to Ernest Hemingway, March 9, 1921, Hemingway Collection, Kennedy Library.

Chapter Eight: SON AND LOVER

1. Hadley Richardson to Ernest Hemingway, June 3, 1921, Hemingway Collection, Kennedy Library.
2. "The Three Day Blow," *Short Stories*, p. 122.
3. Hadley Richardson to Ernest Hemingway, May 25, 1921, Hemingway Collection, Kennedy Library.
4. *88 Poems*, p. 32.
5. Baker, *A Life Story*, p. 78.
6. Hadley Richardson to Ernest Hemingway, March 30, 1921, Hemingway Collection, Kennedy Library.
7. Hadley Richardson to Ernest Hemingway, [April 2, 1921], Hemingway Collection, Kennedy Library.
8. Florence Wyman Richardson, "The Revolt of Wives," *The New Republic*, 3 (June 5, 1915), 122. See also obituary "Mrs. F. W. Richardson, Suffrage Leader, Dies," St. Louis *Post-Dispatch*, August 21, 1920, p. 3.
9. Hadley Richardson to Grace Hall Hemingway, April 8, 1921, Hemingway Collection, Kennedy Library. This letter is with the

collection of Hadley letters and not with the Grace Hemingway collection where it should have been. At the University of Texas there is a letter from Hadley to Grace dated May 20, 1921, which Grace annotated as "1st letter from Hadley."

10. Hadley Richardson to Ernest Hemingway, February 7, 1921, Hemingway Collection, Kennedy Library.
11. Hadley Richardson to Ernest Hemingway, April 8, 1921, Hemingway Collection, Kennedy Library.
12. *A Farewell to Arms*, p. 139.
13. Hadley Richardson to Ernest Hemingway, April 11, 1921, Hemingway Collection, Kennedy Library.
14. Hadley Richardson to Ernest Hemingway, April 8 and May 20, 1921, Hemingway Collection, Kennedy Library.
15. Hadley Richardson to Ernest Hemingway, April 8, 1921, Hemingway Collection, Kennedy Library.
16. Ernest Hemingway to Emily Goetsmann, July 13, 1916, Hemingway Collection, Kennedy Library.
17. Anthony Rhodes, *The Poet as Superman* (London: Weidenfeld & Nicolson, 1959), p. 157.
18. Many of the insights on d'Annunzio derive from Nicholas Gerogiannis, "Hemingway's Poetry: Angry Notes of an Ambivalent Overman," *Ernest Hemingway: The Papers of a Writer* (New York: Garland Publishing Co., 1981), pp. 73–87.
19. Toronto *Star Weekly*. December 11, 1920, p. 26.
20. *Selected Letters*. p. 46.
21. Chicago *Tribune*. October 15, 1920, p. 21.
22. "To Will Davies," *88 Poems*. p. 21.
23. *88 Poems*. p. 39. First published in *The Double Dealer*. 3 (June 1922), 337.
24. Hadley Richardson to Ernest Hemingway, July 14, 1921, Hemingway Collection, Kennedy Library.
25. "Chapter XV," as reprinted in *Short Stories*. p. 219.
26. "Gun-Men's Wild Political War On in Chicago," Toronto *Star Weekly*. May 28, 1921, pp. 21, 22; as reprinted in *The Wild Years*. ed. Gene Z. Hanrahan (New York: Dell, 1962), pp. 46–8.
27. Hadley Richardson to Ernest Hemingway, May 13, 1921, Hemingway Collection, Kennedy Library.
28. May 20, 1921, *Selected Letters*, p. 49.
29. Hadley Richardson to Ernest Hemingway, June 22, 1921, Hemingway Collection, Kennedy Library.

30. Toronto *Star Weekly*, August 20, 1921, p. 22.
31. Marcelline Hemingway Sanford to Grace Hall Hemingway, April 14, 1939, Humanities Research Center, University of Texas.
32. MS Minutes of the Board of Education, Oak Park and River Forest High School, Oak Park, Ill.
33. *Tabula*, 33 (April 1916).
34. See Item 384, Hemingway Collection, Kennedy Library.
35. Ernest Hemingway to Marjorie Bump, [April 1921], Hemingway Collection, Kennedy Library.
36. Item 240, 14pp. MSS, Hemingway Collection, Kennedy Library. Hadley Richardson to Ernest Hemingway, April 20, 1921, Hemingway Collection, Kennedy Library.
37. Y. K. Smith to Ernest Hemingway, n.d. [c. spring, 1921], Hemingway Collection, Kennedy Library.
38. Hadley Richardson to Ernest Hemingway, May 20 and 25, 1921, Hemingway Collection, Kennedy Library.

Chapter Nine: CITY LIGHTS

1. Hadley Richardson to Ernest Hemingway, August 11, 1921, Hemingway Collection, Kennedy Library.
2. *Selected Letters*, p. 47.
3. *Publications of the Field Columbian Museum*, Zoological Series, vol. 8 (1907), A Catalogue of the Collection of Mammals in the FCM; *Field Museum of Natural History*, Reports, vol. IV, Annual Report of the Director, January 1914; Annual Report of the Director, Field Museum of Natural History, Publication 119, vol. 3, no. 1 (January 1907). *Field Museum of Natural History Guide* (Chicago, 1910), 9th edition.
4. *Fieldiana*, Zoology, 1 (6) (1905), 148–9.
5. *Oak Leaves*, rerun in Christmas supplement, December, 1910.
6. *Oak Leaves*, October 12, 1912.
7. *Oak Leaves*, January 4, 1913.
8. *Oak Leaves*, March 1, 22, 1913.
9. *Oak Leaves*, March 1, 1913.
10. *Oak Leaves*, June 7, 1913.
11. *Oak Leaves*, May 31, 1913.
12. *Oak Leaves*, December 7, 1913; January 3, 1914.

13. Ernest Hemingway to Grace Hemingway, August, 23, [1930], Lilly Library, Bloomington, Indiana.
14. "Roosevelt," first published in *Poetry* (January 1923), reprinted in *88 Poems*, p. 45.
15. Hadley Richardson to Ernest Hemingway, June 9, 1921, Hemingway Collection, Kennedy Library.
16. "Three Day Blow," *Short Stories*, p. 118.
17. *88 Poems*, p. 30.
18. Hadley Richardson to Ernest Hemingway, July 20, 1921, Hemingway Collection, Kennedy Library.
19. Chicago *Tribune*, November 16, 1921.
20. Hadley Richardson to Ernest Hemingway, July 14, 1921, Hemingway Collection, Kennedy Library.
21. During the week of General Diaz's visit, one Nicolo Adamo was murdered in Chicago. It seems unlikely that Hemingway used the name for Nick Adams. I assume rather that it is one of those random historical curiosities.
22. Hadley Richardson to Ernest Hemingway, June 16, 20, August 7, 8, 11, 14, 1921, Hemingway Collection, Kennedy Library.
23. Hadley Richardson to Ernest Hemingway, August 22, 1921, Hemingway Collection, Kennedy Library.
24. "Preface," *Nigger of the Narcissus*, reprinted in *Joseph Conrad on Fiction*, ed. Walter F. Wright (University of Nebraska Press, 1964), p. 162.
25. Ernest Hemingway to Clarence Hemingway, March 20, 1925, Hemingway Collection, Kennedy Library.
26. *Green Hills of Africa* (New York: Scribner's, 1935), p. 109.
27. Sherwood Anderson, "New Orleans, The Double Dealer and the Modern Movement in America," *The Double Dealer*, 3 (March 1922), 121-2.
28. Hadley Richardson to Ernest Hemingway, August 24, 1921, Hemingway Collection, Kennedy Library.
29. "Divine Gesture," *The Double Dealer*, 3 (May 1922), 267-8.
30. Hadley Richardson to Ernest Hemingway, July 26, 1921, Hemingway Collection, Kennedy Library.
31. Chicago *Tribune*, August 16, 1921.
32. Grace Hall Hemingway to Ernest Hemingway, August 19, 1921, Humanities Research Center, Texas University.
33. Clarence Hemingway to Ernest Hemingway, August 4, 1921, Hemingway Collection, Kennedy Library.

34. Clarence Hemingway to Ernest Hemingway, August 10, 1921, Hemingway Collection, Kennedy Library.
35. Grace Hall Hemingway to Ernest Hemingway, August 7, 1921, Hemingway Collection, Kennedy Library.
36. Ibid.
37. Marcelline Hemingway Sanford to Grace Hall Hemingway, various letters January through May, 1942, Humanities Research Center, Texas University.
38. This medical history has been pieced together from numerous sources, including the Baker biography, but it is primarily based on family correspondence at the Humanities Research Center, Texas University.
39. Ernest Hemingway to William Smith, [July 18, 1921], Hemingway Collection, Kennedy Library.
40. Marcelline Hemingway Sanford, *At the Hemingways*, p. 216.
41. See Bernice Kert, *The Hemingway Women* (New York: W. W. Norton, 1983), p. 74.

Chapter Ten: THE BEAUTIFUL COUNTRY

1. "Wedding Day," *The Nick Adams Stories*, p. 231.
2. "Lovely Walloona," (Walloon Lake, Michigan: n.d.).
3. L. R. Koontz, "My Favorite Subject is Hadley," *Connecticut Review*, 8 (October 1975), 37.
4. See Chicago *Tribune*, October 1–15, 1921, a continuing story.
5. The only surviving issue of the *Co-Operative Commonwealth* is from October 1, 1921 in the Hemingway Collection at the Kennedy Library. The ice-berg story has no by-line, but the typed draft for it is in the manuscript collection. Hemingway's duties for this issue are also in note form.
6. Item 576, Hemingway Collection, Kennedy Library; the October 8 issue is not available. It has been reported that the *Co-Operative Commonwealth* was a monthly publication; however, the October 1 issue says it is "the weekly magazine of mutual help."
7. Ernest Hemingway to Grace Hall Hemingway, December 22, 1920, *Selected Letters*, p. 43.
8. Charles Fenton, *The Apprenticeship of Ernest Hemingway* (New York: Farrar, Straus & Young, 1954), p. 108.
9. *Oak Leaves*, October 8, 1921, p. 42.

10. Ernest Hemingway to John Bone, draft, March 2, 1921, Hemingway Collection, Kennedy Library.

11. Ernest Hemingway to John Bone, October 29, 1921, Hemingway Collection, Kennedy Library.

12. This money, $9250, was so mismanaged by George Breaker that it was reduced to less than $3000 by 1926. It was not, however, the bulk of Hadley's estate. Her various trust funds remained intact throughout the Twenties, lasting longer than her marriage to Hemingway. Thus, their divorce in 1926 had nothing to do with the money lost by George Breaker.

13. All of the Paris observations come from Anderson's Paris Notebook, 1921, published as *France and Sherwood Anderson,* ed. Michael Fanning (Baton Rouge: L.S.U. Press, 1976), pp. 23–52.

14. Sherwood Anderson to Helen and Felix, July 6 and 7, 1921, Newberry Library, Chicago.

15. Sherwood Anderson to Paul Rosenfeld, March 10, 1921, *Letters of Sherwood Anderson,* ed. Howard Mumford Jones and Walter B. Rideout (Boston: Little, Brown, 1953), p. 72.

16. Fenton, *The Apprenticeship,* pp. 115–16.

17. Chicago *Tribune,* November 18, 1921.

18. *Oak Leaves,* November 5, 1921, reprinting material from the Chicago *Journal*; for sources on the Italian war too numerous to list here see Michael S. Reynolds, *Hemingway's First War* (Princeton: Princeton U. Press, 1976).

19. See Items 734 and 734a, Hemingway Collection, Kennedy Library.

20. *Oak Leaves,* November 26, 1921.

21. Gregory Clark, "Hemingway Slept Here," *Montreal Standard,* November 4, 1950, p. 14. Note: Clark remembers this as happening in 1920, clearly another case of memory collapsing time.

22. Sherwood Anderson to Alfred Steiglitz, June 30, 1923, *Letters of Sherwood Anderson,* p. 100.

23. See Denis Brian, *Murderers and Other Friendly People* (New York: McGraw-Hill, 1972), p. 35.

24. Preface, dated 1960, *A Moveable Feast* (New York: Scribner's, 1964).

25. *Letters of Sherwood Anderson,* pp. 82, 85.

26. Clarence Hemingway to Ernest Hemingway, September 22 and 25, 1923, Hemingway Collection, Kennedy Library.

27. See Bill Horne to Ernest Hemingway, November 29, 1927, Hemingway Collection, Kennedy Library; Horne remembers these two stories from the fall of 1920.

28. Fannie Biggs to Charles Fenton, 1952, Fenton Collection, Beinecke Library, Yale University.

29. Friends of American Writers Collection, Chicago Historical Society.

30. *Oak Leaves*, October 28, 1932.

INDEX

INDEX

INDEX

287